ABOUT THE AUTHOR

Dr David Delvin is Medical Editor of *General Practitioner* and Medical Consultant to the Family Planning Association. He has appeared in hundreds of radio and television programmes, chatting about health matters, and has been Medical Adviser to such BBC television series as *Pebble Mill at One*, *Medical Express*, *Inside Medicine*, *The Afternoon Programme* and *Aspel and Company*, as well as to Anglia's *On Call*.

He writes regular columns for national newspapers and women's magazines, and for various medical journals. His books have been translated into eight languages, and one has recently won the Best Book Award of the American Medical Writers' Association. He was narrowly defeated in a recent series of BBC-TV's *Mastermind*.

His wife – who is a nurse and midwife – helps him with his books and articles.

*By Dr David Delvin and available
from New English Library:*

THE BOOK OF LOVE
CAREFREE LOVE
HOW TO IMPROVE YOUR SEX LIFE
TAKING THE PILL: A GUIDE FOR EVERY WOMAN

HOW TO IMPROVE YOUR SEX LIFE

With special sections on Sex Problems
and the Magic Female G-Spot

Dr David Delvin
Medical Editor of *General Practitioner*
Medical Consultant to the
British Family Planning Association

NEW ENGLISH LIBRARY

ACKNOWLEDGEMENTS

My sincere thanks to Ms Rita Cooper of BBC-TV
– who typed out nearly all of this without getting
too excited.

My thanks also to the splendid Ms Shere Hite
for her advice – over tea at the Ritz – about the
interpretation of the statistics in her two *Hite
Reports*.

A New English Library Original Publication, 1983

Copyright © 1983 by Dr David Delvin

Illustrations © 1983 by New English Library.

First NEL Paperback Edition May 1983
Reprinted February 1984
Reprinted September 1984

Illustrations by Claire Davies and Jennie Smith

NEL Books are published by
New English Library,
Mill Road, Dunton Green,
Sevenoaks, Kent.
Editorial office: 47 Bedford Square, London, WC1B 3DP

Photoset by Rowland Phototypesetting Ltd,
Bury St Edmunds, Suffolk
Printed and bound in Great Britain by
Cox & Wyman Ltd, Reading.

British Library Cataloguing in Publication Data

Delvin, David
   How to improve your sex life.
   1. Sexual intercourse
   I. Title
   613.9′6   HQ31
   ISBN 0-450-05576-0

CONTENTS

Dedication

To the memory of John Donne (1572–1631): great poet, great clergyman, and one of the most entertaining of the early sexologists.

License my roving hands, and let them go,
Before, behind, between, above, below.
O my America! My new-found-land,
My kingdom, safeliest when with one man manned,
My mine of precious stones, my empery,
How blest am I in this discovering thee.
To enter in these bonds is to be free;
Then where my hand is set, my seal shall be.

FOREPLAY

Don't Forget Romance, Laughter – and Love

QUITE RECENTLY, the world-famous *New England Journal of Medicine* published a study of the sex lives of 100 randomly-chosen 'well-educated and happily-married couples', living in Pittsburgh, Pennsylvania. Incredibly, 50 per cent of these 'normal' men and no less than 77 per cent of these 'normal' women told the investigators that they had difficulties with sex!

I can't help feeling (as a bit of an old cynic) that this could indicate that nowadays we've all got things a little out of proportion where sex is concerned. Too many people have the impression that they ought to be living up to some kind of special 'standard' in bed (like: 'x orgasms per week, with multiple ones on Tuesdays, Thursdays and Saturdays').

A lot of novels – and sex textbooks too – reinforce the idea that if you don't have a specified number of Earth-shattering climaxes, you're somehow inadequate, or have a sexual problem. I think that's a load of nonsense. The fact is that people vary wildly in their capacity for sex, and especially in the number of orgasms they can have. So nobody should feel worried because he or she isn't experiencing the number that some sexologist says is the norm.

Therefore, if you're totally happy with your sex life (even if you're not having any orgasms at all) then you don't need to read this or any other 'textbook of sex'. On the other hand, if – like most men and women – you'd just like to know a bit more about sexuality and sexual techniques, then I hope this book will be helpful for you. If you genuinely *do* have a sexual problem, there are special sections of the book in which you'll find advice. And if you want information about some difficulty with contraception, or about today's all-too-common sex infections, then there's a chapter about these topics too.

But the one message that I'd like you to take away from this book is that sex isn't an Olympic event (yet). Sex is actually supposed to be about:

★Romance   ★Laughter   ★Love

If you can bring those three priceless things into your bed, you're unlikely to have to worry very much about your orgasms.

CHAPTER ONE

Sex Is Fun

Let's face it: sex is great! ● *Here's what to do if you've got minor sex difficulties* ● *Or major ones* ● *Making sex even better* ● *It pays to increase your sexual knowledge* ● *Keeping it safe* ● *Doing it fairly often* ● *Understanding your partner.*

Let's face it: sex is great!

There's one thing that most human beings think of more than anything else – and that's sex. Many people don't like to admit that fact, but I think it's better to be honest and accept that sex is one of the most powerful driving forces of our lives. After all, the four billion people on this planet didn't get here because their Mums and Dads spent the evenings playing tiddlywinks.

In fact, the human race owes its continued survival to sex – to the fact that men and women feel this colossal (and sometimes quite irresistible) attraction for each other. We are all here due to the strange fact that most men feel a wild and powerful urge to drive the male penis into the female vagina – and because of the equally strange fact that most women feel the warm, tender desire to take that thrusting penis into the vagina and to receive its precious cargo of life and love. (*Steady on! – Editor*)

The great thing about all this is that it's so nice. How marvellous that the activity which can plant the seed of new human beings is so delightful, and that the act of love between man and woman creates a few minutes of sheer Heaven upon Earth!

If you follow the advice given in this book, there's no reason why those few minutes shouldn't be even more Heavenly, and, with a bit of luck, full of laughter too.

There's no reason, either, why you shouldn't extend those few minutes to thirty or forty – or even (on occasions) to a few *hours* of mutual bliss . . . for the motto of this book is 'Make Love – Have Fun – and then Make More If You Want To.'

Here's what to do if you've got minor sex difficulties

But – and it's a big 'BUT' – the fact has to be faced that love-making isn't *always* a success for everybody. Groucho Marx once said about sex: 'When it's good, it's very good. And when it's

1

bad – it's still very good!' That's good Groucho Marxist stuff. But the truth is that a lot of people do have problems with sex. Instead of being beautiful, for them it's lousy. What should be one of the most wonderful experiences on Earth turns into a sordid – and even painful – disaster.

And it's a sad fact that such problems are very common. One recent survey showed that almost six out of ten twenty-five year old adults (some married, some not) had difficulties or worries with sex. (Admittedly, that may reflect the fact I mentioned right at the start of this book: that these days people often have unrealistically high expectations of sexual performance.) Happily, many of their anxieties were pretty mild – the kind of things that a chat with a sympathetic nurse or doctor could probably help sort out – while other difficulties were of the type which could very possibly be put right by an understanding, loving and sexually experienced partner.

Most people experience these *minor* sex worries at some time or another in their lives – specially when they're young. I've tried to deal with these lesser difficulties as fully as possible in Chapter 6. On the other hand, don't just read Chapter 6 if you've got one of these relatively trifling sexual anxieties or problems. Read the rest of the book as well, because most of those minor sex worries result very largely from lack of knowledge.

When I say 'lack of knowledge', what I mean is that most people – though they may pretend otherwise – don't actually know very much about the anatomy and physiology of their own sexual organs – or anybody else's either.

Despite all the rubbish we read in the papers about everybody having had lots of sex education ('The youngsters know it all today . . .'), the truth is that the average human being's ignorance about sex is truly colossal.

Why else do you think we get all those hundreds of thousands of unwanted pregnancies each year? (One out of every *six* US babies is now born out of wedlock.) And why do you think that the Family Planning Clinics are full of women who don't know their clitoris from their elbow?

So if you've got some minor sex worry, read through the book and get the *facts*. I hope that Chapter 6 will be particularly helpful in aiding you to sort things out. If not, you'll find in Chapter 21 the names of Counselling Agencies and Advice Centres throughout the world who can help you get it together.

What to do if you've got major problems

What are more *serious* difficulties? Well, these are pretty common too. That's why psychosexual counselling clinics are overflowing with patients who are suffering from male disorders like:

★impotence (difficulty in getting the penis stiff enough to go in)
★premature ejaculation ('hair-trigger trouble' or 'coming too soon')
★loss of libido ('lack of interest')

and female ones like:

★vaginismus (painful intercourse)
★inability to reach a climax
★so-called 'frigidity' (better termed 'loss of female sex drive')

To give you an idea of just how common these more serious problems are, let me just point out that even in these 'enlightened' days well over 10 per cent of women cannot reach a climax at all – and though some of them make light of the fact, and aren't really worried by it, others are desperately frustrated.

The incidence of the other difficulties listed above is pretty high too, and this is so all over the Western world. In Canada, two doctors recently claimed that premature ejaculation ('coming too soon') is actually the commonest disease of adult males. I think they were exaggerating a bit, but there's certainly a lot of it about. In the US, the world's leading sex researchers Masters and Johnson state that major sex problems threaten 40–50 per cent of American marriages. I find that a bit hard to believe – but if it were true, this statement would go a long way towards explaining the astronomically high US divorce rate (a rate which is now being approached by Britain, Australia and some other countries).

Anyway, if *you* have a major sex problem like one of those listed above, I suggest you read the whole of this book – because increasing your general sexual knowledge will help you to cope with your problem. You'll find specific advice on dealing with the major problems in Chapters 17 to 21.

Making sex even better

What most people are interested in is making sex even better than it is already. That's the main object of this book – to help you and your partner (husband, wife, boyfriend or girlfriend) to have a more enjoyable sex relationship than you've got at the moment.

For let's face it; there's no such thing as a totally perfect sexual union. It can always be improved a little. And if you say to yourself: 'Oh, no: my wife/husband is *completely* satisfied with the way I make love,' then beware! All too often, people who think their partners are totally satisfied in bed are quite wrong.

Take the case of Harry. He thought he was a great lover and that nobody could teach him anything about what to do. He fondly imagined that his wife Sheila found him absolutely wonderful between the sheets, until, that is, Sheila – totally out of character – went off and had an affair with a more inventive, sympathetic and skilled lover. What Harry hadn't realised was that for ages Sheila had been bored to tears with his unadventurous and unromantic love-making.

It happens the other way round too. There are countless wives who think that they're 'giving their husbands what they want' – but in reality those same husbands are quietly slipping off to topless massage parlours in order to get the kind of thrills that aren't being served up at home. So it's a good insurance policy to make sure that your love-making techniques are fresh and varied and inventive, so there will be no need for either of you to look elsewhere for satisfaction. Apart from all that, I hope that if you use the techniques which are outlined in this book, you'll find that – for both of you – love-making is much more rewarding and a very great deal more fun.

It pays to increase your sexual knowledge

The first thing to do if you want to make your sex life better is to learn as much as possible about the facts of sex – and as much as possible about the techniques of love-play and love-making. If you really know next to nothing about such things, then you'd do better to start with the first volume in this series *The Book of Love* (UK, New English Library: USA, St Martin's Press) which explains the basic facts of sex from the very beginning. Later, you can move on to *this* book – which is really for rather more advanced students. If you already know quite a bit about sex, but want to increase your skill, improve your performance, and generally give more pleasure to the one you love, then read on.

Keeping it safe

Here's a vital point. It's very difficult to enjoy sex to the full unless it's *safe* sex – in other words:

4

★sex which is safe from the fear of unwanted pregnancy
★sex which is safe from the fear of VD

Tragically, many beautiful sexual experiences are followed by the disasters of unwanted conception – or by the arrival of the symptoms of venereal disease, or some other genital infection. People often find these facts unpalatable, which is why the sexy magazines so rarely mention such topics. But the truth is this:

★In Britain, there are several hundred thousand unwanted pregnancies a year, and out of *all* pregnancies, about one in five ends in abortion. In the USA (with its much larger population) there are now 1¼ million abortions per year. In Australia too, about one pregnancy in five ends in termination.
★In Britain each year, nearly half a million people attend a VD clinic – though happily many of them do not turn out to have the more serious forms of infection. In the USA, there are an incredible 1,000,000 cases of gonorrhoea and syphilis each year – plus many millions more cases of other infections. In Australia, (thanks to the legacy of the Vietnam war) the VD figures have increased greatly in recent years – including a lot of penicillin-resistant strains imported from South-East Asia.

Unwanted babies, abortions, and venereal infections can ruin people's lives. It's crazy that so few 'sex manuals' tell you how to avoid these dangers.

However, I've given a brief guide to evading these risks in Chapter 22. More information on VD and other sex infections is given in *The Book of Love*, and much more detail on the many ways of avoiding unwanted pregnancy is given in the other companion volume of this series *Carefree Love – The Home Doctor Book of Safe Sex and the Pill* (New English Library). So there's no excuse not to keep it *safe* as well as keeping it happy! Remember the slogan which a lady reader of my advice column suggested should be emblazoned on the doors of all Family Planning Clinics. The simple words she chose were these:

'Don't trust to luck,
When you have a fuck'.

A wise motto indeed: I commend it to you.

Doing it fairly often

There's another couplet that's worth remembering, and that's a little two-liner which I think originated with the US psychiatrist Dr David Reuben, author of *Everything You Always Wanted to Know About Sex (But Were Afraid to Ask)*. Its message is this:

> 'Use it –
> Before you lose it!'

In other words, don't let the Heaven-sent and laughter-filled gift of sex go to waste. Many people – especially those who are older – seem to decide not to bother about love-making for a long while: they neglect their partners (perhaps because of tiredness or overwork or too much booze) and dismiss the whole idea of making love to them from their minds for weeks or even years at a time. Then (particularly if they're middle-aged or elderly), when they decide to 're-start' sex again, they often find they seem to have lost a lot of the ability. Sometimes too, the neglected wife/husband just doesn't seem interested any more.

So – keep in practice. The best way of maintaining a good sex life is to make love fairly regularly. Not only is regular love-making good for keeping your sex drive in tip-top condition, but it's also good for keeping a loving relationship in tip-top condition too. How can you expect your loved one to appreciate you when he/she is frustrated and feels that you don't physically desire him/her any more? (Of course, that doesn't mean that you have to try to break any world records.)

Understanding your partner

Don't kid yourself that you're going to fulfil your partner's deepest needs by leaping on him/her at every conceivable opportunity. And don't kid yourself that the astonishing size or beauty (in your own eyes) of your sexual equipment will thrill him or her to the core. Nor should you fool yourself that the kind of skill in sheer mechanical sexual technique which you can learn from a book such as this will necessarily make the Earth move or fill your lover's soul with stars. A little more is required: in a word, *understanding*: understanding of the fact that the other person is a human being, not a sex object.

Men in particular need to bear this fact in mind, for far too many of them forget all about the necessity for romance and love. They forget that every woman needs to be carefully and lovingly wooed each time you want to make love to her. It's no good just taking her acquiescence for granted, and climbing aboard every time you feel like a bit of sex. Also, beware of these all-too-common male misconceptions about the female of the species:

★The myth that Anglo-Saxon females (British, Australian, New Zealand, WASP Americans and so on) are embarrassed by romancing, and don't want men to pay them a lot of compliments before, during and after love-making.
★The myth that all women are interested in is the size of your penis.
★The myth that they just want you to ram it in as hard and as fast as possible.
★The myth that they like you to reach a climax quickly (in reality, most ladies prefer it slow and sexy).

But – like men – women also very often fail to understand the emotional needs of their partners. Men *do* have emotions – and are just as partial to a spot of romance. Don't spoil things for your husband/lover by making remarks which take away the romantic glow for him. You'd be surprised how many ladies ruin inter-course for the men who love them by suddenly saying things like:

★'Oh God, I've left the washing machine on'.
★'I think I can hear the children'. (Fit a bolt on the bedroom door, choose your moment and *forget* the children.)
★'Finished, dear? Then pass me a tissue, will you, 'cos I'm bound to be *awfully* messy'. (Wow, what a put-down!)
★Worst of all is the expression which the French claim that Anglo-Saxon girls use just after a man has reached a shatter-ing climax: 'Feeling *better* now, Charles?'

Instead, *much* nicer things for a lady to say before, during and after sex are:

★'Gosh, you're sexy'.
★'You do that marvellously – and it'd be even better if you did it a little more to the left' (or whatever).
★'You look beautiful while you're coming inside me'.
★'That was tremendous. Kiss me'.

And *both* sexes should remember that by far the sexiest phrase you can use in bed (providing you mean it, of course) is the simple phrase:

★'I LOVE YOU'.

CHAPTER TWO

Women's Sexual Areas

'Know thyself' ● *Woman's sexiest areas* ● *Her breasts* ● *Her vaginal area: what you can see* ● *The goodies inside her* ● *Sexually arousable organs nearby* ● *Her cervix* ● *Her womb* ● *Her ovaries* ● *Her 'waterworks' areas* ● *Her secret 'G-spot'* ● *Her bottom.*

'Know thyself'

Recently I had a rather sad letter from a reader of the advice column I run in a British women's magazine. It said:

'Dear Dr Delvin,
   I just can't seem to reach a climax. I know that I should direct my husband's attention to my clitoris.
   But the trouble is that neither of us knows where my clitoris is . . .'

Oh dear! Yet the awful fact is that there are millions like her – both men and women – who aren't too sure where their own (let alone their loved one's) sexual organs are. (And if you don't know how to tickle your wife's ovaries, you could be depriving her of a rare and exotic pleasure.) More seriously, it is of course quite dotty that so many of the population are literally groping around in the dark without any real idea where the clitoris is. For it's quite true that, as the lady above implied in her letter, the clitoris (pronounced 'CLIT-or-iss') is the main (though not the only) key to a woman's sexual pleasure. No wonder that so many poor souls who don't know where to find it have unsatisfactory love lives. If you really know nothing at all about where to locate the nearest clitoris, you'd probably do best to go back and read the preliminary volume of this series, *The Book of Love*. However, I will be touching on the clitoris (so to speak) in the anatomical exposé that follows. First I'll deal with the sexy parts of ladies – and in the next chapter I'll turn to the men.

Women's sexiest areas

It's very important to realise that ladies have all sorts of sexy areas

– so-called 'erogenous zones' – scattered all over their body. Many men don't appreciate this fact, and make the bad mistake of lunging straight at their poor old partner's vaginas without devoting time and attention to these other erogenous zones *first*.

I stress that word 'first', because as a general rule it's necessary for at least some of these other areas to be caressed *before* approaching the vagina. Most women have a real dislike of a 'frontal assault' on the vagina without preliminary caressing of other sexy areas. If a man neglects to stroke and kiss these other parts first, he'll probably find that his lady's 'tunnel of love' is unprepared and unresponsive. Indeed, when couples come to doctors complaining that 'the vagina is too dry, doctor', it very often turns out that the real problem is that the man hasn't been paying anything like enough preliminary attention to their various other sexy zones, and so hasn't stimulated the love juices to flow.

So what are these sexy areas? Well, I'm almost tempted to say that a woman is one great throbbing erogenous zone all over – because really skilful caressing of almost *any* part of her body can get her going, and even make her have a climax. But the main non-genital sexy areas (which, please note, *vary a bit from woman to woman*) are these:

1. Her lips.
2. Her tongue.
3. Her ears.
4. Her neck.
5. Her shoulders.
6. Her armpits.
7. Her spine.
8. Her breasts.
9. Her navel and tummy.
10. Her buttocks.
11. Her thighs.

Also, some women do respond to gentle caressing behind the knees (and there's an old medical student tradition that because the nerve supply of the back of the knee joint is linked with that of the vagina, a quick tickle behind the knees was supposed to make a chap's advances irresistible!)

In addition, some women do like having their feet caressed or, better still, massaged. However, quite a lot of others are so ticklish (or embarrassed about corns or smelly feet or whatever) that they don't like their feet being touched at all. In the chapters on love play, we'll be looking in detail at just what you can do to stimulate these erogenous zones. But meantime, let's move on to the breasts.

Her breasts

Breasts are marvellous things, but the only trouble about them is that these days, people have become almost too obsessed by them. All over the world, there are millions of women who think that their boobs are 'not good enough' or 'absolutely pathetic' – all because they've seen pictures of film stars or pin-ups whose jutting, thrusting mammaries seem to have been designed and built by the same firm who gave you the Colosseum. Sadly, a few husbands take this demeaning viewpoint of their wives' boobs too – and as a result they do stupid things like going off with some other woman just because she has vast cantilevered tits that you could hang your hat on.

Now all this is quite ridiculous! In fact, it's true that your average pin-up photo looks like the girl in Figure 1. But very often this amazing pneumatic appearance is completely falsely achieved. For instance, the pin-up may be:

★ pregnant (it's believed that several 'Playmates of the Month' have been in this condition)
★ a nursing mum (being 'in milk' expands the breasts marvellously too)
★ a girl who's had special silicone bags put into her bosoms by plastic surgery.

FIG. 1

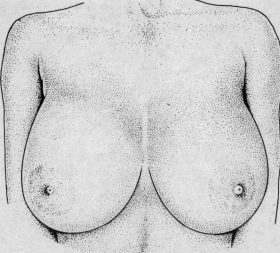

Furthermore, by judicious use of photographic tricks, the photographer may make her seem far vaster than she really is. For instance, he may use a padded stick (cunningly hidden behind the chest) to push a boob further forward. Or he may use transparent sticky tape to give an amazing – but quite unnatural – uplift to the bosom. Or he may just photograph the poor girl on her hands and knees – but with a 'backcloth' which gives the impression that she's upright. This means that sheer gravity makes the breasts stand right out from the body!

Anyway, to cut a long story short, the average breast size in Britain, the USA or Australasia is far, far smaller than most people who've looked at pin-ups imagine. A typical lady's bosoms – when she's feeling fairly sexy – actually look like the ones in Figure 2. If you've got more than that, you're an exception to the rule. What if you've got *less* than the lady shown in Figure 2? No cause for alarm. Bear in mind that:

★Many men actually *prefer* small boobs
★Small ones are *just* as sexually responsive as large ones.

FIG. 2

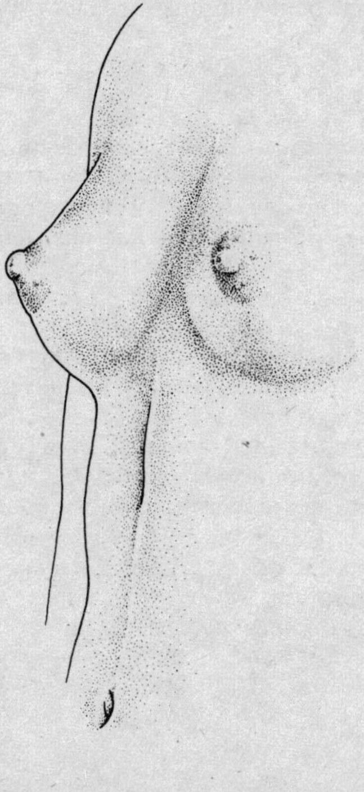

FIG. 3

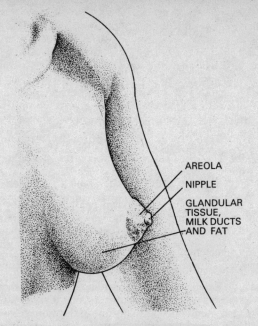

AREOLA

NIPPLE

GLANDULAR
TISSUE,
MILK DUCTS
AND FAT

That brings us to the question of sexual response in boobs. You can see the basic anatomy of the breast in Figure 3. In fact, the whole area is very sensitive to the stimulating techniques described in Chapter 8 – and that's a very fortunate thing. (One woman who'd been unable to reach a climax found that she could do so every time, provided that her husband did what he'd previously failed to do, and caressed her breasts during intercourse. 'Nowadays,' she said later, 'I'd "come" in Trafalgar Square if somebody touched my breasts!')

Though the whole substance of the breast is very susceptible to erotic caresses, it's the central part that is really well supplied with sensory nerve endings. I mean the circle called the areola, and the central projecting part called the nipple. (Many people think that the word 'nipple' means the whole thing, but it just means the bit that sticks out.) The nerves which supply the areola are connected to a special arousal area of the brain – which is why gentle stimulation of this area pays off. And it *must* be gentle – see Chapter 8. The nipple too has rich nerve connections, and it's also got the property of being 'erectile' – which means that when a woman gets excited, it stands up in the same way as a penis does. It's always well worth stimulating the nipple in the ways explained later in the book, in order to make it erect. In general, the more a man can make it stand out, the more his lady will like it. Incidentally, I understand that another trick used by the pin-up photographers mentioned above is to rub (or get the girls to rub) the nipples just before a photo is taken, so as to make them stand out. And they call it 'work'!

Vital Note: Lumps in the breast or sudden inturning of the nipple can mean trouble. *See a doctor within a couple of days if you notice such symptoms.*

Her vaginal area: What you can see

Now to the delicious areas 'down below'. And they really *are* delicious too. I'm appalled at the way in which so many women think that their vulvas (i.e. the visible openings of their vaginas) are 'ugly', 'nasty' or 'dirty'. The vulva and vagina are none of these things. In fact, together they form one of the most remarkable – and beautifully-designed – structures on Earth.

Some men too have this extraordinary idea that there's something 'unpleasant' about the vulva, or that it's 'not hygienic'. Of course it's hygienic! It's normally one of the more germ-free areas of the body, and I think that your average bacteriologist would rather eat his lunch off somebody's vulva than off, say, somebody's nose – any day of the week.

Feminists have quite rightly attacked the demeaning attitude which so many people take to the vulva and vagina, and they've protested about the fact that it's the worst possible insult to call someone a 'cunt'. (True: but it's also a fair-sized insult to call him a 'prick'.) I think that the folly of this stupid and demeaning attitude to the beauteous female organ is all summed up by this poem, composed by an anonymous bard of yesteryear:

The portions of a lady that appeal to Man's depravity
Are fashioned with considerable care;
And what at first appears to be just a modest cavity
Is really an elaborate affair.

Now doctors who have studied these feminine phenomena,
With numerous experiments on dames,
Have looked at all the items of the gentle sex's abdomina,
And given them impressive Latin names.

There's the vulva, the vagina, and of course the perineum,
And the hymen (that is sometimes found in brides),
There's a multitude of little things – you'd love 'em if you saw
*   'em –*
The clitoris, and Lord knows what besides!

What a dreadful pity 'tis, then, that when we people chatter
Of those mysteries to which I have referred,
That we use for such a delicate and complicated matter
Such a very short (and rather vulgar) little word. . . .

Anyway, let's get down to the details of this wonderful structure. And you can see the external details very clearly in the 'full
frontal' in Figure 4. Every man and woman ought to have been
taught where these various bits and pieces are (preferably before
they leave school). But few people have much clue about them –
and that's one reason why so many adults are catastrophically and
even dangerously inept in bed.

Here are a few points of interest about this delicious area,
starting from the top of the drawing.

FIG. 4

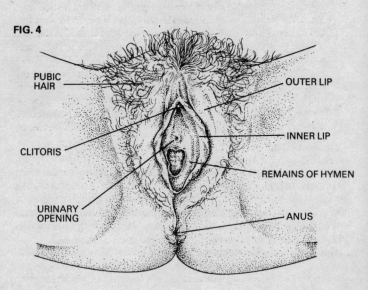

PUBIC HAIR

OUTER LIP

INNER LIP

CLITORIS

REMAINS OF HYMEN

URINARY OPENING

ANUS

THE PUBIC HAIR   This is nice, sexy stuff, and there are ways of stimulating it to arouse your loved one (see Chapter 8). Most books – and all pin-up pictures – show it as a neat triangle, but this is rubbish! Anyone who has seen Glenda Jackson's films knows that it can look more like a long, sexy brush. And in many, many women it spreads far beyond the confines of a triangular shape, so there's not the least need to be embarrassed if *your* 'pubes' spread up towards your navel or down towards your thighs. You can of course *shave* the hair into a triangle if you wish (or use hair-removing creams or electrolysis) but this really isn't necessary.

Some women shave off all their pubic hair to excite their lovers, and this certainly produces an unusual and intriguing appearance. (It also tends to make you a bit prickly and it itches when it grows back.) Anyway, the practice is quite harmless so long as you mind what you do with the razor.

THE OUTER AND INNER LIPS   You can see these in the picture. Their medical names are *labia majora* and the *labia minora*, but the word 'lips' is equally good, because that's what they are. You need only know two things about them:

★Like a man's scrotum (to which the outer lips are the female equivalent) they respond nicely to gentle, sensuous stroking.
★They vary wildly in shape and length from woman to woman: ladies are always getting upset because they think that the size of one or other lip is 'abnormal'. The problem is that they haven't seen many other women stripped, so they don't realise that it's quite OK for the labia to project a very considerable distance. (Incidentally, ladies who go in for nudism aren't troubled by such worries, because they've viewed so many other people's vulvas toasting in the sun that they appreciate that a spot of individual variation is perfectly normal.)

THE CLITORIS   You can see from Figure 4 that this is located *just where the two inner lips (labia minora) meet*. In other words, it's just in front of the opening of the vagina, round about the apex of the pubic triangle of hair – if yours happens to be triangular – and on top of the hard bone which you can feel through the skin at this point.

The fact that it's located over the firm pubic bone is important, as it acts as a really hard base on which to stimulate the clitoris. The recent work of that splendid US sex researcher Ms Shere Hite has made clear that the reason why many women are so sexually dissatisfied is that their partners don't 'grind' the clitoris hard enough against the underlying bone during intercourse (and during love play too).

We'll be coming to techniques of stimulating the clitoris in later chapters of the book. But just in case anybody who's read this far still doesn't realise it, let's make it absolutely clear that THE CLITORIS IS THE **MAIN** KEY TO SEXUAL PLEASURE IN WOMEN. It is so because it's very like the male penis in structure and in sensory nerve supply. Incidentally, some people who've read this statement in books expect the clitoris to *look* like a small penis, and are disappointed (or wonder if things are abnormal) when they find that it doesn't.

Mostly it just looks like the little 'button' shown in Figure 4. Even when it's erect – and it does get erect under stimulation – it never gets much bigger than the tip of a nipple. So don't be alarmed if your clitoris is just a little pink bump. That's what it's supposed to be.

We'll be saying more about the clitoris in the chapters about climaxes and about love play. But just let me stress that – contrary to what so many women have been taught in recent years – there are *other* keys to sexual pleasure apart from the clitoris. And latest research indicates that not all climaxes have to be 'clitoral' ones. For instance, you can have a purely emotional or a vaginal climax too – all will be revealed later in the book!

THE URINARY OPENING   You can see the urinary opening in Figure 4 too. This orifice, I should stress, is *clean*, because (contrary to what so many people think) it's a medical fact that urine is normally a germ-free fluid. So your partner won't catch anything by touching the urinary opening. But one word of warning: *don't shove anything up it* (yes, people are sometimes daft enough to do this!) Popping things up the waterworks will probably introduce infection into the bladder from the outside. Furthermore, the object may disappear up you! This means embarrassing explanations at the hospital, plus an operation to get the object out of the bladder, so forget it.

Similarly, take great care not to put *dirty* fingers on the urinary opening. Many people now seem to go in for such exotic games as fingering the loved one's bottom (i.e. the anus) – but if you do this and then stick the dirty finger over the urinary opening, then a painful bladder infection may follow. The only other thing to be said about the urinary opening is that at moments of climax, it may

16

squirt a jet of urine. (Women who have this tendency may find it easier to make love with a towel under them, especially in hotels.) It can also squirt other things, as will be revealed later in the book.

THE 'VIRGIN'S VEIL' The tattered remnants of the virgin's veil (or 'hymen') are also shown in Figure 4. This is the thin membrane which partly closes off the way to the vagina in virgins. There's nearly always a small hole in it, to let the periods through. Traditionally, this membrane is swept away at the first intercourse, and rude novels make a great old song and dance about this big psychological moment and say how dreadfully painful it is. (Heaven knows what harm has been done to women who've heard that myth!) In fact, the hymen is usually very thin, and in most (not all) cases, breaking it is virtually painless. There may be a few spots of blood. Some 'tags' of the hymen – as in the picture – are left for years afterwards.

These days, many girls' hymens seem to have disappeared by the time they first come to a doctor for examination. It appears likely that many hymens have been broken by use of tampons, or by masturbation or petting, rather than by actual intercourse. Also, some doctors think that the energetic sports which so many teenagers go in for at school may painlessly break the hymen.

Only very, very rarely does an unusually thick hymen prevent intercourse. In such cases, a surgeon can easily 'nick' the membrane and so unblock the passage. But in fact, a large number of the women who are alleged to have had 'thick hymens' have really been suffering from a blockage caused by a very common involuntary contraction of the muscles around the opening of the vagina – see the section on 'vaginismus' in Chapter 19.

Incidentally, once your hymen is gone, it's *gone*. This fact causes great problems for girls from certain countries, where it's expected that a bride will be a virgin – and woe betide her if there aren't a few drops of blood on the nuptial sheet! This difficulty can be overcome, however, and in London, Sydney, New York and other cities a flourishing surgical industry has sprung up – recreating lost virgins' veils! Girls who have loved unwisely in the big city can go to a plastic surgeon and have a new 'hymen' fashioned in a simple operation which at present costs about £250 in Britain and $1000 in the US. Whether it's worth it is another matter, since there are very few males who would have the faintest idea whether they were making love to a virgin or not! In many cases, a little 'maidenly' resistance, a few shrieks, and perhaps even a drop or two of blood on the sheet – from a discreet pin-prick in the finger –

17

may be more than enough. But I ought to make it clear that the 'hymen' created by a surgeon is not a real one. One can scarcely restore true virginity with a surgeon's knife – for, to quote a graffitologist who operates in one of our local girls' schools:

> **'Virginity is like a balloon –**
> **One prick and it's gone.'**

The goodies inside her

Now, on to what lies *inside* the vulva – in other words, the vagina. You can see what it's like in Figure 5.

The word 'vagina' (pronounced 'vaj-EYE-nah', for those many people who are embarrassed about the fact that they can't pro- nounce it) is Latin for 'a sheath'. And that's what it is. It's really a nice, pink, warm, well-cushioned sheath which is admirably de- signed to hold the male penis.

Unfortunately, a lot of people don't realise this, thinking it's a narrow, tight passage up which a penis can only be forced with great difficulty. That's quite untrue! There's really a vast amount of room in the vagina, especially as it 'balloons' out in the most remarkable way during sexual excitement. However, it can also *contract down* in a very nice and sexy way during a climax – hence the popular name of 'the spasm chasm'. (Other names for the vagina include the very apt 'tunnel of love'.)

FIG. 5

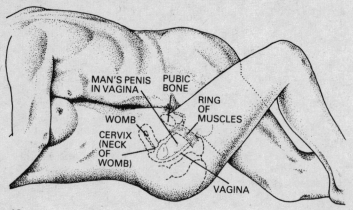

MAN'S PENIS IN VAGINA
PUBIC BONE
RING OF MUSCLES
WOMB
CERVIX (NECK OF WOMB)
VAGINA

The vagina is also *longer* than many men and women think, and unless you have very long fingers, it can be quite difficult to reach the very topmost part of it, which lies behind the cervix (as you can see from Figure 5). When a woman's vagina *lengthens* during sexual excitement, it may be almost impossible to reach the top. What all this means is that almost any woman in the world can 'accommodate' almost any man's penis. Don't believe two common myths about the vagina:

★That a couple don't know if they're 'compatible' until they've tried intercourse – in other words, they don't know if his penis will fit into her vagina.

As a result of the existence of this myth, some men have been known to persuade women to have intercourse 'because I can't marry you unless I know that we fit'. That's crazy! As I've said above, the design of human beings is so remarkable that virtually all men fit into virtually all women (unless the man happens to be a one-in-a-billion anatomical freak, like the gentleman described in the next chapter).

★The second myth is this: that many women are 'small made'.

Lots of ladies believe this about themselves. They find that intercourse is often painful, and they also experience pain when they have a vaginal examination by a doctor. Unfortunately, a few old-fashioned doctors have been known to make things worse by saying, 'Ah yes, m'dear – you're small-made.' In fact, these poor women are virtually *never* 'small-made' at all. If you look again at Figure 5, you'll see the reason for their difficulty: there are muscles which make a circle round the opening of the vagina. These muscles are fairly necessary (for instance, to keep the bath water from getting in), but in order to enjoy good sex, you have to be able to *relax* them. As a rule, ladies who think that they are 'small-made' in the vaginal department simply can't relax these muscles easily. This difficulty – which I've already mentioned briefly above under the heading 'The virgin's veil' – is called 'vaginismus'. It can be treated, and the methods of putting it right are discussed in Chapters 17 to 21.

The muscles can also play an important part in increasing mutual pleasure during love-making, and a woman who is really skilled in bed can use them to 'milk' her loved one's penis. The technique of doing this is explained later in the book. If you think your vaginal muscles are too slack (which is often the case after having children), then have no fear: for I'll be describing ways of toning them in Chapter 13.

To sum up, the whole of the vagina is a nice, warm, pink, moist and very sexually responsive area. Though the clitoris – which we've discussed above – is the most sexually sensitive part of a woman's body, a tremendous amount of sensation comes from those delightful and welcoming vaginal walls. Please see the special note about one newly-discovered part of those walls (the 'G-spot') later in this chapter. I'll be describing how to get the best out of the vagina (so to speak) in the chapters which are devoted to love play and to secret erotic arousal techniques.

Sexually arousable organs nearby

Now on to some interesting sexy bits which are located near the vagina – and which a man can stimulate to give his loved one pleasure, or, indeed, which she can stimulate for herself during love-making – or when she's by herself, if she's feeling sexy and her loved one's not around.

Her cervix

If you don't know where the cervix is, look back at Figure 5. It's also known as 'the neck of the womb'. In fact, if you look at Figure 6, you'll see that it's really the 'tip' of the womb. The cervix can just about be touched by the fingers – and it's easier to feel it if you slip two fingers in *gently*. It's like a soft nose or the top of a thumb to the touch. And you may notice that there's a sort of dimple or dip in the middle of it – this is the opening of the narrow channel that leads up into the womb itself.

Cervixes are funny things. Some seem to be very rich in nerve endings, while others aren't. When a lady has an IUD (coil, loop, etc.) put in, the doctor usually has to put a small clip on the cervix for a minute or so. Some women find this very painful – while others appear to have no nerves in the area and can't feel a thing. Similarly, some ladies seem to have little or no sexual sensation from the cervix. Others derive a lot of pleasure from having it touched – and these are the girls who derive particular pleasure from *deep thrusting* at the end of intercourse, as they feel the tip of the man's penis hitting the cervix. So it's well worth gently stimulating your loved one's cervix with one of the techniques outlined later in the book, and seeing what happens.

Caution: a few women experience *pain* when the cervix is touched, and this is frequently a symptom of some gynaecological

20

problem which needs sorting out. Most commonly it's just an erosion (raw patch) on the cervix, but *always* see a doctor and have it checked.

Bleeding after intercourse or *bleeding between the periods* is often due to disorders of the cervix. One of these disorders can be very serious indeed – so a vital rule that everyone should know is this: UNEXPLAINED BLEEDING AFTER SEX IS A SYMPTOM WHICH SHOULD ALWAYS BE INVESTIGATED BY A DOCTOR, PARTICULARLY IF THE WOMAN IS OVER THIRTY. It may well be nothing serious – but don't take chances.

Her womb

The womb (or uterus, to give it its medical name) is a pretty sexy organ. It contracts violently during a woman's climax – and a lot of ladies reckon that they can actually feel this rhythmic spasm at the height of their pleasure. So it's not surprising that gentle (once again, repeat *gentle*) manipulation of the womb can give quite a few women a very nice feeling indeed.

This technique – which really should only be attempted by advanced lovers who know how to approach the upper reaches of a woman's vagina without hurting her – is described later in the

FIG. 6

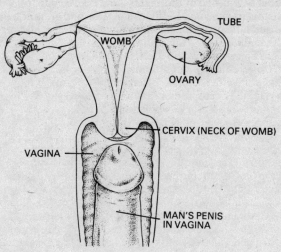

TUBE
WOMB
OVARY
CERVIX (NECK OF WOMB)
VAGINA
MAN'S PENIS
IN VAGINA

book. You can see where the womb lies (in relation to the vagina and the ovaries) in Figure 6.

Her ovaries

Two more sexually arousable organs lying near the vagina are the ovaries – the pair of sex glands which produce lots of female hormones, and also the monthly 'egg' (ovum). Their position is shown in Figure 6. The ovaries are actually very, very like a man's testicles (balls). They're formed from exactly the same sort of tissue, and so they're very sensitive to the touch. Of course, most women are unaware of this because the ovaries, unlike a man's testicles, are deep inside the body, and therefore protected from the occasional flying knee or pubic uppercut to which men are so vulnerable in sporting (or, indeed, sexual) activities. But in addition to being sensitive to pain, the ovaries – just like the testicles – are also *sexually* sensitive, and can therefore be a source of considerable pleasure to a woman.

However, have a care, gentlemen. If you use the technique of stimulating the ovaries which I describe later in the book, you must do it very delicately – with the same care and consideration that you'd wish a lady to use when she takes *your* two most prized possessions in her hands.

Her 'waterworks area'

You can see from Figure 7 that the bladder and urethra are in very close and intimate proximity with her vagina. Her bladder is just

FIG. 7

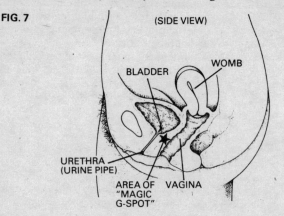

(SIDE VIEW)

WOMB

BLADDER

URETHRA
(URINE PIPE)

AREA OF
"MAGIC
G-SPOT"

VAGINA

above and in front of the upper part of her vagina. And the urethra runs down immediately in front of the front wall of the vagina. There's no doubt that quite a lot of women derive sexual pleasure from these areas of their bodies – and I hasten to say that there's nothing 'kinky' or wrong in that. I'll be describing the technique of stimulating them in later chapters, but basically all you need to know is that if you gently slip two fingers into the vagina and stroke the *front* wall of it with the pads of your finger-tips, this will very likely produce pleasing sensations for your lady-love.

Her secret 'G-spot'

Very recent research carried out in the USA and Canada has shown that in many women there is an extraordinarily sensitive sexual area at the point shown in Figure 7. It's called the 'Grafenberg spot' or 'G-spot' for short – after an early sexologist named Ernst Grafenberg. (No, this is not a hoax!)

At the moment, no-one is quite clear whether the 'G-spot' is really located deep in the front wall of the vagina – or perhaps in the urethra (urinary pipe) itself. But the really important things about it are these:

★It's easy to stimulate
★Stimulating it can help women who can't have orgasms
★It seems to give some women a 'vaginal' (rather than a clitoral) orgasm – which is a nice alternative for them.

At the moment, very few people even know of the existence of the 'secret G-spot'. When the technique of stimulating it becomes better known, this should help a lot of anorgasmic (i.e. non-climaxing) women throughout the world.

I'll be dealing with the Grafenberg spot more fully in Chapter 4 (which is mainly about climaxes). And I'll be describing the technique of stimulating it in the chapters on love play and intercourse.

Her bottom

And now, to finish off the list of 'sexually arousable organs near the vagina', I come – with some diffidence, as befits the subject, – to the lady's rear end. Why diffidence? Well, let me say to begin with that I feel this is a subject which *has* to be dealt with, simply because of the fact that so many couples these days go in for 'bottom play'. A recent British Medical Association booklet estimated that one in five married couples had tried actual inter-course up the *derrière*, and it's quite obvious to me from my postbag that a far higher proportion of adults regularly go in for such games as tickling the loved one's backside and so on. The 1983 *Playboy* Sex Survey showed that such practices are incredibly widespread.

But the big problem is this. The bottom – unlike the area of the vulva and vagina – is certainly NOT a clean area of the body (as more perceptive readers will doubtless have noticed). The buttocks themselves are generally quite OK from a hygienic point of view, so stroking or slapping your loved one's rounded *derrière* is perfectly safe. But it must be admitted that the anus and rectum (the anus is the actual hole, while the rectum is the tube inside – see Figure 8) are usually contaminated with some sort of germs.

FIG. 8

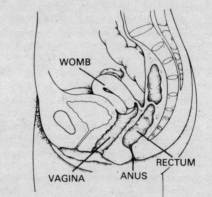

That applies to *any* human being, no matter how hygiene-conscious she or he may be. The only exception might be when a person has just had a warm bath – or perhaps a soapy session on the bidet. Even then, however, there's a certain risk that the anus may have dodgy germs on it. (This is, I'm afraid, the reason why rather a lot of gay blokes get various infections like hepatitis.) But in a world in which popular novels and films – like *Last Tango in Paris* – unblushingly mention love play involving sticking butter up the bottom, and in which sex shops openly sell rectal vibrators and 'bum beads' (you pull them out of the lady's *cul* just as she reaches her climax), it's important that we should discuss such matters. And I'll be doing just that – and telling you how to avoid health risks – in the chapters on love play.

CHAPTER THREE

Men's Sexual Areas

Knowing what men are like ● *Man's sexiest areas* ● *His penis* ●
Sexually arousable organs nearby: His testicles ● *His pubic hair* ●
His perineum ● *His bottom* ● *His prostate.*

Knowing what men are like

There's a story about a biology class at a US women's college. The
lecturer asked one of the group – a very sexy blonde – to come up
to the blackboard and draw the male organ. The blonde took the
chalk and very confidently drew a most uncompromisingly erect
penis. 'Er . . . fine,' said the lecturer, looking slightly embarrassed. 'But don't you think we'd better start by drawing it . . . uh
. . . the other way?' The blonde's blue eyes filled with puzzle-
ment. '*What* other way?' she demanded.

That story is probably totally bogus – but it does illustrate the
point that, just as men don't know as much as they should about
the way ladies are made, the female of the species often knows less
than enough about the male. A true illustration of this fact is
provided by a recent medical survey which was designed to find
out whether wives gained any health benefits if their husbands had
undergone circumcision. The whole study foundered because it
turned out that a very high proportion of women hadn't the
faintest idea whether their menfolk were circumcised or not. A
more extreme case of female ignorance about the male genitalia
was that of a girl of about twenty who had seen some classical
statuary – and who seriously believed that men had a sort of
'fig-leaf' down below!

But even the most well-educated and sophisticated
people have some rather odd misconceptions about the way that
men are built. So let's do our best to provide an advanced course
in male sexual anatomy.

Man's sexiest areas

Man's sexiest area is, of course, his penis, of which more in a
moment. But it's important for a woman to realise that there are
lots of other areas where he likes to be stimulated too. Top of the
list come his lips and tongue, which are very vulnerable to sexual

25

stimulation, using some of the techniques described in the chapters on love play. But you'll also find that your man derives considerable pleasure from gentle feminine stimulation of these areas:

★ His nipples – yes, these are sexy parts in men too!
★ His muscles – even if he's no Charles Atlas, he'll like to have them stroked and admired.
★ His arm-pits – these are very primitive erotic sexual areas, so kiss and nuzzle them. (Let's hope your man uses a reasonable amount of soap, water and maybe deodorant – though in fact, the armpits produce a special chemical called a 'pheromone' which is a turn-on for the female, so often it's a good idea for men *not* to over-do the deodorant.)
★ His neck – nuzzling and snuggling up to him around his neck area will turn him on, and also make him feel masculine and protective (the old Male Chauvinist Pig!)
★ His ears – gentle blowing and kissing inside his ears is good too, particularly when accompanied by murmurings of sweet nothings, whether romantic or rude (or preferably both).

More details of how to caress these sexy areas appear in the chapters on love play.

His penis

A man's most important sexual part – probably the most precious part of his body to him – is his penis. Whole volumes have been written about this remarkable organ – indeed, there's an elegant and erudite monograph on the subject by a well-known and appropriately named British GP, Dr Dick Richards. It's simply called *The Penis* (New York: Valentine Products, Inc). And it's an indication of the public's passionate interest in this subject that Dr Richards' book has sold in such vast numbers in the USA that he was able to buy a Rolls-Royce out of the proceeds. Anyway, I'll try to encapsulate what you need to know about the penis (whether you're male or female) in just a few pages.

First thing to realise is that it's a very cleverly-designed organ – and a very beautiful one too. '*Beautiful?*' I hear you cry. 'Is this man Delvin gay, or something?' No, he isn't. But I long ago rejected the crazy convention that the human body is wondrous in its beauty – all except for its sex organs.

I referred to this absurd Victorian idea in the last chapter on female anatomy, when I made the point that it's pretty foolish to think that women are beautiful everywhere except their vulvas. In precisely the same way, it's daft to say that almost the entire male body is magnificent, aesthetically satisfying and a fit subject for great artists – all except for the penis.

Of course the male organ is beautiful! Curiously enough though, there's also something inherently *humorous* about it. That slightly bizarre curved shape (all too reminiscent of bananas and sausages and cucumbers) has been a wonderful source of laughter for comedians for hundreds of years.

Indeed, this quaint combination of attractiveness and humour in the shape of the penis is so extraordinary that it almost makes one feel that it really *was* 'designed' to give both pleasure and laughter to the human race. Perhaps – to borrow Shakespeare's words – 'there's a Divinity that shapes our ends . . .'

However, though the penis is extraordinarily attractive to women, men have to bear two things in mind:

★The attraction is a subtle one: women don't really think to themselves 'What a vast penis! I must have it!!!' – as men so often imagine. In fact, many ladies much prefer a smaller – and more easily-accommodated – penis.

★As I've indicated above, lots of women – like lots of men – have wrongly been conditioned to regard the penis as 'ugly' or 'revolting' ('Don't look, Clarissa – it's not a pretty sight!'). It often takes a girl some time to overcome these Victorian attitudes, and to learn really to like her man's penis. For instance, even today some women can't bring themselves to touch their husband's 'John Thomases' until many months after they get married – if at all!

THE ANATOMY   Now to the actual anatomy of the 'cock', 'prick', 'dick', or whatever you prefer to call it. (Incidentally, I think it's important that a couple should have words for their sex organs which they can mutually use – far too many husbands and wives who've been married for years can only say embarrassedly to each other 'Would you like me to . . . uh . . . rub your . . . uh . . . uh . . . you know?')

The penis is a fleshy organ, which in its non-erect or limp state is usually about 3 in to 4 in (7.5 cm to 10 cm) long. But length varies very greatly – depending on such factors as whether it's a cold day, or whether he's had sex the night before, or whether there's a nice-looking or friendly girl in the same room with him. In the erect condition, as the great US sex researchers Masters and

Johnson have demonstrated, most men's penises are roughly *the same length* – about 6½ in (or 16.5 cm). Most men don't realise this, since (unless they're gay, or go to orgies) they've rarely seen another man erect. They only see other males in the 'limp' condition – in changing-rooms and so on. And very often, the other guy in the changing room will look much bigger than you – simply because you get a 'foreshortened' view of your own cock.

Another source of male confusion over average penile size is the current boom in blue movies/videos. These often feature strangely-deformed gentlemen whose phalluses (I suspect) have been artificially stretched to abnormal lengths by hanging weights on them for long periods. In Britain, a man known as 'King Dong' has made a thriving career for himself in the porno industry, simply because he has a penis which is about *two feet* long in the limp condition. One of the medical journals where I work was recently sent a photo of this man sitting astride a lady's hips. His penis stretched up her tummy and chest to just under her chin – and she was looking distinctly apprehensive (as well she might).

In the accompanying volume in this series, *The Book of Love*, I've explained at great length (sorry!) that men worry far, far too much over the measurements of their penises – so much so that a fair proportion of the male sex would give almost anything to have an extra inch or two of length! Some idiots, I suppose, would like to be like King Dong.

Women will know how stupid all this is, and that you couldn't care less whether a man has five inches or nine inches, provided that he's loving and tender and considerate. But be sympathetic to us poor males and our phallic fantasies – and if your man obviously wants you to tell him that he's got an absolutely enormous cock, then do him a favour and tell him so.

THE INTERNAL STRUCTURE The interior of the penis is made up of a large number of cavities which can fill up with blood during sexual excitement. It's this 'filling-up' (tumescence) which causes erection and makes the penis stiffen. In full erection, some men come up to the near-vertical angle shown in Figure 9, while others come up to about a horizontal level. Either way, the state of being erect or 'stiff' enables the man to penetrate the lady.

In practice, many men have considerable difficulty in achieving erection. This is mainly because of anxiety. When a fellow is worried – and especially if he's worried about his sexual performance – his nervous system releases hormones including adrenaline (known in the USA and some other countries as epinephrine). These are chemicals which prepare the body for 'fight, flight or fright'. Unfortunately, while this stuff is great for getting you geared up for battles and races and arguments, it has the sad side-effect of giving you a very, very limp 'dick'. We'll come to ways of dealing with this widespread difficulty in the chapters on sex problems.

FIG. 9 FORESKIN
WHICH HAS
ROLLED BACK IN ERECTION

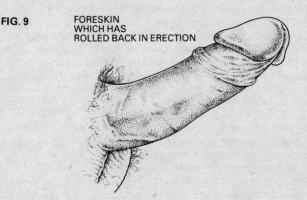

THE SKIN OF THE PENIS The nice thing about the soft skin of the penis is that it's terrifically sensitive sexually. Almost anything a woman does to it – from tickling it with a feather duster to giving it a good rub-down with warm, soapy water – will be very pleasant for her man. A list of exotic things you can do to your partner's organ is included in the chapters on love play. Incidentally, the tip of the penis – known as the 'glans' – is exquisitely sensitive, and there are nice things you can do to that as well. But ladies should take it just a little bit easy with this purplish-coloured 'head' of the penis, because it's probably the most sensitive part of a man's body – and you don't want to hurt him. Follow the instructions in Chapters 9 and 11, and you'll be OK. But don't be afraid to stimulate the glans, because that's what men really love. And – as a medical friend of mine once sagely remarked – 'the Devil makes work for idle glans. . . .'

THE FORESKIN I've dealt with the basic facts about the foreskin and circumcision very fully in the previous volume in this series, *The Book of Love*. However, I find that even advanced lovers are a bit confused about where the foreskin (prepuce) is attached, and what happens when it's removed. We've tried to make this clear in

Figure 9a. In the USA, most men are still circumcised. In Britain, very few now are. In Australia and New Zealand circumcision is still fairly popular, depending to some extent on the parents' religion. But from a *sexual* point of view, the important thing to grasp is this: it doesn't matter whether a man is circumcised or not.

FIG. 9a

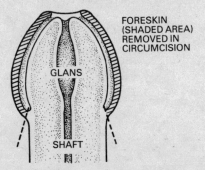

FORESKIN
(SHADED AREA)
REMOVED IN
CIRCUMCISION

GLANS

SHAFT

Way back in 1966, the US sex researchers Masters and Johnson showed with tests involving pinpricks that there was no difference in sensitivity between the glans of the circumcised penis and the glans of the uncircumcised one. However, I think that there's one important exception to this rule. That great and courageous American Dr Alfred Kinsey found that quite a substantial proportion of uncircumcised adult men have one big problem: *when they're erect, their foreskins don't go back*. You can see what I mean by looking at the poor bloke whose erect penis is shown in Figure 10.

So, in this significant minority of men, the glans isn't ever exposed. This certainly makes intercourse less satisfactory. Perhaps more important, it means that things are much less hygienic than they should be.

An uncircumcised man needs to pull back his foreskin more or less every day to wash. If he doesn't do this, an unaesthetic cheesy material called 'smegma' accumulates under the foreskin, and irritation may well develop. It's thought that in the long term this irritation could lead to cancer of the penis (admittedly, a rare disease). But there's also some evidence that chronic irritation under the foreskin could possibly be a factor in giving a man's sexual partner cancer of the cervix. Sadly, this is a moderately common – and often fatal – disease of women.

So, the message is clear. If an adult male's foreskin doesn't 'go back', he should get himself circumcised. (This is a fairly trivial operation for an adult.) In addition, let me stress that every man – particularly every uncircumcised man – should try and wash himself 'down below' once a day. I'm constantly amazed at how fellows who keep their penises in the most appalling hygienic condition seriously expect women to 'go down' on them – i.e. give them oral sex.

FIG. 10

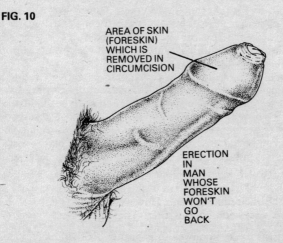

AREA OF SKIN (FORESKIN) WHICH IS REMOVED IN CIRCUMCISION

ERECTION IN MAN WHOSE FORESKIN WON'T GO BACK

Remember, gents – it's an insult to a woman to offer her your penis – whether to put in her mouth or her vagina – if it isn't tolerably clean. Would *you* want something unwashed, un-pleasant-tasting and unhygienic pushed into *your* mouth? (If the answer's 'yes', then I suggest you try the food at one of our local hospitals.)

Sexually Arousable Organs Nearby

Although a man's anatomy isn't nearly as complex as a woman's, it's important for a lady who wants to be a skilled lover to remember that the penis isn't everything where male sexuality is concerned. As is the case with women, the richness of the sensual nerve supply in the whole pelvic area means that there are various parts near your loved one's penis which are well worth stimulat-ing. And these are what they are:

31

His testicles

A man's testicles (or 'balls' as they seem to be generally known throughout the English-speaking world) are the equivalent of the female ovaries. In other words, they're the sex glands and they produce the male 'seed' (sperms). They are sexually sensitive, and men do like their ladies to hold them in their hands and make idiotic complimentary remarks about them. ('Heavens, but they're lovely, Cedric.')

But don't forget that they're also more sensitive to pain than any part of a man's anatomy. So treat them gently: many a promising bed-time session has been halted when a lady has inadvertently lifted a brisk knee into her loved ones *balles*, with all the subtlety of a Welsh Rugby forward.

Incidentally, if your fellow has been unlucky enough to lose a ball through disease or injury (don't worry, bed-time injuries are never *that* serious – I mean sporting or road traffic or industrial injuries), it's now a fairly easy matter to get a urological surgeon (urologist) to fit a plastic replacement which feels just right. The operation can be quite expensive, especially as the plastic 'balls' are themselves quite pricey, but it may be well worth it because of the help it'll give the man's self-esteem.

His perineum

The perineum is the area of skin between the testicles and the anus. In British Commonwealth countries, it's still sometimes spelt 'the perinaeum'. In the past, this is said to have led to marvellous confusion with the Athenaeum – an ecclesiastically-orientated gentlemen's club which I gather offers a good deal less fun than the perinaeum, though one does tend to meet rather more bishops there.

Anyway, the perineum is very sexually sensitive, and all you need to know about it is that it's very nice for a bloke if you tickle/caress/kiss him there. It's generally accepted that that's what pop star Sylvia meant in her famous hit *E Viva Espana* when she sang of kissing your favourite matador 'behind the castanets'. However, the perineum is in quite close proximity to the bottom and you certainly shouldn't kiss it unless your chap is clean and hygienically-minded. How wise the French were to invent the *bidet*!

His bottom

And now we come to your man's bottom. If you've read what we've said about ladies' backsides in the last chapter, you'll know that:

★ It's now very common for lovers to go in for 'bottom play'
★ *Avant-garde* marriage manuals cheerfully advise this sort of thing as though it were completely harmless
★ Films like *Last Tango in Paris* take it for granted – there was even a French cinematic successor with the appalling title of *Coupez vos ongles et passez le beurre* ('Cut your fingernails and pass the butter').

But, but, BUT – there are certain very real hygienic dangers in mucking about with your man's backside. The common practice called *postillionage* (which simply means putting your finger in his anus) will probably give him pleasure – but could cause infections if you're not careful. This subject is discussed further in the chapters on love play – and I reckon that you certainly should not engage in these techniques without reading the hygienic advice given in those chapters.

Incidentally, I ought to say that – despite the hygienic risks – there's nothing kinky or perverted about either a man or a woman deriving pleasure from bottom stimulation. The design of the human body is such that the nerve supply of the bottom makes it quite inevitable that skilfully applied stimulation in that area can produce sexual responses in the spinal cord and brain. (If you don't like this fact, I'm sorry: complain to the Designer.) In practice, many women can reach a climax through bottom stimulation alone. This doesn't usually seem to apply to men – but most of them do enjoy being 'attacked in the rear' by a pretty woman with a well-lubricated finger, provided that they're not too hung-up about the whole idea to enjoy it, or not suffering from a sore anus at the time. Deriving pleasure from this region doesn't imply homosexuality, as some folk imagine. However, I repeat that caressing the bottom can be very dodgy from a health point of view. Don't do it unless you've read Chapters 10 and 11 and considered the implications.

His prostate gland

Every man has a sex gland called the prostate – which half the world's English-speaking population think is called 'the

FIG. 11

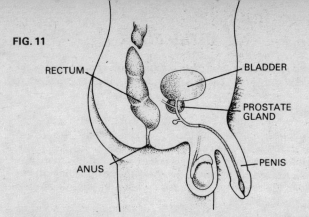

RECTUM

BLADDER

PROSTATE
GLAND

PENIS

ANUS

prostrate'. It isn't – the word is 'prostate'. (Pronounced 'PROSS-tate'.) The prostate's main function is to add a contribution to the seminal fluid – a contribution which probably helps to 'nourish' the sperm as they set off on their journey to fertilise an egg. The fact that the secretion from the prostate increases the volume of a man's seminal fluid is probably a factor in increasing the intensity of his climax – a subject discussed further in the next chapter.

You can see where the prostate gland is located in Figure 11. It's about the size of a horse chestnut, and the urinary pipe runs straight through it (which is why enlargement of the prostate in middle and later life often gives men waterworks trouble).

However, what concerns us here is the fact that the prostate is another sexually-arousable organ. Stimulation of it can give a man intense pleasure – and even make his seminal fluid 'leap' much further at a climax. This is good news, I hear you cry! But now comes the *bad* news.

Look again at Figure 11, and you'll see that, alas, the only access to the prostate is through the bottom. So, though it is quite easy for a lady to reach her man's prostate in the way explained in Chapter 11, and to massage it in such a way as to give him a fairly exotic sensual experience, nonetheless once again this is a technique which carries hygienic risks – unless you know what you're doing. Harold Robbins' best-sellers have popularised all over the world the idea of a dusky maiden stroking the hero's prostate and bringing him to a shattering climax, and I must admit that the technique has a certain value – especially if your man has problems with getting aroused, with getting an erection, or with reaching a climax. But please do *not* use it until you've carefully studied the hygienic advice given in Chapter 11.

CHAPTER FOUR

How Everything Works – Or How To Get To A Climax In Four Easy Stages!

What's a climax? ● Don't forget romance ● The four stages in both sexes ● Multiple climaxes: the truth ● A woman's climax ● What makes her climax? ● The great 'Do women ejaculate?' controversy.

What's a climax?

It's very hard to describe the climax, or moment of orgasm, in either men or women. Often, doctors say to female patients: 'Do you ever have a climax?' – to which they get the hesitant reply: 'Well, I'm not sure . . .' To put it bluntly, if you're not sure whether you've ever had a climax, then you've never had one. It's usually such a shattering and mind-blowing experience – in both men and women – that no-one can really be in much doubt as to whether they've just had one or not. A whole lot of nerve circuits fire off deep down in your pelvis, causing rhythmic spasms in the sexual parts of the body. In time with these violently pleasurable contractions, nerve impulses rush upwards from the sex organs to the spinal cord – and thence to the brain, where they should produce an overwhelming sense of delight. Indeed, the ecstatic experience may sometimes be so powerful that some people practically pass out at that wonderful moment when 'all the fuses blow'. No wonder that Jacobean poets like John Donne used the euphemistic word 'die' when they meant 'reach a climax'.

As Hemingway said in *For Whom The Bell Tolls*, there really are a few occasions when this experience is so extreme that it feels as if (to quote his famous phrase) 'the Earth moves'. But such moments of almost mystical ecstasy are frankly rare, even between those who are very much in love. And sadly, I must admit that when things aren't going right for a couple, and particularly when a relationship is grubby or sordid, or when it was once loving but now seems to have turned sour or stale, there are times when a climax really isn't very satisfying: when it's more of an *anti*-climax in fact. We'll be looking at ways of improving this situation in subsequent chapters. The first way of improving matters is discussed in the next section, entitled 'Don't forget romance'.

Don't forget romance

You may remember that the foreword of this book was also called 'Don't forget romance and laughter – and love!' I'm just repeating that message here because it applies with such importance to the subject of climaxes. There's far too great a tendency these days to regard orgasm as the be-all and end-all of love and love-making. Couples tend to settle down to a session of love-play and intercourse as though they were embarking on the Olympic marathon. Grim-faced Jim is determined to 'hold on' as long as possible and not to reach his climax until his missus is herself on the orgasmic heights; while up-tight Ethel, his poor wife or girlfriend, is lying there in a state of monumental anxiety, wondering if tonight she'll be able to 'come' – or whether all the techniques which Jim is using so doggedly on her will once again fail. This is a recipe for disaster.

Couples in this situation really need to *relax*. The secret of reaching a good climax at the right time is not even to try. Instead, just devote yourself to the romance and love of the moment. Gently and lovingly explore the mutual pleasure which you can give each other. Take delight in the reactions you can evoke in one another – and relish the sensations that your loved one's fingers or lips (or just *words*) can produce in you. There's help later in this book for those who have trouble with their climaxes. But if you begin by following the advice above, you'll find that the whole business of 'coming' – and 'coming' at the right time – will soon (with a bit of luck) be very much easier.

The four stages of a climax

There are actually four basic stages of a climax in both men and women. This was worked out some years ago by the great US sex researchers Dr William Masters and Mrs Virginia Johnson (nowadays Dr & Mrs Masters), who got up to some truly amazing laboratory experiments, with cameras inside the vagina, artificial penises and Heaven knows what else. Though some people disapproved strongly of the Masters' experiments on the hundreds of volunteers who cheerfully had climaxes in the lab. for them, the fact is that this work taught us far more about the human orgasm (male and female) than we ever knew before. Out of the Masters' work grew wonderful new methods of treating the various sexual disorders – particularly disorders of orgasm – to which there had previously been no medical answer.

Now let's look at the four stages of orgasm, as revealed by the Masters' work. They're shown graphically in Figure 12 (the male

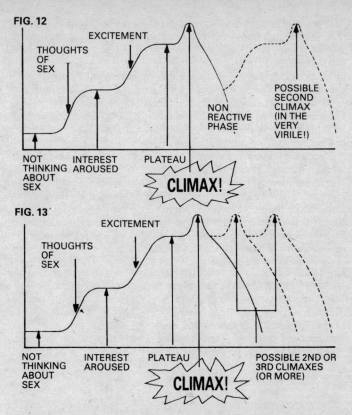

FIG. 12

EXCITEMENT

THOUGHTS OF SEX

NON REACTIVE PHASE

POSSIBLE SECOND CLIMAX (IN THE VERY VIRILE!)

NOT THINKING ABOUT SEX

INTEREST AROUSED

PLATEAU

CLIMAX!

FIG. 13

EXCITEMENT

THOUGHTS OF SEX

NOT THINKING ABOUT SEX

INTEREST AROUSED

PLATEAU

POSSIBLE 2ND OR 3RD CLIMAXES (OR MORE)

CLIMAX!

climax) and in Figure 13 (the female climax). You can see that in both sexes before anything happens, there's a stage of 'general interest'. Many men – and quite a few women – are basically in this stage a fair amount of the time: in other words, they have a pleasant awareness of the opposite sex.

Note: failure to get into this pleasant preliminary stage of potential excitability is termed by famous US sexologist Dr Helen Singer Kaplan 'disorder of desire'. Ways of treating it are described later in this book.

First stage As you see from the two diagrams the first stage is the *stage of excitement*, when the person's sexual drive really starts building up, as the possibility of intercourse begins to impinge on the deep emotional centres in the brain. Naturally, skilled love

37

play and a romantic atmosphere help the man or woman to enter this 'excitement phase'. In fact, many people need a good deal of manual love play to achieve it – specially if they're past the first flush of youth.

In men, the stage of excitement is characterised by erection of the penis. In women, it's characterised by a sudden and noticeable increase in lubrication of the vaginal walls – leading to a certain pleasing honeyed dampness 'down below'. It's also characterised by a relaxation of the vaginal muscles which (as already explained in Chapter 2) form a sphincter at the opening of the vagina.

Research seems to indicate that this stage of excitement is at least partly due to the release into the bloodstream of chemicals which are formed by what is called the 'parasympathetic nervous system'. The 'parasympathetic' is the antagonist of the better-known 'sympathetic nervous system'. The 'sympathetic' is the one which releases the well-known 'fright, flight, fight' hormone called adrenalin (or epinephrine) and similar chemicals into the bloodstream. Figure 14 may make this clearer. In fact, the very

FIG. 14

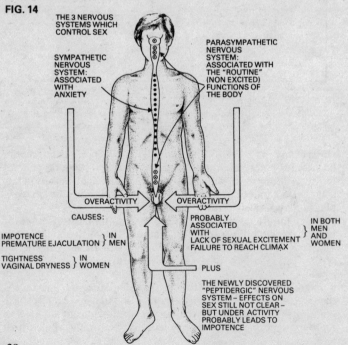

THE 3 NERVOUS SYSTEMS WHICH CONTROL SEX

SYMPATHETIC NERVOUS SYSTEM: ASSOCIATED WITH ANXIETY

PARASYMPATHETIC NERVOUS SYSTEM: ASSOCIATED WITH THE "ROUTINE" (NON EXCITED) FUNCTIONS OF THE BODY

OVERACTIVITY OVERACTIVITY

CAUSES:

IMPOTENCE PREMATURE EJACULATION } IN MEN

TIGHTNESS VAGINAL DRYNESS } IN WOMEN

PROBABLY ASSOCIATED WITH LACK OF SEXUAL EXCITEMENT FAILURE TO REACH CLIMAX } IN BOTH MEN AND WOMEN

PLUS

THE NEWLY DISCOVERED "PEPTIDERGIC" NERVOUS SYSTEM – EFFECTS ON SEX STILL NOT CLEAR – BUT UNDER ACTIVITY PROBABLY LEADS TO IMPOTENCE latest research indicates that there's a *third* nerve network (the 'peptidergic nervous system') which is also closely involved with sexual arousal – through releasing a hormone called 'VIP'. When we get the chemistry sorted out, it may be possible to use drugs acting on this newly-discovered nerve network in order to treat serious disorders like impotence.

It's a little complicated, but it is worth going into such detail, because if the excitement phase (which prepares your penis or your vagina for intercourse) is at least partly under the control of the parasympathetic nervous system, then overactivity of the sympathetic will foul you up badly.

In other words, *if you're over-anxious, tense or frightened, the chemicals released by the sympathetic nervous system will screw up your excitement phase completely*. Thus:

★If you're a man, you won't get a decent erection
★If you're a woman, your vagina will remain unlubricated and tight.

So, fear and tension – and also certain tablets which you might be taking with or without medical advice – can make the sympathetic overpower the parasympathetic, and so ruin the excitement phase. We'll deal with ways of countering this later in the book.

Second stage   Happily, most lovers pass pleasurably through the excitement phase and on to the second stage, which, as you'll see by turning back to the two diagrams (Figure 12 and Figure 13), is called the 'plateau phase'. Basically, this is the very nice stage when the lovers have got going, and are in a high stage of sexual excitement but are in control of themselves. That's the vital thing, particularly where men are concerned. If a man only has a very, very short 'plateau phase' he'll fire off much, much too soon.

In other words, he'll be a 'premature ejaculator' – and there's no ways he's going to satisfy his loved one. The problem of premature ejaculation (or 'hair trigger trouble', as this all-too-common disorder is often called) is discussed later in this chapter. Happily, sufferers will find that it's easily treatable today, and treatment is explained further on in the book.

It's nice for a woman to stay in her 'plateau phase' for a while too. Indeed, many couples happily remain in this phase – either caressing each other or having actual intercourse – for perhaps half an hour at a time. (To my surprise, I was once quoted in a French magazine as saying that '*aujourd'hui, toutes les femmes anglaises demandent une bonne demie-heure.'* Not quite true, but a nice idea!) But – in contrast to men – it doesn't matter quite so much if the woman gets carried away rather sooner than she meant to, and goes 'over the top' into actual orgasm. Admittedly, if she's a lady who only has one climax a night (and if she was hoping for a simultaneous orgasm with her lover) then she definitely won't want to move on to the actual climax quite so soon. If she feels herself going, she can just tell her partner to take it easy with his caresses for a bit. If she herself then takes a few really deep-down relaxing breaths right down into her tummy, then the need to reach an immediate climax will go away.

However, lots of women do actually have *multiple* climaxes during a love-making session – as we'll see in a moment. And for them it clearly doesn't matter a hoot if they have an orgasm (or a dozen orgasms) while their lovers are still in the plateau stage.

Third stage If you just look back at those two diagrams again (Figures 12 and 13), you'll see that the third stage is of course that of orgasm itself. In both men and women, this marvellous moment seems – according to latest research – to be largely under the control of the sympathetic nervous system.

You'll remember from what I said above that that's the nerve system that's concerned with 'fight, flight and fright'. It's the one that produces adrenalin (epinephrine). And it's the one that is *opposed* by the parasympathetic nervous system. Once more, there's a point to this complex explanation.

If a man's got too much of his sympathetic going (in other words, if he's nervous and het up) then he'll have far too much adrenalin (epinephrine) whizzing round his bloodstream, and he won't be able to stop himself 'coming'. This is the condition that I referred to earlier: premature ejaculation. There's unfortunately a lot of it about – literally millions of Americans, Canadians, British, Australians and indeed Europeans ejaculate as soon as they get inside their partners' vaginas. Not much chance of a '*bonne demie-heure*' there! Still, as I've said above, treatment is now highly successful – see Chapters 17 to 21.

To recap: *excessive sympathetic nervous system stimulation* (normally caused by anxiety, but sometimes by pills) has two effects on men.

1. It gives them trouble in getting an erection – in other words, it helps to keep them 'floppy' or impotent.
2. It makes them 'come' too soon – in other words, it makes them premature ejaculators.

So it's no surprise that many poor chaps who have 'PE' (premature ejaculation) also have difficulties with their potency. I repeat: both *can* be treated.

Conversely, there are a much smaller number of men who seem to have plenty of parasympathetic drive – but very little adrenalin (epinephrine) coming from the sympathetic nervous system. These chaps often seem to me to be of a rather phlegmatic, non-excitable disposition. They're the reverse of the over-excitable, finely-triggered premature-ejaculator. Instead, their problem is that *they can't reach a climax*. It may seem incredible, yet this is a well recognised medical condition (which can also be caused by over-the-counter or prescribed drugs), and it goes by the curious name of 'ejaculatory incompetence' (EI). Once again – a successful treatment for this is available, and we'll be discussing it later in this book.

Orgasm problems in women. If men's orgasms can go wrong because of an imbalance between the sympathetic, the parasympathetic and peptidergic nervous systems, can the same thing happen to women in this 'third stage'?

In fact, an overactive 'sympathetic' (caused by fear, anxiety or pills) just doesn't make a woman 'come too soon' – as is the case with the male premature ejaculator. (In fact, as we've said already, it's a bit hard to see how a woman could really 'come too soon'.) The reasons for this difference between the sexes aren't entirely clear yet.

On the other hand, inability to reach orgasm – possibly caused in part by excessive parasympathetic influence over the sympathetic – is *extremely* common in women. Just like the 'ejaculatory incompetence' problem of males who can't reach climaxes, there are millions of ladies who simply cannot reach a climax.

This is a very big, and – for some people – a tragic problem – for at least one in eight younger women, and an awful lot of more mature ones, can't reach a climax. (Admittedly, there are lots of well-adjusted women who don't reach a climax – and simply don't mind at all.)

However, there are successful treatments for this problem, and these methods will be explained later in the book.

The fourth stage   Let's turn to the happier subject of the fourth (and last) stage of orgasm – often known as the 'resolution phase'. This is a very pleasant, happy phase, in which the couple are slowly 'coming down the other side of the mountain together', locked in each other's arms, warm, comfortable, and (I hope) very much in love.

If you find your way back to the twin male and female orgasm diagrams (Figures 12 and 13), you'll see that in this phase there's a *very* big difference between male and female. And it's this: most men – particularly those who are past their teenage years – have to wait a long time before they can get another erection and have another climax. To take some examples, in one middle-aged man, it might be half an hour. In another, it might be half a day. (Kinsey showed that by age forty, only about 50 per cent of men had the strength even to try for a second climax in a session.) But women are different.

Multiple climaxes – the truth

Certainly, there are lots of women (and it's vital to realise that they're in a very big majority) who just have one nice climax in a night – and are happy and fulfilled with that. Good luck to them: they certainly needn't feel inadequate. But there are also lots of others (one in seven, according to Kinsey) for whom one single climax is really just a sort of *hors d'oeuvre* – insufficient to satisfy the appetite. Many of these really prefer about six or seven orgasms in a session, and feel a bit cheated with less.

There is even a small minority of delightful and *very* highly-sexed women who're like the lady whose responses are shown in the right hand part of the chart in Figure 13. They can just reel off orgasm after orgasm after orgasm – certainly twenty or so in a session, though I have heard unconfirmed reports of up to 100. All this tends to leave them rather tired and rather sore – but very, very satisfied. They are hard work to handle for a man, and only a skilled lover is really going to give them what they want. But to bring a beautiful women to twenty orgasms in a night is a memorable experience indeed. Incidentally, I must say that women's vastly superior abilities to ours in the field of multiple orgasm make nonsense of any 'MCP' ideas that males are some-how 'better' than women. This is just one of many fields in which they triumph over us.

A woman's climax

Having got all that scientific stuff out of the way, let's get down to the pleasant practicalities of what actually happens to you at a climax.

We'll start with women. The studies of American sexologists (together with the less academic observations of various amorous-minded gentlemen around the world) have made this fairly clear.

Basically, what happens is that at her supreme moment of pleasure, most of the muscles of a woman's body go into a splendid and quite uncontrollable spasm. Her eyes become wonderfully dreamy, with big pupils (this is the effect of the sympathetic nervous system and its adrenaline – or epinephrine – again). Her face contorts into an expression which may be like the widest of smiles, or which may be almost like a grimace of pain. Of course, it's not pain she's feeling: it's ecstasy.

Even her toes curl up with pleasure – one of the most reliable signs that orgasm has taken place, if – of course – you happen to be in the region of her feet at the time. (Not usual, I admit – but it can happen.)

What else? The mouth of her vagina – which has become swollen into a sort of 'collar' to fit snugly around the base of the penis, starts to contract in a series of immensely pleasurable waves which happens at about the same rhythm as the man's orgasmic surges – roughly one contraction every 1½ seconds. Muscular surges also take place in the womb, and when I wrote *The Book of Love*, I thought that women couldn't feel them. Nowadays I'm inclined to believe the women who tell me they can.

Anything else? A woman's breasts change at orgasm, and we've tried to show you what these changes are like in Figure 15. In fact, the 'sex flush' which occurs on the breasts can be seen on much of the rest of the body during orgasm. It's a pink rash – sometimes described as being 'measles-like' – and it disappears shortly after the lady has had her climax. Clearly, it's more obvious in fair-skinned women.

I think a lot too much fuss has been made about the 'sex flush' or 'orgasm flush' in women's magazines and so on in recent years. I've even had letters which said 'My boy friend doesn't believe I'm having a climax because I don't come out in this measles rash!' Frankly, that attitude is very stupid. The sex flush is *not* very distinct in most women, and the lover who's wasting his time looking for it should be devoting his mind to other things.

Far, far more important – and useful – as a sign that a woman is reaching a climax is 'the cry'. Most women conclude the ever-quickening breathing of sexual arousal with an involuntary cry or scream at the supreme moment. This cry is very hard to stifle – save by stopping the lady's mouth with kisses – so be careful not to make love where somebody else can hear you! (Actually, it's quite agreeable hearing somebody else making love. Twice recently, while staying at hotels in Austria and Cannes, I've heard the unmistakable night-time sound of a lady giving the shrill cry of a climax. And very nice it was too.)

FIG. 15

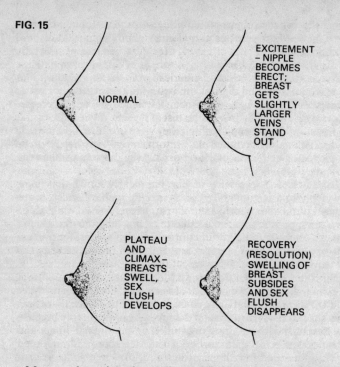

NORMAL

EXCITEMENT – NIPPLE BECOMES ERECT; BREAST GETS SLIGHTLY LARGER VEINS STAND OUT

PLATEAU AND CLIMAX – BREASTS SWELL, SEX FLUSH DEVELOPS

RECOVERY (RESOLUTION) SWELLING OF BREAST SUBSIDES AND SEX FLUSH DISAPPEARS

More to the point, the really useful thing about the woman's 'climax cry' is that it gives her partner a clear indication that *now is the moment*.

Since so many couples have such difficulty in reaching simultaneous orgasm (see below), the 'sex cry' is a great help to the poor man who's not quite sure whether his partner is there yet or not.

There's one final thing that some women may do in a climax – and that is *ejaculate*. But this is a highly contentious subject – and we'll come to it in a moment.

What makes her climax?

The intriguing question of what makes a woman climax is not as easy to answer as you might think. Back in Freud's day (i.e. between 1900 and 1940) it was generally felt – at least among those doctors who admitted that women could reach climaxes (and there are still one or two who *don't* admit it!) – that orgasm should come purely from stimulation of the vagina. The Freudians went even further and announced that although they knew that some women reached orgasm by having their clitorises rubbed, this sort of orgasm was *immature* and therefore *to be disapproved of*! As a result, a whole generation of American women (for Freud's works were popular in the US) grew up believing their clitoral orgasms were wrong, 'babyish', immature. Fortunately, these Freudian views didn't spread to a lot of the rest of the world – because by the 1950s and 1960s it turned out that they were a load of old rhubarb!

As I've said in Chapter 2 the clitoris *is* generally the key to a woman's sexual pleasure. That's usually the 'button' you have to work at if you want to make your loved one 'come' – and the splendid US researcher Shere Hite has clearly shown that there are countless women who greatly prefer to have much more clitoral stimulation during intercourse. What Ms Hite wants is for men to make much more considerate efforts to 'grind' their pubic bones – that's the bone behind the pubic hair – against the 'pubes' of their loved ones. Unsubtle as this sounds, it's actually a very effective way of stimulating the clitoris to orgasm.

With the realisation – in the fifties and sixties – that clitoral orgasm was *in*, even the greatest of sex researchers began to forget that there might be other types of orgasm. The 'official' line was now that all sexual intercourse achieved its effect simply because the thrusting of the man's penis pulled on the vaginal 'lips' – and therefore pulled on the clitoris too. This viewpoint was reinforced by the fact – mentioned earlier in this book – that some women seem to be curiously lacking in nerves inside their vagina, and appear to feel very little pain there. (Others most certainly *do*.) So, in a complete about face, lots of folk now believed that all orgasm was clitoral – not vaginal.

Back in the 1970s, I began to think that this reasoning had some flaws. If all orgasms came from the clitoris, why was it that:

★Many women could reach a climax just through having their breasts rubbed?

★Others seemed to be able to do it just through seeing their loved ones reach a climax in front of them?

★A very few could actually 'come' if the man they loved whispered a few sexy words to them *down the phone*? (He hadn't much opportunity to get at the clitoris from there!)

So, clearly orgasm was a more complex business than just being something that *always* originated in the clitoris. And in the early part of the 1980s came what seems to be confirmatory proof that orgasms *can* be started in the vagina after all – without the clitoris being involved.

The area of the vagina which is particularly involved is called the 'Grafenberg spot' or 'G-spot'. In fact, as I've explained in Chapter 2, it's not yet clear whether this little patch is actually in the front vaginal wall, or in the area of the close-by urinary pipe (the urethra). Anyway, the general region of the vaginal 'G-spot' is shown back in Figure 7 on p. 22. Stimulate it properly, and your lady love will most probably have a rather different sort of orgasm to the clitoral one she's used to. If by chance she can't usually achieve a climax, stimulation of this newly discovered area might perhaps pay rich dividends and get her there.

Ways of stimulating the magic 'G-spot' are discussed later in the book. But now on to something which is very relevant to the 'G-spot' – the controversial question of 'Do women ejaculate at a climax?'

The great 'do women ejaculate' controversy

Until very recently, I believed it was a complete myth that some women ejaculated (i.e. squirted a sexual fluid, just like men) at their moment of orgasm. Certainly, half the rude books written through the centuries, including the highly-influential *Fanny Hill* (1744), spoke glowingly of the heroine 'letting her lover know that she had reached the very Olympian summit of her most exquisite pleasure by gushing forth her precious love fluid'. (After this, she usually 'swooned', as well she might.)

I admit I thought this was complete rubbish. I knew that Masters and Johnson had put their intra-vaginal cameras up 500 or so obliging ladies – and had found *no one* who ejaculated. However, one or two of their 'subjects' had involuntarily passed urine at the moment of climax. And my own researches indicated that really quite a lot of women accidentally did the same – hardly a surprising fact when you consider the powerful spasm of a climax, and the fact that even a sneeze or a laugh will make so many ladies leak a little urine. I recently mentioned this in the British women's magazine *SHE*. And the result was uproar!

I was flooded (sorry) by dozens of letters written by irate ladies who said that they *did* produce a sexual fluid at the moment of climax. When I told a colleague this, he said bewilderedly, 'But where from?'

'Oh,' I said, 'from Manchester, Oxford, West Germany, Canada. . . .'

Eventually I grasped that he wasn't asking where the letters were from. What he meant was *where was this fluid coming from?* The only possible anatomical structure seemed to be the opening of the urethra (the urinary pipe – turn back to Figure 4, p. 14). And that suggested that the fluid these ladies were getting indignant about really was just urine – especially as we knew that certain men who went in for oral sex had reported being hit in the eye by a quick jet from the urinary pipe.

I asked *SHE* readers to send in samples of this fluid for analysis, but alas the only container I received – from a lady in Tunbridge Wells – cracked in the post, leaving me with nothing but a stained though pleasantly fragrant envelope.

Then came the above-mentioned report of the discovery in America of the 'G-spot'. American and Canadian doctors wrote their work up in a US medical journal, and that work appears to show that if you stimulate a woman's 'G-spot' in the way I'll be describing in the chapters on love-play, it can sometimes happen that at climax she produces a fluid which is *not urine*. It does come from the waterworks pipe, but it seems, according to biochemists who analysed it in Canada, to be a fluid rather similar to that squirted out by men at *their* moment of orgasm. All this only goes to show you that doctors can sometimes get it wrong!

CHAPTER FIVE

More About Male Climaxes – And About Simultaneous Orgasms

How climaxes happen in men ● How to delay a man's climax ● What makes a climax feel so good? ● How much fluid should he produce? ● How often do men have climaxes? ● Simultaneous climaxes: the truth.

How climaxes happen in men

I've already said a good deal about the male climax – and how it compares with the female one – in the previous chapter (in which I also explained the basic reasons for two sex problems connected with the male climax – 'premature ejaculation' and 'ejaculatory incompetence'.) But now let's be more specific about the male climax. What actually *happens* during it? And is it easy to synchronise it with your loved one's climax, so that you achieve the fabled goal of 'simultaneous orgasm'?

The male climax is pretty well always due to direct stimulation of the penis. Unlike women, men can't normally reach an orgasm purely through stimulation of various different bits of their bodies – though it's certainly a help if his lady stimulates other areas (especially if – like so many men – he's having a bit of trouble in 'performing'). But basically it's got to be direct stimulation of the penis that brings a man to orgasm. (The only exception I know of is the very common situation where a man reaches a climax in a 'wet dream' – but even here, it seems likely that the friction of the bedclothes, or his pyjamas, against his penis is a major factor in making him 'come' while he's asleep.)

Direct stimulation of the penis can of course be by the hand, by the lips, by the tongue, or by almost anything else – but best of all – of course – by the vagina of the woman you love. This stimulation takes the man through the 'phase of excitement' (see Figure 12 on p. 37) and onto the 'plateau phase' – where, if he's a skilled and considerate lover, he'll probably want to remain for some considerable time while he 'pleasures' his partner. But eventually there comes a point when the man feels a different (and highly pleasurable) sensation in his penis which tells him that orgasm is near. A skilled lover can easily take himself up to the brink of this moment again and again – and then 'change down a gear' so that he's in complete control again. Learning this skill is an enormous help in making you a successful lover.

How to delay the man's climax

It's important for women who want to be experts in bed to realise that it's not always easy (even for experienced men) to do this quick 'change down' at the last moment. Why? Because if a man is hovering on the brink of a climax and doesn't want to go over the top, the woman must help him by refraining from thrusting her pelvis at him, or from 'milking' his penis with her vaginal muscles, or from saying rude and sexy things that might 'bring him off'! In these circumstances, women should be prepared to give their partners half a minute's respite – they'll soon be ready for action again.

If you're not sure how a skilled lover can pull himself back from the brink, the main thing I'd say is that it needs a lot of practice. However, deep, rhythmic breathing, right down into the tummy, is helpful in counteracting the effects of the sympathetic nervous system – which, as I've said earlier in the book, is the excitement part of the nervous system which produces the adrenaline (epinephrine) and related chemicals which tend to make men fire off into a climax. Turning your mind to other things for a minute is also a help in drawing back from a climax – there's nothing like a brief cogitation about the price of fish (or the difficulty of reaching the eighteenth green in two) to take a man's mind off orgasm!

Note: if you can't control your climax, see the comments about *premature ejaculation* in the previous chapter. As you'll discover in Chapters 17 to 21, this very common condition can be cured.

What makes a climax feel so good?

Eventually comes the moment when the man, voluntarily or involuntarily (though I hope it'll be *voluntarily* after reading this book), blasts into phase three – the climax itself. This begins with a fraction of a second (called by US sexologists 'the moment of ejaculatory inevitability') when the man realises that *that's it*. It's going to happen now, and there's nothing on Earth will stop it. This feeling actually occurs at the moment when the seminal fluid floods into the lower part of the urethra – the long pipe which runs upwards through the penis. A little of the fluid is discharged from the balls, but the majority of it is squirted from higher up – including the prostate gland. (If you're not sure where that is, go back to Chapter 3 and look at Figure 11 on p. 34.)

It's the sudden flooding of fluid into the lower part of the urinary pipe (distending it to several times its normal diameter) which produces such intense pleasure. (You can see what I mean from Figure 16.)

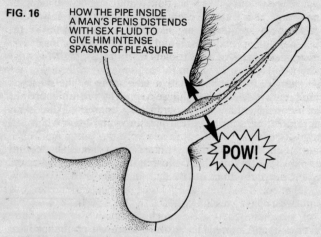

FIG. 16   HOW THE PIPE INSIDE A MAN'S PENIS DISTENDS WITH SEX FLUID TO GIVE HIM INTENSE SPASMS OF PLEASURE

POW!

The rapid distension of the pipe near the base of the penis provokes a tremendously powerful series of muscular contractions in the wall of the tube – with great spasms occurring about every 1½ seconds. It's these powerful muscular contractions which so pleasurably drive the fluid straight out of the tip of the penis in a series of about half a dozen surges, blasting this remarkable, life-bearing liquid far into the upper reaches of your loved one's vagina.

How much fluid should he produce?

The average is about a teaspoonful – or 5 ml. Considering all the effort involved, that doesn't sound very much, does it? Indeed, many blokes insist that they produce 'far more than that, doctor' – and clearly think they're turning out about half a gallon at a time. This just isn't true: for the sperm count reports which doctors get back from hospital labs almost invariably quote volume figures of between 2 ml and 7 ml. (Indeed, if you produce 7 ml, you're doing very, very well!) So unless all these chaps are missing the specimen jar with their first 'squirt', then clearly 5 ml is about average.

But the volume does vary a lot from day to day, and it's likely to be reduced – sometimes to virtually nil – by repeated climaxes. And as is well-known, if a man abstains from sex for a few weeks (not an easy task, I grant you), the volume of 'stored up' fluid which he produces will be much greater.

Though the volume of seminal fluid is quite small in all men, the point to remember is this. Unless you've had a vasectomy (or are infertile) there are something like *500 million sperms* in the seminal fluid you produce each and every time you 'come'. This certainly makes those little droplets worth regarding with some respect.

Incidentally, if you *have* had a vasectomy – like so many hundreds of thousands of men these days – you will not notice any difference in the volume or appearance of your seminal fluid – or, indeed, in the amount of sexual pleasure you obtain when that great gush distends your urethra and you start pumping. This is because, as I've said above, the volume which the testicles contribute to the fluid is very small: most of it comes from higher up, round the prostate gland.

How often do men have climaxes?

It was that great American Dr Alfred Kinsey who announced that the average US male had 2.4 climaxes per week (though I suppose you could say that the odd 0.4 wouldn't be a lot of fun). Seriously, this was an important discovery, because prior to that time people had been able to get divorces on the grounds of their spouses' 'excessive sexual demands' – for instance, twice a week! Kinsey actually found one man – an attorney – who had averaged 33.1 climaxes a week for many years. But most of us aren't in the 33.1 a week league, and about twice a week seems to be about the average in most Western countries. Naturally, younger men achieve more climaxes, and middle-aged and older men less.

However, please, let me stress that there's also great individual variation. You are *not* abnormal if you only have a climax once a fortnight (in fact, 15 per cent of the male population is like you), nor are you abnormal if you need one every day (like 8 per cent of males). It's just like some people being tall and some people being short: be happy with what feels right for you – and for your partner, of course.

Simultaneous climaxes: the truth

Finally, let's turn to the question of simultaneous climaxes. Of course, these are what always happen in novels, aren't they? Like:

'As the crashing wave of his passion broke within her, he knew that she too had – at the same, sweet moment as himself – attained the lofty pinnacle of love's sacred and sweet-scented mountain. "Oh, doctor," she cried, rearranging her crisp, starched nurse's apron, "Oh, doctor – are you going to do another ward round *next* week?"'

Alas and alack, life is only like that for a lucky minority. The plain fact is that most couples *do not* achieve simultaneous climaxes most of the time. Perhaps that statement may put things in perspective for you if you're struggling for a simultaneous climax – and not succeeding.

In addition, to judge by novels and films – and by the way most people talk about their sex lives – you'd think that at the very least, most women reached a climax during intercourse. In other words, if their climaxes weren't *simultaneous* with their husbands, then at least they were fairly near.

All nonsense, I'm afraid. For a tragic and remarkably little-known fact is this: *most women don't usually manage to reach orgasm during intercourse itself.* They may reach it during 'petting' – before or after intercourse – but they don't actually 'come' during intercourse itself. Naturally, this makes simultaneous orgasm a trifle difficult for them.

Now you may not believe what I've just said about most women not reaching a climax during intercourse itself. But in the USA, Shere Hite's surveys of thousands of women have quite clearly demonstrated this point. Ms Hite found that only about one third of all women regularly reached a climax during intercourse. Kinsey had made a similar suggestion many years before – but it was more or less ignored by doctors and psychologists until Shere came along.

Her studies confirmed what previous investigators had shown: that round about 85–90 per cent of women could easily reach a climax through masturbation or love play, or as Ms Hite puts it 'could orgasm in non-coital situations'. (A medical friend of mine expressed this more succinctly by saying that they could 'come unscrewed'.) When Ms Hite's message first began to spread across the world in the late 1970s, few doctors believed it. I repeated her findings at a medical meeting and saw bewildered psychiatrists shaking their heads and saying 'It can't be true.'

After all, some of us had actually been *treating* women who could regularly have a climax through petting but not during intercourse – and now this American lady was telling us that such women weren't sick – but made up most of the female population.

Subsequently, large statistical studies carried out by a pair of British women's magazines (*Woman* and *Woman's Own*) showed that virtually the same thing was true in Britain. Only about 30–40 per cent of women were regularly reaching orgasm through intercourse. For climaxes, they relied mainly on petting. Later, a French women's magazine survey showed that much the same thing was true in France. Furthermore, there was a distinct tendency for Frenchmen to pack up their efforts altogether once they themselves (i.e. *les hommes*) had reached their climaxes. . . . So it looks as if all over the world, most women aren't even getting an orgasm during intercourse, *let alone* a 'simultaneous climax'.

The main exceptions are probably the 14 per cent or so of ladies who can easily manage multiple climaxes and who can therefore very often 'come' almost at will just when they feel a man reaching his own orgasm inside them. Happily, some women who don't have multiple climaxes can 'synchronise' things with their men-folk too – though often they have to have a good relationship for about a year or so before they can 'come together' like this.

But at the moment, the fact is that most couples *aren't* achieving a simultaneous orgasm – indeed, most of the time the poor lady isn't even getting there during intercourse.

If this applies to you as a couple, then there's no need for you to despair: you can still have a lot of fun in bed! Many people who have never 'come together' in their lives have wonderful bed-time relationships – for instance, taking pleasure in watching each other climax.

On the other hand, if you really want to, it *is* possible to change all this. With the right preparation; with the right love play and intercourse techniques; with the right amount of love and under-standing – it is very, very possible for a wife to reach orgasm with her husband inside her. Moreover, it is sometimes practicable to go a stage further – and to achieve that magical moment when both of you, joined by love – feel the beautiful flower of a mutual climax blossom between you.

CHAPTER SIX

Minor Sex Worries

(i) INTRODUCTION FOR BOTH SEXES

How common minor sex problems are in both sexes ● *What are the most frequent minor difficulties?* ● *Why they occur* ● *Not forgetting major sex difficulties.*

(ii) MINOR SEX PROBLEMS IN WOMEN

'I'm losing interest in sex' ● *'I feel guilty about sex'* ● *'I'm worried that I'm not good enough for men in bed'* ● *'I can't always reach a climax'* ● *'I can reach one – but not during intercourse'* ● *'Sometimes sex is uncomfortable'* ● *'I get sore the day after love-making'* ● *'I've got this discharge'* ● *'I bleed after sex'* ● *'I'm always terrified of getting pregnant'* ● *'I feel guilty about masturbation'* ● *'I'm worried that my vulva doesn't look right'* ● *'I'm scared I'm a lesbian'* ● *'I get wind up the vagina!'* ● *'My vagina's too loose'.*

(iii) MINOR SEX PROBLEMS IN MEN

'I'm worried about my performance' ● *'I'm not happy about the size of my penis'* ● *'There was one night when I couldn't manage it!'* ● *'I can only do it once a night'* ● *'I've got this tendency to come too soon'* ● *'I have trouble getting to a climax'* ● *'I feel guilty about masturbation'* ● *'I just feel guilty'* ● *'I think I'm over-sexed'* ● *'I think I'm losing interest in sex'* ● *'I'm afraid I'm gay'* ● *'I think I'm AC/DC'* ● *'I've got this discharge'* ● *'My penis is sore (or swollen)'* ● *'My penis is bent'* ● *'I think I'm bent'.*

(i) INTRODUCTION FOR BOTH SEXES

How common minor sex problems are in both sexes

As you'll have gathered from the above rather amazing catalogue, there are an awful lot of minor sex problems. But a lot of them aren't too serious, really. I'm reminded of the story of the lady who went to the doctor and complained that she'd been losing interest in sex.

'I see,' said the physician. 'And how old are you?'

'I'm eighty-four – and my husband's eighty-three.'

'And when did you first notice the symptoms?'

'Twice last night – and three times this morning.'

Incidentally, I hasten to add that five times in a night is *not* 'par for the course' at eighty-four – or at any other age, either. (2.4 times a week is very roughly average – more when you're young, less when you're not so young. Dr Alfred Kinsey demonstrated this in 1948 – and Shere Hite confirmed in 1981 that it was still true. Highly-sexed people naturally tend to score rather higher, and for folk who are by nature not as interested in sex, it's quite normal to score much lower.)

Though I've been treating this subject a bit light-heartedly, the fact is that these 'minor' sex problems do cause people quite a bit of distress. *And they are common.* As I've said earlier in the book, the famed US sex researchers Masters and Johnson went so far as to say that sex difficulties threatened almost half of all American marriages. Not every doctor would agree with that estimate by any means. But studies in England, Scotland and France have shown that an astonishingly high proportion of men and women who consult doctors actually do have some secret worry about sex which they'd like to ask somebody about – but often daren't! (A pity – because quite often the doctor could reassure them that they're totally normal.) To take just one striking example, we've seen in the previous chapter that Shere Hite found in her first report that most women don't actually reach a climax during intercourse. Many of them would probably like to do something to improve that situation – but they're usually afraid to ask for advice. And to turn to the menfolk, Shere's Hite's second report – published in the US in 1981 and this time on men and sex – showed that *three out of five men don't know whether a woman has reached a climax or not.* Yet they practically never seek expert guidance from doctors on this rather vital subject. No wonder that human beings have such difficulties in getting their organs together!

Happily, things are beginning to change quite a bit. As more and more sex counselling facilities become available in such countries as Britain, Canada, the US and Australia, people are slowly beginning to be less inhibited about coming to doctors, psychologists or counsellors for advice about the problems that have been troubling them. Indeed, if an expert – or even a self-styled 'expert' – sets up a sex clinic these days, he or she will soon be inundated with sexual problems, both major and minor.

What are the most frequent minor difficulties?

I get a pretty good idea of what sort of minor difficulties affect the average man and woman from studying the huge amount of mail which comes in to my health, family planning and sex medicine columns in various British and overseas newspapers and magazines. But one of the best *scientific* estimates I know of was carried out by the distinguished English sociologist Michael Schofield – who showed that well over half of all twenty-five-year-old adults (married or unmarried) had some minor sex worry or difficulty. He sets out the details in his famous book *The Sexual Behaviour of Young Adults* (Allen Lane). The figures were very little different for men (56 per cent) and women (59 per cent). Schofield's study of the incidence of minor sex problems accords very well indeed with my none-too-skilled statistical analysis of the letters I get in my various postbags. In fact, I've tried to summarise some of his most important findings in Figure 17 and Figure 18. Figure 17 is a 'block diagram' which shows the incidence of minor sex problems in the large group of twenty-five year old women studied by Schofield. You'll see that:

★Female worry No. 1 is 'losing interest in' or 'being bored with' sex (23 per cent of all women).
★Female worry No. 2 is guilt (this includes moral and religious worries).
★Female worry No. 3 is 'fear of poor sexual performance'.

FIG. 17

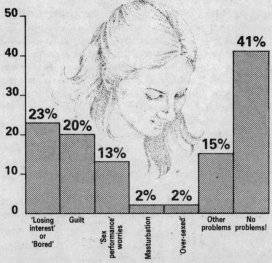

56

Now, let's turn to the men. According to Schofield (as you can see from Figure 18):

★Male worry No. 1 – rather surprisingly in this so-called 'permissive age' – is guilt (more than one in four men).
★Male worry No. 2 is that eternal masculine fear about 'performance' (of which more later).
★Male worry No. 3 is about masturbation – and isn't it crazy that in this day and age, mature twenty-five year old adults should be worried about having masturbated?

I'm going to try to deal with *all* the common minor sex difficulties in this chapter.

Why do minor sex difficulties occur?

Minor sex difficulties mainly occur for the same reasons that major difficulties do:

★Because of ignorance;
★Because of guilt and shame inculcated into a person in childhood.

In short, the vast majority of sex difficulties – both major and minor – are not physical. Lots of people seem to be surprised by this, probably because human beings like to attribute symptoms

FIG. 18

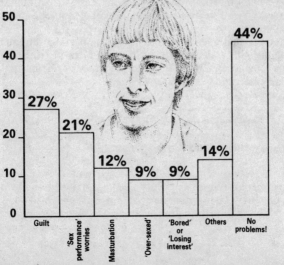

Guilt	Sex performance worries	Masturbation	'Over-sexed'	'Bored' or 'Losing interest'	Others	No problems!
27%	21%	12%	9%	9%	14%	44%

57

to good, solid, physical causes – rather than ones stemming from the emotions, or from sheer lack of knowledge. But the fact is that there is *no* physical factor in most sexual problems. There are certainly exceptions to this rule – for instance, the case of the woman who finds love-making painful because she has a vaginal infection, or perhaps a poorly-healed vaginal tear (or episiotomy incision) after childbirth. Also, there's the not-uncommon case of the man whose sex difficulties are really due to pills prescribed by a doctor for some health problem, like blood pressure.

However, most sex problems – minor and major – lie in the mind. There's no shame or blame in this, as some folk think – after all, we're all creatures of our emotions, and we can't help it if our emotions screw our sex lives up for us.

But the great thing is that, because these minor difficulties are largely due to emotional stress or plain lack of knowledge, they can very easily be cured.

And if *you* have a minor sex worry or problem (just like over half of all younger adults, as I've said), then I hope that this book will help you and your loved one to solve it together.

Not forgetting major sex problems

This chapter is about minor and relatively trivial sex difficulties which – as I've said – can as a rule easily be put right with a bit of commonsense advice, plus preferably the help of a loving partner. But I haven't forgotten the (literally) millions of people who have really *major* sex difficulties: for instance, the many poor souls who've been married for years and have never yet managed to have sex. (Yes, I'm afraid there's still a lot of 'non-consummation' about.)

All these really serious – and, as a rule, marriage-threatening – problems will be dealt with in Chapters 17 to 21. But now, let's discuss how to cope with the dozens of minor problems that worry so many men and women.

(ii)   MINOR SEX PROBLEMS IN WOMEN

'I'm losing interest in sex'

This, as we've seen above, is a very common complaint, with almost *one in four* of all twenty-five year old women having this kind of worry. To my mind the first thing to realise is that the sheer size of that figure (one in four) indicates that women aren't the insatiable lusters after penetration that many films and 'Harold Robbins-type' novels make them out to be. It seems to me to be quite normal for some women not to be terribly interested in (or just plain bored with) sex *some of the time*. Such times would include:

★ When they're tired, run-down or over-worked or concentrating on exams, or over-burdened with kids;
★ When the guys they're seeing are boring – or just plain sexually inept.

Remedies are fairly obvious. Look at the causes of the problem – and if necessary talk it over with a doctor *and* with your partner.

If you're just tired, run down or busy, then accept the fact. Accept that sex won't be great till you're on top form again. If, in addition you're depressed, see your doctor and get some help. If the problem is that your fellow is either boring or sexually clumsy – well, then either ditch him, or (if you love him) get him to wake his ideas up. For a start, he could read the chapters in this book about how to romance (and how to excite) a lady.

Note: if your loss of interest in sex really seems to be pretty serious, then excuse the light-hearted approach I've taken above. Consult the chapters on serious sex problems later in the book.

'I feel guilty about sex'

As we've seen above, about one in five young adult women have this feeling. The reasons are not far to seek. Both women and men are still far too often brought up with a set of sexual repressions – with either parents or teachers (or both) giving them the idea that sex is 'dirty' or 'nasty'. Many parents tell the child *nothing* about sex – yet somehow manage to make the poor child feel that it's all 'filthy'. Try and rid your mind of these Victorian ideas. *Sex is beautiful*. Sex with someone you really love (and who loves you) is arguably the most wonderful experience on Earth – in my view, only rivalled by seeing the children who are brought into being by this magical act of creation.

Sure, if you're having some rather seedy, messy affair with somebody else's man, then it's *natural* that you should feel guilty. But sex in itself is not 'wrong' or 'dirty'. If you're religious, bear in mind that the God you believe in would scarcely have invented a nasty or a sinful way of continuing the human race – surely, a divine being would have made the whole process beautiful, aesthetic and fulfilling: which is what it is.

'I'm worried about not being good enough for men in bed'

Relax – you're probably a lot better than you imagine. If you're warm, cuddly and loving; if you hold your man's penis and make appreciative remarks about it; if you're usually willing to try something new in order to give you both pleasure (for instance, love play and intercourse techniques described in the middle chapters of this book), then you're almost certainly doing just fine. Don't worry if:

★You don't reach a climax every time;
★You have trouble reaching one during intercourse itself (this is statistically normal);
★You don't have 'multiple climaxes' (most women don't).

As I explained in the previous chapter, all these things can be – and usually are – quite normal. And if you love your man and do your best for him in bed, then you usually need have no worries about your performance. It works both ways, and as you'll see later, he's supposed to do his best for you too!

'I can't always reach a climax'

All women sometimes have trouble reaching a climax. At times, 'it's there but it just won't come' (if you'll forgive the phrase). This is OK. It's just like a singer or a cook having an off day. Such off days are common when you're tired, or tense about something, or perhaps suffering from pre-menstrual tension (PMT). Accept the situation, and just tell yourself that things will be better next time. But – and it's one of those big BUTs – make sure that next time your partner knows exactly what you want him to do to make you 'come'. Far too many men just haven't a clue as to what to do to make a lady reach an orgasm. And – as Shere Hite revealed in her report on men – three out of five men don't even know whether their partners have 'come' or not, and unfortunately, some of these characters don't even *care*. So make sure your man reads the advice on climax-inducing techniques outlined in the middle chapters of this book.

'I can reach a climax – but not during intercourse'

If you haven't read the earlier part of this book, let me explain briefly that studies done in the US, Britain and France show the rather disappointing fact that most women don't reach their climax during actual intercourse – only during petting. If you're happy with this situation, then fine. But if not, then you and your man should read the middle part of this book which is all about:

- ★pre-intercourse techniques that will get you prepared for orgasm;
- ★techniques during intercourse that will help to get you there while your man is actually inside you.

'Sometimes sex is uncomfortable'

In young and inexperienced women, love-making is often a bit uncomfortable – though, contrary to popular myth – it should not really hurt. (If it does, consult the later chapters.) But as you get more used to sex, your vaginal muscles relax better. Furthermore, your vaginal fluids flow more freely and increase your natural lubrication. Also of major importance is the fact that if your first lover is inexperienced and knows little about how to stimulate ladies, then it is going to be very difficult for you to relax and lubricate. When you establish a loving relationship with a man who has learned what to do, then everything will be fine because his skilled fingers and lips (and words) will make your vagina moist, relaxed, welcoming and comfortable. In addition, read the advice about artificial lubricants in the next section. These often help a young couple to get over initial problems of discomfort.

Note If, however, you're so tensed up that intercourse is a nightmare – or even downright impossible – then read Chapters 17 to 21, which are about *major* sex problems.

Two special situations in which sex may be uncomfortable, and in which the cause is physical:

- ★It's very, very common to have a dry, sore vagina after the menopause: hormone cream prescribed by a doctor will usually cure this almost at once.
- ★Millions of younger women become sore, and so find sex uncomfortable, because they have one of the common vaginal infections, such as thrush (candida) or trichomonas. These are usually quite easily cured – see the section on 'Discharges' later.

'I get sore after love-making'

It's quite normal for both men and women to feel rather pleasantly sore after an intense and prolonged session of love-making. Indeed, women in particular often enjoy the sort of reminder of last night's fun which next day's sweet and pleasurable sensation of friction produces. But *real* discomfort isn't, of course, a pleasure. If you're very uncomfortable the day after sex, then that suggests one or more of these possibilities:

★His love-making techniques are too rough, and/or not skilled enough. Get him to read Chapters 7, 8 and 10.
★You weren't relaxing enough last night, and therefore your vagina wasn't adequately lubricated. (Next time, a little artificial lubricant obtained at a pharmacy or family planning clinic may help – UK brand names are KY Jelly and Durol. Not so good, but of use if you're desperate are Vaseline and good, old-fashioned saliva!) In America, baby oil is often used.

'I've got this discharge . . .'

Discharge – often associated with soreness of the vagina, making intercourse difficult or impossible – is one of the commonest of all symptoms which cause women to consult a doctor. Indeed, in an analysis of the letters I get in my postbag at the British women's magazine *SHE*, I found that 14 per cent (that is, almost one in seven) were from women who were worried about discharge. However, this isn't a textbook of gynaecology, but a guide to good sex, so I shall just summarise a complicated subject in this way:

1. Many women don't realise that to have a good deal of vaginal secretion (which they may think of as a 'discharge') is normal. In fact, it's very good from the sexual point of view because it lubricates things so nicely. Don't go in for douching or excessive bathing to try and get rid of these natural love juices.
2. If your vaginal secretions are *brown* or *blood-stained*, you should have an internal check-up by a doctor as soon as possible.
3. If you have a discharge that is *irritant* (i.e. sore or itchy), then you almost certainly have one of the common vaginal infections which affect literally millions of western women – and especially the sexually active ones.

I'll deal with these infections more fully in Chapter 22. But meantime, you should know that the two really common infections which cause discharge and irritation are:

★ **Thrush** (or Candida or Monilia) – a very troublesome little fungus which causes a whitish discharge plus soreness and itching. It's commoner in pregnancy – and in those on the Pill. It loves nice warm, moist places – like women's vaginas – but your partner may sometimes have a reddened and slightly sore penis too.

Treatment: go to a doctor, have a swab taken to check the diagnosis, and get a prescription for one of the many anti-thrush pessaries (that is, vaginal tablets) plus an anti-thrush cream or ointment to use on the outside. There are also some new oral tablets available. Your partner should also use a cream in my view. It's *vital* to have the full course, otherwise thrush will exercise its well-known propensity to recur! Don't have sex till you're cured. Good hygienic ploys for helping prevent recurrence of thrush are:

  (i) Avoid warm baths – remember thrush likes warmth and moisture – have cool showers instead;

 (ii) Don't wear nylon or other synthetic pants, which are also too hot;

(iii) Likewise, don't wear pantie-hose or tights – except the open-crotch type;

(iv) Don't sleep around – although thrush isn't *necessarily* caused by sex contact, it certainly can be passed on in this way:

 (v) If you're having real trouble with recurrent thrush, it's worth trying the yogurt cure. Get a pot each morning from your milkman – and with the aid of a 'Bendy-straw' and perhaps a helpful friend, you should be able to do daily vaginal irrigations with yogurt for a week.

    Incidentally, I call this the 'Women's Lib' cure, because it was pioneered by feminists in California. When police broke into one of their clinics, found a lady with a pot of yogurt in her hand, and tried to charge her with 'practising medicine without a license', she explained that it was 'just her lunch'!

★ **Trichomonas vaginalis** (or 'TV' or – in North America – 'trich') – also a very common little bug. This one tends to produce a yellow or yellowy-green discharge, plus intense vaginal soreness. Your man may occasionally have symptoms (such as a slight discharge), but usually doesn't.

Treatment: again, go to a doctor, and have a swab taken. He'll probably give you a prescription for a drug called metronidazole (called Flagyl in the UK and many other countries) or a related product. This drug is taken by mouth – and it is essential that *both you and your partner* take it. Failure of treatment is very often due to failure to treat the male. Don't have sex till you're cured – though frankly 'trich' is so painful that unless you're a masochist you're not likely to!

It's also worth following the commonsense anti-recurrence hygienic precautions outlined above under the heading 'Thrush'. In particular, don't sleep around – specially if 'TV' is widespread in your area, as it is in many communities. Research, particularly in the USA and the UK, is identifying other germs which have caused women much discharge, distress and discomfort (and spoiled their sex lives), and treatments for these conditions are becoming available. Please see also the section on VD in Chapter 22.

'I bleed after sex'

Bleeding after sex *may* just be due to a small 'flesh wound' caused (say) by ragged finger-nails or inexperienced efforts at love play. Where this is *clearly* the case, just press a clean cloth (e.g. a freshly laundered handkerchief) or some cotton wool over any obvious bleeding point till the haemorrhage stops. If the injury seems to be internal, put in a tampon. Very heavy bleeding can be arrested by cutting a sanitary pad in half and *gently* inserting it into the vagina. Naturally, you must see a doctor if an injury caused during love play causes heavy bleeding.

And now one of those big BUTs. If bleeding occurs after intercourse and has clearly *not* been caused by a finger-nail, then you must bear in mind that it could be due to a gynaecological disorder. Some such disorders are trivial (e.g. erosions of the cervix); others are not. Either way, unexplained bleeding after sex means you need a check-up from a doctor within a week or so.

'I'm always afraid of getting pregnant'

Very sensible. Sex *does* lead to babies – a fact which so many sex books (and sexy novels, TV plays and films) so often seem to forget. The result of this rather basic fact of life is that:

★in Britain 150,000 women a year have abortions – and hundreds of thousands more have babies they didn't really want.
★in the USA, there are now 1¼ million abortions a year, or more than one for every three births.

- ★ in Australia, the Royal Commission on Human Relationships recently estimated that one in five pregnancies is terminated.
- ★ in New Zealand and Canada, abortion figures have sky-rocketed recently – despite attempts to jail physicians who have carried out legal terminations.
- ★ even in Soviet Russia, unwanted pregnancy is so common that there are more abortions than childbirths.

My advice? Unless you're actually trying for a baby – which is after all not a common situation except for those unlucky couples who have fertility problems, *never let a bloke have sex with you unless one or other of you is using a safe method of contraception.* Details in Chapter 22.

'I feel guilty about masturbation'

Don't. Masturbation is *normal*, and all available surveys indicate that the majority of women have done it at some time. In fact, there's an increasing feeling among doctors and sex therapists that masturbation is actually *good* for you. Why? Because:

- ★ It relieves tension;
- ★ It aids young women to get accustomed to their own vaginas (something that very few of them are!), and so helps to avoid sexual hang-ups later on.
- ★ It helps to get you on the right route for having a climax – which so many women cannot manage.

In fact, many sex therapists now openly advocate a spot of 'do-it-yourself' for ladies who're having sexual difficulties – like trouble in reaching a climax or just general lack of libido. I agree with this trend. Let me stress that masturbation has *no* ill-effects (ignore those daft myths which have been circulating for decades about 'wanking' driving you mad or making you blind!) Further-more, you can't get pregnant by masturbating.

'I'm worried that my vulva doesn't look right'

This is a very common one in my postbag. And it's linked to the last fear I mentioned, because many of these ladies are afraid that they've somehow altered the appearance of their vaginal openings by masturbating – which is impossible. Vast numbers of women are worried half to death because of such fears as these:

- ★They think their labia (lips) are too long;
- ★They think that one lip is much too big compared with the other;
- ★They think that their clitorises aren't large enough;
- ★They think that their vaginas 'gape' too much;
- ★They think that 'the hair doesn't look right'.

The trouble here is that so few women have ever seen other women stripped, so they don't realise that vulvas vary a great deal – just as people's faces do. The real incidence of gross structural abnormalities of the vulva and vagina is *very* low – in a five-year period, I saw one case (which was easily put right by a surgeon).

Girls who go in for naturism (nudism) rarely have these worries. They see other girls, and older women, leaping around in the open air each summer, and they get to know what the human vulva looks like. So they don't start thinking that they've got some dreadful abnormality. I must say that I do applaud the naturist movement for the good it does in this respect. I also applaud the American feminist organisation who recently made a film – intended for showing to women – which consisted entirely of a long series of shots of ladies' vaginas. OK – it sounds a bit 'pseud'. But many of those women who saw the film expressed great relief afterwards that it had showed them that they were normal! If, despite what I've said, you're still worried about the shape or size of your vulva, then go and see a doctor (a female one if you like – in Britain and some other countries, their advice is readily available and *free* at Family Planning Clinics) and get her reassurance that you're OK.

'I'm scared I'm a lesbian'

Well, perhaps you are; if so, the best thing to do is to go ahead and be one. But do bear in mind that many young women go through a bisexual phase for a while, and then 'settle down' as heterosexuals. Furthermore, there's a well-known tendency for women who are lonely or frightened or (perhaps most important) away from home to turn to another woman for a reassuring cuddle – which may, quite frankly, be a sexual cuddle. For instance, Dr Alfred Kinsey, who startled the medical world by his findings in 1948–1953, discovered among many other things that almost one in three US college girls had had a lesbian relationship – the obvious factors being that they were away from home, and under some stress. In our own time, we've seen a similar phenomenon on the top pro tennis circuit – where so many stars (away from

Mum and under all sorts of pressures) succumb to lesbian seduction.

Another factor, incidentally, is that most younger men are totally incompetent and thoughtless lovers. Many gay women are very, very good at sex play – and naturally, they know *exactly* what a woman likes, and can go on doing it for hours. Clearly, most women who have lesbian affairs eventually turn out 'straight'. If this seems to apply to you, then don't feel guilty about your past lesbian frolics – just regard it as part of growing up. But – as I've said – if you're genuinely sure you're lesbian, then there's no point in fighting it or, in my view, in seeking 'treatment' – which is not very likely to be a success in the confirmed lesbian (though it might work in the woman who's borderline). Sex comes in rich varieties, and – for whatever reason – lesbianism is part of it. If you're gay, then forget your guilts – go ahead and enjoy it.

Note: Counselling organisations which can help gays/bisexuals/floating voters are discussed in Chapter 21.

'I get embarrassing wind up the vagina!'

When this problem first turned up in my postbag, I thought the sender had a very unusual problem. But once I'd mentioned it in print, I found how wrong I was. Hordes of letters came in from ladies whose vaginas make rude noises when they're making love – because of trapped air leaking out, of course. One woman even said she had the same problem in her yoga class!

It seems to me that this embarrassingly noisy problem is commoner in women who've had children, since their vaginas are laxer (see next section) – and so let air in (and out) more easily. But in fact vaginal 'wind' is also a problem for many ladies who've never been pregnant. I must confess that I've not been able to come up with an entirely satisfactory answer to this one. You could try filling your vagina with a contraceptive aerosol foam, such as the one marketed in the UK and elsewhere under the brand name Delfen. But that may not work. Operating to tighten up a vagina made a bit lax by childbirth (see next section) seems a bit drastic just in order to try to stop a few rude noises during love-making, and it may fail to stop the noises anyway. So I think that the best thing is if you and your man (or even your yoga class) can just regard vaginal 'wind' as a joke – one of those rich and rather vulgar jokes which so often bring the priceless gift of laughter into our sex lives!

Incidentally, there are certain African tribes who prize this noise very highly, and who try to urge on newlyweds by imitating it outside the bridal hut (using a stick dipped in a muddy hole). You could always go and join them, though I don't know if they do very much in the way of yoga.

'My vagina's too loose'

A common problem this, since the birth of every child tends to make the 'tunnel of love' a little wider – and may strain the muscles which support the female sex organs. Laxity around the vagina (I hasten to add that I speak in the muscular rather than the moral sense of the word) is not too good from a sexual point of view. To sum it up, when things are not so tight, they may not be so nice – for either party. Husbands tend to be more worried by this laxness of the vaginal muscles than wives are. This is because a lot of a man's pleasure depends on him being firmly gripped around the penis. On the other hand, much of a woman's *direct* sexual pleasure (as opposed to the more general pleasure she gets from the whole experience) comes from two areas:

  (i) Her clitoris;
  (ii) Her vagina – especially the newly-discovered 'G-spot'.

If you're not sure where these two points are, go back and read Chapter 2. The point is that a woman's sexual satisfaction is only dependent to a rather limited extent on how tight the vagina is round the penis, which is why, as explained in Chapter 3, the idea of a large penis does not necessarily fill a woman with the ecstasy which so many men think it ought to do.

Of course, some men don't care if their partners have wide vaginas. But others find that they even have a bit of trouble keeping an erection going because the vagina is no longer snug around it. One man whose wife had had five children rather sadly remarked that making love to her was 'like throwing a small banana up the Simplon tunnel'. The trouble is that if matters get to this stage, husbands are often silly enough to go off and have affairs with younger ladies with no children and tighter vaginas. Alternatively, they may encourage their wives to go in for inter-course up the rectum – since *that* particular orifice is so much tighter than the vagina, and grips the penis very firmly indeed. Incidentally, be very wary about doing this: if you haven't read the hygiene warnings situated (appropriately enough) at the bottoms of Chapters 2 and 3, then please do so.

The cure. But in fact, the important thing to realise is that a 'loose vagina' can be cured. In serious cases, there are various types of 'repair' operations available – and they're very commonly performed by gynaecologists – not only to improve people's sex lives, but for health reasons too. If a woman has severe laxness of the pelvic muscles, she tends to get 'descent' or 'prolapse' of the womb and of the bladder down towards the vaginal opening, which can lead to serious problems. The operation, which is usually a sort of general 'tightening up' of the muscles and tissues round the vagina, doesn't *always* cure the sex difficulty, but usually it does.

However, *most women with lax vaginas don't have to go as far as having a surgical operation*. Very often, the job can be done by toning the pelvic muscles up through exercises. These muscles are called the 'pubo-coccygeus' musculature – so in Canada and the USA, the exercises are often termed 'PC exercises'. The basic exercises are very simple, but they must be performed regularly – preferably for twenty minutes three times a day over a period of at least twelve months. The two main exercises are these:

(i) Strongly and powerfully, tighten up your FRONT pelvic muscles as if you were trying to stop the flow of urine. (In fact, you can try it first time when you're peeing, if you like, to make sure you've got it right.) Hold the contraction for seven or eight seconds, then relax and repeat . . . and repeat . . . and repeat.

(ii) Likewise, strongly tighten up your REAR pelvic muscles as if trying to hold back a bowel motion. Maintain the contraction in the same way – then repeat . . . and repeat . . . and repeat.

In my view these valuable 'Kegel' exercises, as they're often called, should be taught to all post-natal mums. You can do them while lying in bed, or sitting down, or working – or whenever you like. It's also very good to do them *while you're actually making love*. Once you've got the knack of contracting the muscles properly, your man will greatly appreciate the delightful 'milking' sensation which this sexy muscle contraction produces. (See also Chapter 13.)

An advance on these exercises has been made by a Welsh sex expert. He has invented a specially shaped device which you can put into your vagina, and practise contracting the muscles round it. In this case, you do the exercises on all fours – and the extent to which you can retain the device within your vagina without it falling out (please try not to laugh) helps you assess how you're getting on. An invention with slightly less sense of humour to it is the perineometer – an inflatable gadget connected to a dial, and used by many US and Canadian gynaecologists to assess the progressive increase in power of the vaginal muscles. Another device available in North America is a mild electrical stimulator called the Vagitone. It can be ordered (through your physician) from Techni-Med, Inc., 3400 West Lomita Bvd., Torrance, CA90505. It was invented by Dr Edwin A. Rudinger. But you don't have to use these devices to tighten up your muscles if you follow the exercises described above. Incidentally, a *temporary* solution to the problem of 'looseness' during sex can be achieved by making love with your thighs together.

(iii)   MINOR SEX PROBLEMS IN MEN

Now, after all those minor female worries, let's run through the commonest minor *male* difficulties, one or other of which affects most men at some time or another. (Can I remind you that if you have a MAJOR sexual difficulty that's really making your life hell, then you'll almost certainly find it and its treatment discussed, not in this chapter, but in Chapters 17 to 21.)

'I'm worried about my performance'

Men are *always* worried about their 'performance' or their 'virility'. Our culture has made most men feel that they should be 'super-lovers': muscular lions with magnificent penises, ever ready to spring to an erection, ever ready to satisfy a woman – and to satisfy her again, and again, and again. . . . Frankly, that's a load of _____ . . . I'll avoid the obvious sexual metaphor. Men are *not* supermen; they get tired, and over-worked, and over-stressed, sometimes even ill; they are *not* always ready for sex, and they *can't* always produce an erection just like that. When they do produce one, they sometimes lose it. Sometimes they 'come' more quickly than they meant to – and sometimes they're so 'knackered' (to use an old and very accurate English/Australian/New Zealand expression) that they can't manage to 'come' at all – and perhaps even fall asleep in the midst of trying to make love! And, while many – probably most – women intuitively understand these things, most men do not.

All too often, men seriously believe that if they don't present a woman with an immediate erect penis, they're somehow 'insulting' her attractiveness. This is of course nonsense. Lots of men – particularly those who are over thirty – don't produce a massive erection at will, so there's nothing to be ashamed of if you take your clothes off and reveal to your loved one that you're still limp. If she loves you and desires you, she'll soon put that right. If she doesn't know how to, ask her to read the chapters of this book which are about love play and about turning a man on – especially Chapters 7, 9 and 11.

'I'm not happy about the size of my penis'

I couldn't care *less* about the size of your penis, and neither should you, for as I've explained in Chapter 3, women share my view: they do *not* want you to have some great enormous 'dick' which would be uncomfortable to get inside – and which wouldn't give them any extra pleasure. Indeed, if anything women are turned off by huge great penises. As I've indicated in Chapter 3, men tend to think that their penises are smaller than those of other men – because each of us only sees our own in a foreshortened view – i.e. looking downwards. Conversely, if you see another guy's 'cock' in the sports changing rooms or wherever, you don't see it foreshortened – so it usually looks bigger than yours! (And remember that he's probably thinking that yours is bigger than *his*.)

If the above doesn't convince you, and you still want an extra half-inch or so – well, there are things called 'penis-developers' these days which you can buy from sex shops. They're usually vacuum tubes – that is, tubes into which you put your penis, and then pump the air out – in the hope that this will draw your penis out a bit. I once had as patients a couple who accidentally bought one of these things when I'd told them to buy a vibrator. For some obscure reason, they phoned me up in great indignation – to complain that the penis developer's instructions were in Danish!

Since then, I've been unable to take penis-developers very seriously. But I do know one doctor who practises in this field, and who believes that they can help a man who genuinely feels that he's sexually inadequate because he needs a tiny bit more length or girth. Incidentally, the devices are usually prescribed along with a set of sexy exercises, which I suppose must be quite good fun to do if you've got the time. Indeed, I wonder if any success achieved by this 'régime' couldn't be explained by the fact that the exercises could give the patient confidence in his sexual ability.

'There was one night when I couldn't manage it'

Every man has an occasional night when he can't 'manage it'. Like many other doctors, I've often said this at medical meetings, and so far no one has leapt to his feet and said: 'You're wrong: I've always managed it whenever I wanted to!' So, most men do 'fail' occasionally – especially when they're:

★nervous – because, for reasons I've explained in the earlier part of this book, the hormones produced by tension effectively block erection;
★tired – for obvious reasons;
★guilty – ditto;
★drunk – because alcohol – except in moderation – is a great enemy of erection. (Just as well – think of all the poor kids who'd have been conceived otherwise.)

If you're having serious troubles with erection – i.e. more than once in a while – then consult Chapters 17 to 21. Otherwise, don't get up tight about it. The best thing to do by far is to make a joke about it with your lady love; as I've said, women tend to be more understanding about this sort of thing than men themselves. Get her to massage your penis and – most important – to guide it in with her hand at that tricky moment of entry. (There's no shame in rubbing it yourself if you want to.) Above all, do *not*:

★Make ridiculous excuses ('It must have been the mulligatawny soup, dearest');
★Turn away bitterly, convinced of your own disgrace;
★Get angry with the lady (incredibly, murders have quite often been committed under these circumstances when stupid men have felt that a woman is somehow laughing at their lack of virility).

If you enlist her help, everything will probably be OK. And if it's not – relax and *laugh* about it: given reasonable luck, things should be fine next time.

'I can only do it once a night'

James Bond may have been supposed to do it ten times in an evening (though Ian Fleming never said so), but you almost certainly *can't*. Quite a few teenage men can have sex (say) six times a night, if they really try, but they'll be awfully tired and sore in the morning. But few men in their twenties can often manage more than twice or three times in an evening – and they rarely do even this, because of tiredness from work or study (or because of the grog they've consumed while romancing the lady in question).

Once past thirty, you can feel that you've 'done your stuff' if you just manage one climax in a session – two is a distinct bonus. And over forty, most men are 'one shot guys', as the Americans have it. A two or three shot man deserves a medal (especially as he'll probably feel pretty shattered next day).

Over fifty? You may well find that sometimes you're satisfied with an evening's love-making without even reaching a climax.

The above figures are rough averages; if you're doing better, then good luck to you! If you're not scoring quite so well, then relax a bit more, try to get more sleep, don't work too hard – and avoid excess alcohol. But sex *isn't* an athletic event, you know. So if you and your loved one are happy, who the hell cares how many climaxes you have?

'I've got this tendency to "come" too soon'

Yes – as explained in the searing, in-depth study of the climax to be found in Chapters 4 and 5, the 'anxiety hormones' of the body (like adrenalin) not only affect a man's stiffness – they can also make him 'come' too soon. In fact, most younger men – who are in the main fairly finely-triggered sexually – tend to have their climaxes much sooner than they mean to. With the years one develops control, so by the early twenties, most men should be able to delay their orgasm for as long as they want to. If they aren't selfish, they'll delay it for anything up to half an hour or so, till they're sure their partners are really satisfied. But if you've got a tendency to 'come' a bit too soon (and nothing more serious than that) try these ploys:

★Have a drink – not too much – before love-making: it helps to calm slightly over-anxious types.
★When you feel a climax getting near, immediately turn your mind to other things: Einstein's Special Theory of Relativity, the possibility that Sebastian Coe will break the world record for the mile, the best bait for catching cod, the imminence of the new Ice Age, the place of Man in the Universe, or whatever.
★Pinch yourself or bite the pillow – these 'distraction techniques' often work in cases of mild over-excitability.
★Try the 'Valsalva manoeuvre' – this is a medical trick in which, when you think you're getting near a climax, you close your mouth and blow hard against the closed lips so that your tummy is puffed out. (Don't go on too long, or you'll make yourself faint.)

73

★ *Most important* – tell the lady that you're trying hard not to come! Get her to stop wriggling, squeezing, making sexy remarks, and all the other nice things that women do – otherwise, she'll shoot you over the top!

★ At all costs, treat it light-heartedly with her. If you can get her to help you slow down, then that's great. But if you *can't* avoid ejaculating too soon, then apologise – but do make really sure you then make up for it by then stimulating her to whatever heights she wants with your fingers and lips. (Regrettably, far too many men just go to sleep when they've 'come' too soon – a recent survey showed that this was one of the main complaints of Frenchwomen about Frenchmen as lovers!)

★ If things aren't too good, you could try diminishing the sensitivity of your penis with a local anaesthetic jelly, cream or ointment. Your doctor might be willing to prescribe this stuff – and you can certainly buy it at a sex shop. It may not work, but it's worth a try – though you'd better bear in mind that local anaesthetics can give you – or your lady – soreness because of 'sensitivity' reactions.

★ But if things are so bad that you need these preparations, your case of 'premature ejaculation' is fairly severe. These days it's easily curable. To find out how, read the chapters on more serious sex problems (17 to 21).

'I have trouble getting to a climax'

Not so common in men as in women, but – as I've indicated above – a lot of men have this trouble when they're tired or ill, or have had too much to drink. If this has only happened to you *occasionally*, then don't worry about it. Get your loved one to do a few more sexy things to you (see Chapters 9, 11 and 13) and to say a few loving words to turn you on. But if it's happening often or always, then things are more serious – though, once again, curable. See Chapters 17 to 21.

'I feel guilty about masturbation'

For Heaven's sake, forget it! 98 per cent of men have masturbated, and the other 2 per cent are probably suffering from some hormone deficiency, or are too busy taking degrees in sociology. Unless you have plans to be a saint (and even then I'm sure the Good Lord would forgive you) then just accept that masturbation is part of life. Naturally, the habit gets less common when a man settles down in a stable relationship with a lady. But even many married men masturbate, especially when they're away from home, and there's nothing wrong with that. Just look back to the second section of this chapter – the one for women – and see what we said about masturbation there. It doesn't make hair grow on your palms, or harm your eyesight, or screw up your future sex life. All it does is to relieve sexual tension in a natural and healthy way. It can also do good things like help promote sleep when you've got insomnia – much better than sleeping pills, and much more fun! The great thing about masturbation is that it's like the old saying 'If wishes were horses, beggars would ride'. In the sort of cheerful masturbatory fantasy that most men indulge in, you can 'have' any lady in the world whom you fancy – with none of the problems and risks that such a liaison would cause in real life.

'I just feel guilty'

As I said at the start of this chapter, British researcher Michael Schofield's findings indicate that the plain, ordinary guilt about sex is about the commonest worry in twenty-five year old adults. More than one in four young men suffer from it. I suggest you read what I said about guilt in the section of this chapter intended for women – section (ii). I reiterate what I said there: *of course*, it's natural for you to feel guilty if you're doing something wrong, e.g.:

★Treating a girl badly;
★Exposing somebody to the risk of pregnancy or VD;
★'Knocking off' your best friend's fiancée;
★Stealing somebody else's wife;
★Making love to your girl friend's mother (yes, these *Graduate*-type situations DO really occur);
★Having some sordid commercial encounter with a terrible-looking old whore who should be drawing her old age pension.

Otherwise, think about why you feel guilty. Is it just because of what your parents or grandparents or teachers told you years ago – or perhaps *didn't* tell you, but instilled into you by their Puritanical attitudes? If that's all, then chuck their attitudes out of your mind. Sex is why we're all here – and good, loving sex is beautiful, natural and wholesome. Particularly if you're engaged or married to the lady in question, you have nothing to be guilty about.

'I think I'm over-sexed'

I have never met anyone who was genuinely over-sexed – though Schofield's above-mentioned survey showed that 9 per cent of men (and 2 per cent of women) thought they were. What you really mean, I imagine, is that you just like sex. That's fine – it's a super activity. If you really enjoy having ten or twenty or even (like one of Dr Kinsey's patients) thirty-three orgasms a week, then good luck to you. If you take precautions against pregnancy and VD, then the only side-effect I know of that you might get is a very sore and swollen penis.

The only thing to bear in mind is this. If you're having sex very often in order to prove something, then that's just stupid. You should have sex because you like it (or because your partner likes it) – *not* because you're trying to prove how great you are in bed. If you think you fall into this latter category, then you're like a male version of those so-called 'nymphomaniac' girls who keep on having man after man after man in a desperate effort to seek fulfilment. Get medical advice or counselling – if you're young, you could go to a Youth Advisory Service or similar organisation if there is one in your area (see Chapter 21).

'I think I'm losing interest in sex'

Far fewer men than women have this problem. Likely causes include:

* ★You're over-working;
* ★You're depressed (see your doctor);
* ★You're drinking too much;
* ★You've fallen out of love with your present lady;
* ★You're not really very highly sexed – which is a perfectly honourable state (after all, we're not all mad-keen on football or golf – why should we all be crazy about sex?)
* ★You're really *gay* – read the next section.

'I'm afraid I'm gay'

At least 5 per cent of men *are* – maybe 10 per cent. It could be that you're one of them. But read through what I said about homosexuality in the section of this chapter intended for women – Section (ii). Much the same remarks apply to men, many of whom go through a transient bisexual phase especially in their early teens – but then become straight.

Dr Kinsey showed that an incredible one third of American teenagers had had a homosexual experience to the point of orgasm. And even in adulthood, the odd homosexual fantasy or dream *doesn't* make you gay. If in doubt, seek counselling – see Chapter 21. But if you're *sure* that you're gay, then don't risk messing up some girl's life – as a few homosexuals still do – by having a heavy affair with her or even marrying her. Just accept that you're gay – and enjoy it.

'I think I'm AC/DC'

I'm almost tempted to reply 'Aren't we all?' – because psychologists now feel that no one is absolutely and entirely heterosexual or homosexual. When I first published a statement like that a good few years ago, I used to get letters like this:

> 'Dear Dr Delvin,
> What rubbish! I personally am *entirely* heterosexual. Stop standing up for those goddam "pooves" and "fairies".
> Yours sincerely,
> Disgusted of Tunbridge Wells.'

Nowadays, if I say in print that no one is 100 per cent 'hetero' or 'homo', the letters I get read like this:

> 'Dear Doc,
> I take real exception to what you say. Personally, I'm 100 per cent *gay* – and there's not a drop of heterosexual blood in my body. How *dare* you suggest otherwise?
> Yours furiously,
> Indignant of Hampstead.'

(Seriously, I'm not making this up! I really do get missives like that.) My view of the spectrum of human sexuality has been greatly changed by the years during which I worked in VD clinics, where I discovered just how much bisexuality there is around.

I've summed up my view of the sexual spectrum in Figure 19. As you'll see, far more men (and women) than is generally realised are attracted to both sexes at times – especially during the early years of adulthood, and when the person is under a bit of stress. I can't help acknowledging my old-fashioned feeling that AC/DC relationships are a bit disruptive of family life and of what's often called 'the fabric of society'. But if you seem to be a bit of a 'floating voter' in early adulthood, then don't worry: you'll prob-

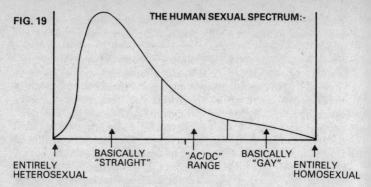

FIG. 19 THE HUMAN SEXUAL SPECTRUM:-

ENTIRELY HETEROSEXUAL | BASICALLY "STRAIGHT" | "AC/DC" RANGE | BASICALLY "GAY" | ENTIRELY HOMOSEXUAL

ably soon choose which way you want to go. Whichever way it is, good luck to you.

'I've got this discharge'

Discharge in men nearly always means either

    (i) Non-specific urethritis (NSU), or
   (ii) gonorrhoea ('clap')

Both are curable, but both need prompt treatment. *Don't* have sex till you've completed the course of therapy. Fuller details – Chapter 23.

'My penis is sore (or swollen)'

A sore (or swollen) penis is often just due to over-use, in which case give it a bit of a rest, or next time, use a gentle lubricant like baby oil. These days, however, lots of men get sore penises because they've picked up one of the infections that literally millions of women get each year – particularly thrush. See the ladies' section of this chapter – section (ii) – for full details. A simple anti-thrush cream from your doctor will rapidly cure you.

    P.S. It's not the lady's fault; in fact, you may have given it to *her*. And bear in mind that thrush can often arise without any sexual infidelity between the partners. More details in Chapter 22.

'My penis is bent'

Few guys have totally *straight* penises. For a start, when erect, it's natural for them to bend towards your stomach – a bit like a

78

banana. But many penises bend a bit in the other plane – that is, to the right or to the left. Slight bends of this sort do not matter – and anyway tend to straighten out during erection. There is no truth in the famous poem about the chap whose penis twisted to the right – but whose wife unfortunately had a left-hand screw. There is, however, a fairly uncommon though important condition in which the *erect* penis develops a strange kink in it – angulating sharply to the right or left. This is called 'Peyronie's syndrome' or 'chordee', and although it provokes people to all sorts of brave jokes like 'I dunno whether I'm coming or going, doctor', it's really no laughing matter. In severe and untreated cases, love-making is impossible. If you think you have this condition, see a urological specialist (a urologist) as soon as possible so that treatment can be started. One problem is that the angulation of the penis may not be apparent when it is limp – and not many people are keen on showing an erect penis to a surgeon so that he can see the bend. A distinguished British urologist has now got round this problem: he issues suspected cases of Peyronie's disease with a Polaroid camera – so they can take a confirmatory photo of the bent penis in the privacy of their homes. Drugs such as Vitamin E and potassium para-aminobenzoate seem to help some.

'I think *I'm* bent'

An awful lot of men – but far fewer women – have 'kinky' ideas involving unusual and exotic ways of making love. These 'kinks' usually seem to have their origin in early childhood. At least, that's what the Freudians tell us – and in this instance, I believe they're probably right. (If you think about it, some of the more common 'kinks' – like being obsessed with being strapped up, or liking to lie on rubber sheets *do* seem to remind one of certain things that happen to every baby, don't they?) The point I want to make here is that the dividing line between what is 'kinky' and what is 'normal' is often not very clear at all. In other words, people frequently worry quite unnecessarily about their sexual preferences.

To take one example, it used to be common, especially among working class men and women, to regard any love-making position except the classic 'missionary' one as 'perverted'. Nowadays, most people – especially men – are quite keen to try out as many positions as possible. During the time I've been practising medicine, we've seen the most amazing changes in attitude towards what's considered to be 'bent'. Twenty years ago, many doctors thought that oral love-making was 'perverted' – nowadays it's par for the course. Similarly, as recently as the 1970s you could still find a few medical men who thought that masturbation was a 'perversion' – but I think they've pretty well all died out now.

People should realise that so-called 'kinky' practices are often just exaggerations of behaviour that's fairly normal for the rest of us. For instance, most men and women are agreeable to a bit of gentle bottom-smacking – and indeed many ladies can reach a climax through this stimulation alone! But things have clearly got a bit exaggerated in the case of the man who has to go to a prostitute and have his backside caned if he is to get any sexual satisfaction at all. That is one definition of the 'dividing line'. If you *have* to go in for a particular activity in order to get satisfaction, then you've got problems. You can get treatment from a psychiatrist, and this is often quite successful – particularly when the condition has only come on during a period of stress, as is often the case. (In years gone by, I've seen a number of patients who, at stressful periods of their lives, felt driven to dress up as women or to put themselves in handcuffs – but who dropped these habits when the pressures of life were easier.) But often there's not a lot of point in seeking treatment, provided that your 'special taste' is quite harmless, and that your partner is happy about it. All over the world, for instance, there are men who like their wives to wear plastic raincoats while making love (echoes of babyhood again, I think!). It sounds dotty – but it's certainly harmless as long as the lady doesn't mind having a slightly chilly backside.

WARNING. If, on the other hand, your particular 'kink' is anti-social or potentially harmful to other people (for instance, child pornography, or violent sadism), then **I advise you very, very strongly to seek psychiatric help before the police (or possibly – in some parts of the world – a lynch mob) catch up with you.**

Happily, most slightly unusual or – if you like – slightly 'kinky' activities aren't like that. People go in for them just for fun – and to add spice and variety to their love-making – and also, perhaps, to pep up a sex drive that has been sapped by tiredness, overwork or boredom. Such bed-time frolics which you and your loved one may want to try out some time are discussed in Chapters 14, 15 and 16. These chapters also stress the *dangers* of certain practices.

CHAPTER SEVEN

Understanding (And Loving) Your Partner

You can't do it all just by 'technique' ● *The importance of romance* ●
Is actual love necessary? ● *How common is sexual misunderstanding?* ● *The importance of talking* ● *Looking for things that turn your partner on* ● *Making yourself attractive to your partner.*

You can't do it all just by 'technique'

A lot of this book is about sexual technique – some of it pretty advanced sexual technique too. But let me stress again that all the technique in the world won't make you a good and desirable lover if you're:

★selfish;
★lacking in warmth and tenderness;
★uncaring about your partner and his/her sexual fulfilment.

Of course, if you're a complete and utter bastard (male or female) then you probably won't be reading this chapter anyway! But if you're like most people, you could probably do with showing just a little more tenderness, affection and consideration in bed.

It's mostly women who complain that their partners aren't considerate enough in bed. But Shere Hite's report on male sexuality makes absolutely clear that a high proportion of men have exactly the same feelings about their womenfolk! I agree entirely with what Shere Hite says: because doctors see an awful lot of men who desperately wish that their ladies would show more attentiveness and understanding in bed. 'She just lies there thinking she's doing me a great favour and expecting me to do all the work,' is a common male complaint. For *both* sexes, the message is clear. Try to understand what your partner's basic needs are – both physical and emotional. Does he/she need more cuddling, more murmuring of sweet nothings, more whispered ruderies, more evocation of sexy fantasies – or just more reassurance and more love? It'll pay you rich dividends if you can find out.

The importance of romance

I don't want to labour this topic, but to my mind the most

important aspect of mutual understanding is romance. Yet it's so often forgotten – by both men and women! The things that men do include:

- ★Coming home from work and not bothering to kiss their wives;
- ★Gawping at the TV all evening without talking to their partners;
- ★Getting into bed unshaven – and probably with smelly feet;
- ★Then wondering why they get a frosty reception when they roll over and expect sex!

As for women – well, the things they do wrong from a romantic point of view are best summed up in that wonderfully shrewd song *Time To Get Ready For Love* – in which the lyricist neatly explains how failure to do your hair or fix your make-up may *well* lead to your man being tempted down the primrose path by one of the girls at the office. So watch it, both of you: keep romance fresh, and be considerate and loving.

Is actual love necessary?

This is one of the really big questions. Traditional moralists would say that sexual union between man and woman *without* love is not only wrong – but also totally unsatisfactory and unfulfilling. Though this argument sounds all right – and though I am personally in favour of sex mainly taking place between people who love each other – one has to face facts. Many people have sexual relationships with partners whom they don't actually love – very often these relationships are very satisfactory. If that idea upsets you, I'm sorry, but one can't get away from the truth; as English researcher Michael Schofield has clearly shown, a very high proportion of young adults (both men and women) go through a distinctly promiscuous phase in their lives. (For example, Schofield demonstrated that among unmarried twenty-five year old adults in Britain, 39 per cent had had sex with more than one person in the past year.) Clearly, not all these relationships can involve genuine love – though perhaps considerable affection. But despite that, the men and women concerned often enjoy such relationships very much indeed.

Of course, there are ghastly loveless sex affairs, in which one or both partners has a miserable time – and probably wishes to Heaven afterwards that they'd never done it. (This is particularly likely if as so often happens the two participants were drunk at the time – or if the 'quick screw' leads to VD, or to an unwanted pregnancy.) But though I know I'll anger strict sexual moralists by saying so, I have to admit that lots of women and men do have very rewarding and delightful sexual experiences with people whom they don't actually love. Sometimes such experiences really are just 'one-night stands', in which a couple meet, perhaps go out to dinner – and then go to bed together and have really good sex, before parting in the morning.

But being an incurable romantic, I do feel that even the more casual type of relationship has the best chance of physical and emotional success if the couple feel considerable human warmth, tenderness and affection towards each other – though I must admit that once you reach this stage, you're really not very far away from what is at least a *form* of love.

How common is sexual misunderstanding?

In practice, most couples take quite a while to get to understand each other's sexual needs, and for each to get to know what the other one likes and dislikes in bed. I'd say a year is about average – but even then, the slightly unfortunate fact is that (as I've explained in earlier chapters) statistics show that the great majority of couples don't usually reach a simultaneous climax during intercourse. Still, that's not the end of the world – and most men and women can have a very good and loving bedtime relationship, even if they don't actually 'come' at the same time.

But there are two big troubles, which are:

★Very often, a couple never really 'settle down' at the start and don't try to understand each other's sexual needs;
★Even more frequently, a couple may have had a good, steady relationship for many years – and then seem to grow apart. They get to understand less and less about each other's desires and feelings, and the sex relationship gradually goes up the creek.

Divorce often follows either situation, of course. The truly appalling divorce statistics in western countries (with one in three British marriages likely to end up in the courts, and an even worse state of affairs in North America) are in no small measure related to the commonness of sexual misunderstanding between husband and wife.

In other words:

★*She* doesn't really understand what he wants;
★*He* doesn't really understand what she wants.

Both become increasingly angry with each other, or perhaps more and more indifferent. Sex becomes more infrequent – and less successful when it does occur. She throws herself into her job, into housework, or coffee mornings, or into an obsessive interest with the children – or else takes a lover. He flings himself into his work, or into sport, or else spends every possible evening going 'out with the boys', takes to the bottle, heads for the massage parlours, or perhaps finds himself a mistress. Sounds a bit grim, doesn't it? But it can be prevented. And the remedy is in the next section. . . .

The importance of talking

This may sound a cliché to you, but every marriage counsellor or doctor working in this field will tell you the same: *If a couple can only get talking about their sex lives, there is a hope of resolving the mutual misunderstanding*. It may not work – but it offers a chance.

Let's take one of many, many similar cases. Jayne was American, and got married to an Englishman in a whirl of romance. Within a few years, things were going badly wrong, both in bed and out of it. Matters were so bad that sex only took place about once in two months – 'And even then, I have to remind him' said Jayne indignantly.

Unfortunately, like most people in this sort of situation, Jayne and Peter couldn't talk about it. *She* felt that he was immature and that he wanted to treat her as a mother. *He* felt that she was rejecting him and didn't understand that at the end of a long day, he badly needed to be cuddled by warm, loving arms – and to rest his head on a soft breast.

Fortunately, they brought themselves to seek advice from an experienced marriage counsellor. She got them talking (with great difficulty), and the truth eventually came out – which was:

★Peter had been sent away to an English boarding school at the age of eleven. Ever since, he had felt rejected by his mother;
★When they had met and married, Peter not only liked and loved Jayne – he also felt that this was a girl who would give him the *maternal* love which he had so desperately craved;
★Jayne, on the other hand, had had a rather 'matter-of-fact' mother who avoided demonstrative physical love – and Jayne had tended to acquire her attitudes. *Her* father had never

wanted to rest his head on Mum's breasts, and she couldn't imagine what Peter saw in such 'childish' behaviour.

It took quite prolonged counselling – with the careful stimulation of a lot of talk between Jayne and Peter – to make the pair of them realise that their attitudes were different – and that they were being far too inflexible in these attitudes.

For instance, Jayne came to realise that:

★Most men, however mature, appreciate a bit of 'mothering' now and again.
★It's not an insult to a woman if her husband sometimes regards her as the warm, tender, lady who will welcome him home to her breast when things aren't going well.

And Peter had to learn that:

★Women are quite rightly often very independent-minded and self-assertive these days: they may not take kindly to being regarded as a pair of walking breasts for a man to weep all over!
★Nonetheless, a woman can learn to provide a man with the comfort and reassurance he needs when things are going against him – but only if she understands *why* he needs that help.

Jayne and Peter got it together in the end – entirely due to the fact that the counsellor had got them to *talk* to each other.

It is only if you talk to each other – being brutally frank, using honest sexual language ('You couldn't care less about making me come – all you want is your own goddam climax!') and getting to the stage of tears if need be, that you'll get yourself out of one of these difficult but oh-so-common situations.

Looking for things that turn your partner on

Let's get to something just as important but a little less depressing – finding out what turns your partner on. Far too little attention is paid to this, I'm afraid. For instance, lots of young men think that their girlfriends will be turned on by the same things that turn on men. They tell them dirty jokes, assure them of the amazing size of their penises – and then wonder why the poor girls don't immediately tear off their clothes and leap into bed. (A common male response to a refusal like this is: 'She must be a *lesbian*, I suppose – can't understand it, meself.')

Similarly, women often have little notion about what turns men on – and especially about the *fantasies* they like to indulge in. US women have recently been horrified by Ms Hite's revelation that no less than 99 per cent of their men-folk masturbate – doing so not just because they're not 'getting enough' in the marital bed, but because skilled hand masturbation can give a *very* delicate sensation (and their partners may not have learned the technique of doing this skilfully). Perhaps most of all, masturbation – with all its drawbacks in terms of lack of personal contact, warmth and love – does give very free rein to the rich sexual fantasy life which so many men want to live.

So, learn about your partner's favourite 'turn-ons'. That sterling British institution, *The Sun* newspaper, recently carried out a massive poll in which it set out to find out what its male and female readers' special turn-ons were. In summary, these were the results:

WOMEN

34% turned on by books and pictures.
31%   "   "   sexy clothing.
25%   "   "   candlelit dinners, wine and music.
20%   "   "   bottom smacking, biting, etc.
14%   "   "   vibrators.
13%   "   "   mirrors or cameras.
10%   "   "   acting out fantasies.

MEN

39% turned on by books and pictures.
31%   "   "   sexy clothes.
30%   "   "   candlelit dinners, wine and music.
25%   "   "   vibrators.
20%   "   "   bottom smacking, biting, etc.
20%   "   "   mirrors or cameras.
16%   "   "   acting out fantasies.

The surprising thing about these figures is that the male and female 'turn-on' lists are so similar!

Making yourself attractive to your partner

This should scarcely need saying, but it certainly does! So many people reach an appalling degree of sexual misunderstanding with their partners: 'He/she isn't interested in me,' they cry. And then, when the doctor or counsellor looks at them and examines them, the reason becomes abundantly clear. **They are physically not very attractive** – not through any fault of nature, as a rule, but through sheer general slovenliness. After all, would *you* want to make love to one of the many people who are dirty/scruffy/smelly/badly made-up/possessed of ugly (and dangerous-looking) broken finger nails? Here are a few basic recommendations which should help to improve relationships:

WOMEN:
★Don't for God's sake, go to bed with your hair in rollers;
★Don't go to bed covered in blobs of face cream;
★If you think your complexion isn't great, don't go to bed without at least a modicum of make-up;
★Don't go to bed with scruffy, greasy, unwashed hair;
★Don't go to bed with bad breath: you'd be surprised how common this is – and it's mostly curable in two minutes with a toothbrush;
★Don't go to bed wearing some passion-killing garment that would put off Don Giovanni himself;
★Don't forget perfume.

MEN
★Don't go to bed with a rough chin;
★Don't go to bed without taking reasonable precautions against BO;
★Don't wander around the bedroom dressed in smelly socks – and wash your feet as well;
★Don't go to bed with dirty hair:
★Don't come into the bedroom with jagged nails – these may seriously damage your partner;
★Above all, *don't* come into the bedroom with your private parts in an unhygienic condition. It's amazing how many men don't seem to wash down below very regularly – and then they wonder why their wives won't participate in oral sex.

So wash every night. And here's a good tip – a swift dab of after-shave lotion 'down there' will not only render your most personal part more attractive to your partner – but also, through its dilating effect on the blood vessels – have a certain pleasing effect in stimulating you to rise to the occasion.

CHAPTER EIGHT

How To Make Women Happy With Love Play

Simple things first ● A note about lesbian love play ● Why have love play anyway? ● Should you 'pet' the lady to a climax? ● Verbal techniques of love play ● Caressing her 'erogenous zones' ● Stimulating her breasts ● The key to it all: the clitoris ● Love play techniques inside her vagina ● Cunnilingus (oral love play).

Simple things first

In this chapter and the next one, we'll be dealing with the more simple and straightforward love play techniques, which every man and woman should know about (but which lamentably few can carry out with any great skill). In subsequent chapters, we'll be looking at much more *exotic* methods of love play which can be of great value to advanced students of the art of love. This chapter devotes itself to the love play methods which a man can and should use on a woman – while the next one (Chapter 9) deals with those which a lady can use on a man.

A note about lesbian love play

Incidentally, these days I keep getting indignant letters in my postbag at *SHE* magazine from lesbians who say: 'You MCP! Don't you realise that it isn't just *men* who do these things to *women*? Love play is for women to use on women too!' So, though I must personally admit to a preference for old-fashioned 'boy-meets-girl' sex, I must also admit that if you happen to be gay, there's no reason why you shouldn't read this chapter. In practice, I understand that most gay women are already exceedingly skilled in love play techniques – for the very obvious reason that they have women's bodies and therefore often know exactly what it takes to really thrill another woman. We men could certainly learn from the care and attention which they devote to exciting and satisfying their partners.

Indeed, the sheer love play skill of experienced gay women, coupled with the fact that – unlike most men – they don't lose their interest in further sexual activity once they've 'come', is one of the reasons why they often find it so easy to seduce a young woman – especially if the young woman in question is fed up with her boy friend's fumbling and inept attempts at love play. A senior member of the Women's Pro Tennis Circuit is reported to say to young women tennis players in the dressing room: 'Why bother with those clumsy boys? We know how to give you a *really* good time.'

Why have love play anyway?

Lots of men seem to think that there's no need for love play – that it's 'silly' or 'cissy', or that it's much better to plunge straight in and start 'screwing'. Well, if that's your point of view, I suggest you re-read the section just above. If you *don't* use satisfactory love play techniques on your lady then – who knows – you may find her going off with a female Wimbledon champion! More seriously, there are vitally important physiological reasons why a man needs to use love play with a woman before 'just plunging in'. The reasons are these:

- ★In the unaroused state, a woman's vagina is relatively tightly closed by the muscles round the vaginal opening.
- ★Similarly, in the unaroused state, a lady's vagina is fairly dry and unlubricated.

It's only when a lady has been properly romanced and complimented, caressed and cuddled and given an adequate amount of love play that two vital changes take place:

- ★The muscles of her vagina open up in a welcoming fashion;
- ★The walls of her vagina start to pour out a lubricating fluid which helps to make intercourse easy and pleasant.

So, romance your lady and give her plenty of love play before you enter. In some women, five minutes may be enough. Others may need up to half an hour – and it's important that during this time the man should *not* fall into the common errors of looking at his watch (seriously), sighing resignedly, or saying, 'Aren't you *ready* yet?' In fact, there's no need for a bloke to get bored or fatigued while he's stimulating his lady, for two good reasons:

- ★He should enjoy and take pride in the pleasure he's giving to her;
- ★At the same time, *she* should be doing nice things to *him*! (See next chapter.)

Should you 'pet' the lady to a climax by love play?

This is a question I'm often asked, and male readers of my columns, especially, are frequently worried by this delicate point of etiquette. If you use one of the 'petting' techniques outlined later in this chapter (and in other chapters), and if you do it skilfully and tenderly on a lady who has no hang-ups and who loves – or at least likes – you, then there's going to come a point when she shows every sign of being about to reach a climax. Do you continue doing whatever you're doing with your mouth or your fingers or whatever? Or do you, as one bewildered US male enquired of the *Playboy Advisor*, 'just sorta leap aboard like a surfer trying to catch a wave, thrust like crazy and hope you'll catch up with her'?

The answer is – *it depends*. If you know perfectly well that the lady is one of that fortunate and talented minority of women who can and do have climax after climax with no difficulty (see the section on multiple orgasms in Chapter 4), then there's absolutely no need for you to stop whatever kind of love play you're using and switch over to intercourse. Just carry on with what's obviously a highly successful petting technique, and enjoy the delicious spectacle of watching her reach a climax in your arms. (Don't forget to tell her afterwards how lovely she looked.) If you like, you can bring her to orgasm after orgasm before she's ready for you to come in.

However, if you're sure she's one of those ladies who don't have more than one climax in an evening, then things are a bit different. In other words, if she shows signs that orgasm is fairly imminent (such as ever-quickening gasps and shrieks of pleasure, ever more intense thrusts of her pelvis, and a tendency to hug you ever-tighter as waves of pleasure sweep through her body), then clearly you should consider putting your penis inside her. Often the lady will make things absolutely clear to you by merrily crying 'Fuck me *now*, Clarence,' or some similar expression. However, even then, do be a bit careful! All too often what happens in these circumstances is that the man 'enters' his partner and – carried away by all this passionate urging and shrieking and wriggling – manages to 'come' himself just that bit too soon. The lady may be left 'high and dry' (so to speak), and unless you're one of the minority of men who can keep thrusting hard after you reach your climax, she can be left frustrated. Happily, however, you can usually remedy this situation if you manually 'pet' her to a climax, just as soon as you've recovered your senses after your own.

There *is* a better way of doing things than this, however, and it's the way used by skilled lovers. What you do is this. When your lady looks like reaching her one and only climax of the evening, by all means 'enter' her. But take it easy: don't go 'over the top' yourself until you're absolutely sure that she is there too. In other words, exercise the control which is the hallmark of a skilled lover. And always remember that you can speed your lady to that last peak by rubbing her clitoris with your finger tips at the same time as you make love to her – as well as by whispering loving words in her ear. (See below.)

Verbal techniques of love play

There are a very few women who can actually be roused to a climax by having 'sweet nothings' whispered in their ears. Some can even do it over the phone! All women place a great deal of value on being verbally complimented in bed. Telling them how beautiful, how adorable, and how sexy they are forms a very important part of love play. Most men are a great deal better at this sort of thing these days than they used to be. Twenty years ago the average US, British or Australian male thought it was rather undignified to say romantic things to a woman – that sort of stuff was strictly for 'foreigners'! Alas, though, a lot of couples still make love in a kind of embarrassed silence, as if they were terrified to say anything to each other. So, don't be embarrassed about saying romantic things. Don't forget to say 'I love you', (assuming, of course, that you mean it) because those three words are probably more erotic than anything else on earth. And though it's not everyone's cup of tea, there's a lot to be said for a more robust form of verbal love play. Many couples quite uninhibitedly use basic four letter words to urge each other on in bed, and there's nothing in the least wrong with this.

However, it's fairly obvious that a man should employ caution when he first tries this. A smart, sophisticated career girl who uses the odd expletive herself now and then will almost certainly enjoy it, but a wife who has been primly brought up may be a little shattered if somebody tells her she has a 'beautiful cunt'. Some men still think that women relish very coarse jokes in bed, but this is rarely so. Many a girl has been turned off by her mate trying to tell her some really obscene story just when she's feeling all warm and romantic! In fact, there's one great advantage in employing basic Anglo-Saxon terms as a form of verbal love play because at least your lady will understand what you're talking about! Few people, even in these so-called enlightened days, know the proper names for the various parts of their sex organs, but most of them

do at least know the rude ones. Your wife may not really understand the word 'vulva' (unless she's read this book), but she'll
probably have heard the Anglo-Saxon equivalent mentioned
above.

Caressing her 'erogenous zones'

I said in Chapter 2 that you could practically consider a woman's
whole body as one great, throbbing 'erogenous zone'. And it's
certainly true that many women enjoy stimulation of almost any
part of their bodies, provided it's skilfully and lovingly done.
However, the main sexy areas of a woman, as I said earlier in the
book, tend to be her lips, tongue, ears, neck, shoulders, armpits,
spine, navel and belly, her buttocks and her thighs. (There's also
her bosom, of course – but we'll come to that in a moment.)
Caressing any or all of these areas long before you make any
approach to her vagina will pay rich dividends – and not just for
the physiological reasons mentioned earlier in this chapter. It is
also emotionally necessary for most women to be caressed in these
non-genital areas prior to intercourse. They may well feel that you
are 'treating them cheaply' or 'just using them' if you make an
immediate lunge for the genitals without a preliminary 'courtship'
that takes in some or all of the erogenous zones that I've mentioned.

What should you do to these areas? Do what comes naturally:

★Stroke
★Rub
★Tickle – but be wary: some women like only a firm touch and
  are irritated by light strokes or tickles
★Pat gently
★Slap a little more firmly in some areas if you like – particularly
  over the buttocks
★Caress with your eye-lashes ('butterfly kisses')
★Nuzzle
★Bite (gently, please)
★Above all, kiss

Kissing is too often forgotten in these crazy days in which men
think they need exotic and bizarre sex aids in order to pleasure a
woman. I'm particularly appalled at how many men completely
forget that you cannot make love successfully to a woman without
kissing her mouth! The mouth, after all, is one of the most highly
charged sensual areas of the body, with both the tongue and the

lips being very rich in sexy nerve endings. Don't confine yourself to just pressing lips against lips, and optimistically making a bit of a squelching noise. Instead, experiment with:

★Pushing your tongue deep into your loved one's mouth;
★Sucking her tongue into yours;
★Turning your head so that the rough *upper* surface of your tongue rubs against the upper surface of hers;
★Running your tongue tip around the space between her teeth and her lips – some women find this intensely erotic.

More exotic things to do with your mouth (and hers) are described later in the book.

Stimulating her breasts

Instinct tells most – though not all – men what to do here. The most popular manoeuvre is simply to cup a breast in each of your hands and to squeeze gently and rhythmically. Stroking the area round the nipple turns many women on, but you should experiment for yourself to see what your partner likes best. Kissing and sucking the nipples is exciting for almost all women – and some can reach a climax just from this stimulation alone. But don't overdo it: the nipple is a delicate part of the body and violent suction or the use of your teeth can hurt! Don't forget to try stimulating the very end of the nipple with the tip of your tongue. If you use these methods of breast love play, your lady's nipples will stand out firm and erect, and indeed her bosom will increase slightly in bulk (though only for a few minutes, alas).

Don't forget to compliment her on her breasts while you're doing all this. In this mammary-conscious age, many women have very real feelings of inferiority about their breasts. So any nice remark you can make will not only increase her enjoyment but may help her to feel proud of her bosoms – probably quite justifiably.

The key to it all: the clitoris

After a variable amount of non-vaginal love play, the time comes when you can make that first approach to her vaginal area. I'd strongly recommend that even now, you don't make a great lunge at your partner's clitoris! It's better by far to brush against it – almost as if by accident – to start with; then go back to caressing her thigh or belly or whatever; and only return to the clitoris after a good deal of titillation of this sort. If you've done your job properly, your lady will now be more than eager for you to turn your attention directly to her clitoris. Indeed, she may well be clasping your hand and guiding it insistently there.

You should find that things are pretty moist by now, since her secretions have had plenty of time to start lubricating the opening of the vagina. If she is still rather dry, you could lick your fingers and use the moisture as a lubricant. It's also possible to buy tubes of lubricant at pharmacies, but the natural 'love juices' are best.

If you look back at the picture in Chapter 2, you'll see where the clitoris lies, and where to put your finger tips. You don't have to locate it exactly – just gently place the pads of your fingers on the approximate spot and rub upwards and downwards, an inch or two either way. Every now and then vary this by stimulating the whole area with the flat of your hand. Note that some women don't like *direct* pressure on the clitoris, but prefer it to come from the side. You can rub moderately firmly, squeezing the soft tissues against the pubic bone (which is the hard surface lying just under the triangle of pubic hair). However do bear in mind that the little clitoris itself (being very similar in structure to your own penis) is usually rather sensitive, so it may be best to move away very briefly from it from time to time before returning with some slightly new technique of rubbing (for example, moving your finger-tips in a circular fashion). Keep 'scooping' up a little moisture from the vaginal opening just below and applying it to the area of the clitoris. Above all, if you're not sure what she likes best, *ask*.

Learning to stimulate the clitoris properly takes time and you will not become expert at it within a matter of weeks, or even months. Early attempts at clitoral stimulation are usually pretty inept, but don't give up – you'll get the technique eventually. If you use it properly your partner will soon be very excited indeed, for the clitoris (like the male penis) is the main key to sexual pleasure, and the source of most orgasms. However, there is another important 'orgasmic key' in the vagina – see below.

Love play techniques inside her vagina

Contrary to what so many sexologists taught over the years, it's now accepted that a lot of sexual sensation *does* arise from inside the vagina. It's not just the clitoris that makes a woman 'come'. But women do vary a lot in how much sensation they feel from inside the vagina – with some getting a tremendous amount of vaginal sensation, and others relatively little. Some women are very afraid of being caressed inside the vagina, because they're scared of having anything inside them. If your partner has this problem – which is called 'vaginismus' – you and she should read Chapter 6 (on minor sex problems) and – if things are really bad – the complete section on sex problems later in the book (Chapters 17 to 21).

If you've started this book at the beginning, you'll be aware that at the beginning of the 1980s it was discovered that there is a special stimulatory area in the front wall of the vagina, called 'the G-spot'. But stimulating it is an advanced and not entirely easy method of stimulation, which I shan't be describing until Chapter 10. In this chapter, I just want to describe the basic love play techniques of vaginal stimulation, since even these take ages to learn. (If you disregard that warning and don't begin gently, you'll probably end up cutting your lady quite badly with your fingernail.) Indeed, there's no point in trying to master the very skilled caresses described in this section until you've become really good at stimulation of the clitoris. However, once you've got to that stage, you'll find that this is an excellent group of techniques, based on the fact that a man's middle finger fits quite neatly into the vagina.

To begin with, use your right hand for these caresses (assuming, of course, that you're right-handed), because to do them properly requires a great deal of coordination and skill. Clumsiness (which is inevitable among the inexperienced) very readily causes bruising or tearing of the delicate vaginal tissues, as well as temporary injury to the urinary passage (with resultant 'honeymoon cystitis'). Do make sure your nails are properly trimmed before you start.

With your palm *upwards*, gently slip your middle finger into your partner's vagina. You may be able to feel the cervix (or neck of the womb) at the top end. You'll find that when the middle finger is right inside, your thumb or the knuckles of your forefinger will rest on the area of the clitoris, as shown in Figure 20.

Begin moving your hand back and forwards, slowly at first and then more rapidly as you get the hang of it. Not only will the movement of the middle finger in the vagina produce delightful sensations for your partner, but the constant friction of your knuckles against her clitoris will give her exquisite excitement.

As you grow more experienced, you can vary the rate and direction of your thrusts, trying (for instance) circular motions; deep, long strokes; or very rapid short to-and-fro movements. In the early stages, beware of drawing the finger too far out at each stroke – this increases the chance of catching the delicate tissues with your nail. Actually, everybody does this at some stage in their early sexual 'careers'. Unfortunately, it's painful – though not dangerous – for the lady, and she may be alarmed if there's any bleeding. Firm pressure with a *clean* handkerchief (not a paper tissue) or a sanitary napkin will stop it. In time, you can try such variations as putting in both the middle and the index finger – more of this in Chapter 10.

FIG. 20

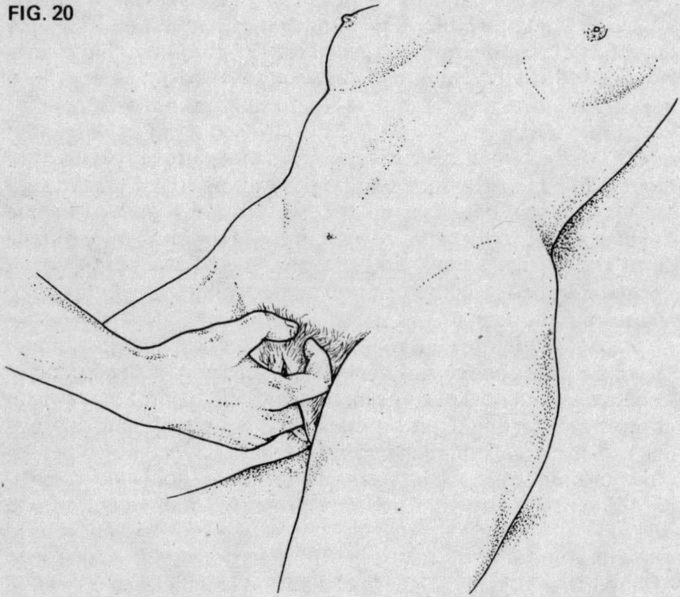

Cunnilingus (oral love play)

No, cunnilingus is *not* an Irish air-line. As I'm sure you know, it means kissing your lady's vulva and vagina. It's sometimes rather strangely spelt 'cunnilinctus' (which makes it sound like a cough medicine), and it's also often referred to as 'going down', 'muff-diving' or – if you're French – '*faire Minette*'. Though a few people are still prejudiced against it, in fact, it's one of the most delightful of all love play methods. Unlike the finger techniques, it is relatively easy to master in a fairly short time.

If you wish, you could begin at the moment in your love play when you've decided that it's time to move from stimulating the rest of the body to concentrate on the vaginal area. Simply bend downwards and apply a few kisses to the upper part of your partner's pubic hair. Gently move your lips an inch or two downwards until you are in the area of the clitoris (your partner's enthusiastic reaction should tell you that you're in the right spot). Then use your lips and tongue to bring her to a high pitch of excitement. Your tongue should slide back and forth over the clitoris in a regular movement, very much as you would do with your finger.

When you have learned to do this, try the effect of actually pushing your tongue into her vagina and moving it rapidly in and out. This is a highly effective method of stimulation that most women enjoy very much. For the inexperienced man, it takes a little getting used to, particularly because it is sometimes difficult to draw breath. (I've even heard it suggested that a snorkel would be a useful accessory.) The woman should therefore take care to keep her thighs well apart so that he can get some air!

This technique works best with one partner (if doesn't matter which) lying on top of the other – the wife can then stimulate her husband's penis using one of the methods outlined in the next chapter. Another way is for the woman just to sit on her partner's face, and wriggle about sexily. Almost as convenient is for the couple to lie on their sides on the bed, with their heads between each other's thighs. This is the famous '69' position – so called because the two bodies are supposed to resemble the figures 6 and 9. Those who have 'the gift of tongues' (sorry) often refer to this posture as 'le soixante-neuf'.

CHAPTER NINE

How To Make Men Happy With Love Play

Women need to know how to 'do love play' too ● Keeping it simple to start with ● Should you 'pet' him to a climax? ● Verbal love play ● Caressing his 'erogenous zones' ● Stimulating his penis: a basic guide to etiquette ● 'Mouth music'

Women need to know how to 'do love play' too

Far too many women think that love play is something men do to women. That's rubbish, because love play is a warm and marvellous part of any sexual relationship between a man and a woman. It's crazy for the woman just to lie there on her back accepting her man's caresses without doing anything for him in return. No wonder that some men get a bit dispirited. Indeed, it came as no surprise to me when I read in Shere Hite's report on the sexuality of US males that a vast number of American men have a pretty low opinion of the average US lady's skill at love play!

Ms Hite's findings agree with what doctors so often hear in the consulting room in Britain or Australia: again and again, men say, 'If only she'd touch me, and caress me. Why doesn't she run her hands all over me? Why doesn't she kiss my penis?' Why not indeed? Usually it's because she is too embarrassed, or has grown up with ideas that it's 'not nice' or 'not ladylike' for women to take the lead. If this is your point of view, think again. For I do assure you that love play is one of the nicest and most generous and most loving things which a woman can do for a man – showing her warmth and tenderness and affection for him and, at the same time, making him feel wanted.

There's another reason too why love play is important – in other words, why a woman should always try and 'pet' her man; a physiological reason – as opposed to the emotional ones we've been talking about. You remember how, in the last chapter, we discussed the fact that preliminary love play is practically a physiological necessity for a woman – because it makes her vaginal muscles relax, and her 'love juices' flow, so that her vagina becomes moist and relaxed and welcoming. You'll recall that without the stimulation of love play to get them ready, many women find intercourse difficult or even impossible. In a way the same is true for many men – specially the older ones. Our crazy

second climax they'll be able to control themselves better, delay things much more, and generally please their partners. But *do* make sure whether you're dealing with a 'one-shot man' or the (far less common) 'repeater man' before you decide to bring him to a love play climax. Obviously, if you judge wrongly, you could be in for a very boring evening.

Verbal love play

As with women, so with men: *verbal* stimulation is a most important part of love play. (One of the few complaints which travelling businessmen make about those mushrooming massage parlours is that 'the girls never say anything nice'. An export salesman told me: 'They just stare at the wall and think about the bloody shopping or something.') Just as a lady likes to be told that she is beautiful and that she is loved, men also like to be complimented in bed. Even today, too many women say next to nothing to their partners during love play – but they're missing out on a valuable bonus by keeping silent. It's amazing how just a quick word of encouragement will immediately increase your man's zest for love-making. So what are you going to say to him?

Telling him you love him (if it's true) is a good start, of course. But you have to remember that a man's mind works in a very different way from yours. In sexual matters men tend to be far more basic than women and they are, on the whole, far less interested in the tender, romantic side of sexual attraction. So to turn your man on, you usually have to say some pretty basic things to him. First of all, compliment him on his body. (However flabby and out of shape he is, he must have *some* good features.) Tell him you love the warmth of him, the strength of his muscles, the curve of his buttocks. Most of all, compliment him on his penis. This kind of thing is of enormous psychological importance to a male. It's very hard for a woman to understand how a man's whole concept of his virility is bound up with his penis. He regards it as the embodiment of his maleness, the symbol of his potency. He tends to be quite ludicrously obsessed with the size of it, often failing to appreciate that it makes no particular difference to you whether his organ is large, medium or small – or that you might even be put off by a huge penis.

So build up his ego. Tell him his penis is beautiful, magnificent, enormous, or whatever descriptions come into your head. Of course, the probable truth is that his organ is little different from anybody else's. Both of you realise that if it were lined up with a dozen others you might not even be able to pick it out from the rest, even if you've been married for twenty years! Indeed, I once briefly investigated a 'sex games' organisation – on behalf of the magazine *World Medicine*, I hasten to add! This outfit specialised in a party game which involved a door equipped with a hole located about hip level. As far as I could make out, all the gents at the party had to go outside – and then they'd take turns to push their penises through the hole. To cut a long story short, the idea of the game was that the wives/girl friends had to guess who the owner of each penis was – and as far as I can determine, most of them had the greatest difficulty in identifying their own gentleman's organ! (PS I didn't actually go to the party.)

Be that as it may, you should try and make your bloke feel that his penis is unique, wonderful and magnificent. It doesn't matter a bit that he knows you're talking with tongue in cheek. The more you can behave as though his penis were some sort of totem pole to be worshipped, the more he'll enjoy it, and you. (I must admit, we blokes have a tendency to be very infantile!)

In your verbal love play, be as frank and as earthy as possible. It seems incredible nowadays, but for generations men and women were afraid to put names to each other's sex organs when they made love. Even today, there are many wives who do try to talk to their husbands in bed, but whose conversation is limited to such embarrassed remarks as 'Shall I rub your er . . . er . . . ?' Remember: love play is the time for being absolutely explicit, and for throwing off *all* your inhibitions. You'll find that it gives your man a great deal of pleasure if you cheerfully use words like 'penis' and 'vagina' as you caress each other. And, if you want, you can use the so-called 'rude' words too. If you've never done this before, you'll probably be astonished at the effect you produce when you use the common Anglo-Saxon words. Seriously: one night, just try saying to your man: 'I can't wait until you're fucking me, my love' – and see what happens.

Caressing his 'erogenous zones'

Fortunately, there are few women who need much instruction on how to cuddle a man. Women seem to have a much better instinct for the technique of tender caresses of the face and body than men do. Make sure that you caress and kiss his lips (put your tongue in and give him a French kiss!), his nipples (most men like having these stroked), his muscles (stroke his biceps and kid him they're great), his arm-pits (assuming he's not got BO), his neck, and his ears. Put your tongue into his ears and wriggle it around. (There's no danger that it'll come out the other side.) And in addition to stroking and kissing, don't forget gentle tickling, slapping and 'butterfly kissing' (that is, with your eyelashes) of his whole body.

On the other hand, bear in mind that your man is probably much more genitally-orientated than you are. While you would very likely prefer to have your limbs and breasts stroked for quite a while before any approach is made to your sex organs, *his* main concern is usually to get you to caress his penis as soon as possible! So tantalise him for a minute or two, tickling, stroking, squeezing and gently slapping his arms, chest, stomach, buttocks and thighs, but don't delay too long before you get to the area of his body where his primary interest lies.

Stimulating his penis: a basic guide to etiquette

Stimulating his penis by hand isn't just something you learn overnight. It's quite a delicate and skilled art that will take you months or even years to master. You have one ally however – your husband or lover. Most women don't think of asking their men-folk exactly what they want done to their penises; how firmly they like to be held, how fast they like to be rubbed, and so on. Do bear in mind however that your partner (unless he is very unusual) probably started masturbating when he was about twelve or thirteen. In fact he's had ample time to become something of an expert on how a penis should be stimulated. So follow his advice on how he likes it done. In general the mistakes that most inexperienced women make are:

(i) Not pressing firmly enough; you won't hurt him by even the firmest pressure, provided you apply it fairly gradually. But don't grab or twist!
(ii) Not rubbing fast enough. A skilled wife can achieve a rate of 300–400 short up-and-down strokes each minute!
(iii) Using an awkward grip.

This last point is probably the most important of all. A lady who is in bed with a man for the first time will usually reach down (often with her left hand, which is normally less skilled than the right one anyway) and grasp his erect penis in her palm in the instinctive way shown in Figure 21a. She can't achieve much speed or sensitivity like this, and she's very liable to produce jerky, irregular movements that hurt the poor man's organ rather than arouse it!

Usually, it's a bit better to reach down and place the right hand in the position shown in the middle picture, with the thumb nearest the man's stomach and the pads of the fingers on the far side of his penis. Up-and-down strokes (anything from half an inch to three inches in extent, depending on his preference) will now produce a most desirable effect on your man. Simple squeezing between fingers and thumb is also very popular.

Even more effective (and particularly valuable if the man's potency is flagging a little) is reversing the hand, so that his partner's fingers are on the side of the penis nearest his stomach, while her thumb is on the curved side. To take up this grip really effectively, she should sit or kneel facing him, between his legs – as shown in Figure 21c. While positioned like this, it's very easy for her to use her left hand when the right one needs a rest, or to use both together at times. A sexy lubricant may be helpful, and this is discussed in Chapter 11.

Those are the basic grips, but there are literally thousands of other ways of using your hands to stimulate your man's penis – for instance, holding it between the flats of your hands and rolling it to and fro; stroking the tip (the glans) with the pads of your fingers; flicking or stroking the frenulum, which is the part on the curved side (furthest from the stomach when erect) that stands out like a bow-string; pulling the penis forward as far as it will go and then letting it spring back so that its tip rubs along your palm, your breasts, or even the sheet; and so on as far as your imagination will extend. In fact, the best thing is to be as inventive as possible – try everything, and see just how much you can discover between you.

Incidentally, apart from using your hands, you can also stimulate your partner's penis with almost any other part of your body.

FIG. 21

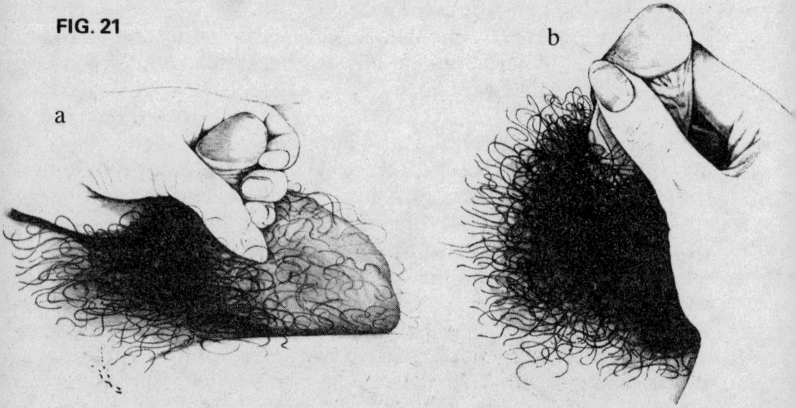

a

b

104

Your breasts are of course ideal for this purpose, even if they're small. Try resting his organ between them and squeezing them together. At the same time, you can either stroke his penis with your finger tips or bend your head forward so that you can lick the tip with your tongue. Figure 22 shows this position – which incidentally, is *very* good for men with potency problems.

'Mouth music'

This widespread but somewhat puzzling term derives from an old Scots musical technique, in which women make a lovely sound rather like that of musical instruments. But in sexual terms, 'mouth music' means using your lips to kiss and stimulate his whole body – including his private parts. Most women don't have to be told how to kiss a man on the lips, but don't forget those other adventurous kisses: putting your tongue in his mouth, kissing with mouths wide open, gently biting his lips, and so on. Don't stop at his lips, either. Kiss his neck, his chest, his nipples, his arms and his stomach, nuzzling, licking and sinking your teeth into the muscular parts of his body.

Most of all, kiss his penis. Oral sex is one of the most delightful aspects of love, and immensely satisfying to both partners. I doubt if many of the readers of this book will have serious inhibitions about mouth-genital contact, but since I still come across women who think that their husbands are being 'dirty' by asking them to do this kind of thing, let me say that this is a completely healthy and natural activity which has greatly enriched many marriages.

c

FIG. 22

If you've never had any kind of oral sex before, you can simply begin by holding your husband's penis and applying kiss after kiss to the tip (the glans). Next, try the experiment of gently taking the tip in your mouth and rocking forwards and backwards. Alternate this with licking the glans, just as you would an ice cream cone. That's all there really is to oral sex – the mysterious activity about which self-appointed moralists have made such a fuss in the past; the completely natural way of expressing love that still carries the risk of a jail sentence for both husband and wife in some states of the USA.

Of course you'll find ways of refining these techniques as time goes by. Swirling your tongue round your husband's penis while it is inside your mouth (the so-called 'silken-swirl') is quite effective. So too is using your tongue to flick the taut bowstring-like frenulum on the outer curved side of the penis. You can combine mouth and breast stimulation by placing your man's penis between your breasts and leaning forward to lick, suck or kiss it. Or you can simply kneel on the floor at your husband's feet while he thrusts his penis in and out. Best of all, you can let your husband excite your clitoris and vagina with his mouth while *you* are kissing *his* genitals. Convenient positions for this kind of mutual stimulation are discussed at the end of the previous chapter under the heading 'Cunnilingus', which is the medical word for kissing the vagina and vulva (kissing the penis is called 'fellatio').

There are only two problems about taking a penis in your mouth. The first is that excessive penetration does worry many women. A man approaches your mouth in just the same way as he does your vagina – he wants to get as far into it as possible. So it's sometimes hard for him to appreciate that thrusting six or seven inches of penis down your throat may half choke you! This problem has increased greatly since the days of porno film star Linda Lovelace, whose renowned ability to take *any* length of penis into her throat was simply due to the fact that – like gay males who practise oral sex – she'd managed to abolish the 'gagging reflex'. When your man seems to be choking you, you've got to make it clear to him that he has to consider your feelings as well as his own, and that he ought to take it easy when you indicate to him that enough is enough.

Secondly, there's the problem of ejaculation. A lot of couples will quite often continue with oral sex until the man reaches his climax. The difficulty is that while the man usually wants to 'come' inside his partner's mouth, many women dislike the idea of swallowing seminal fluid – though others are more than happy to do so. The fluid is actually completely harmless (and can't cause pregnancy by this route, as some women fear) but if you find it a bit messy or downright revolting, the best thing to do is simply to wait for ten seconds or so and then discreetly deposit it in a hanky kept under the pillow. Some couples use a French letter during 'fellatio', but most people would find this a very clinical way of making love. You can of course pull away at the last second, but this is perhaps a trifle unkind to your husband – a bit like the practice of *coitus interruptus*, or withdrawal. However, if you feel you *must* take your man's penis out of your mouth before orgasm, do your best to offer him something else instead so as not to spoil his moment of ecstasy. As he comes out, you could take him in your hand and rub furiously for the last few seconds. Or you could swing your body across his, and thrust him into your vagina.

Alternatively, you could let him reach his climax over your breasts or any other part of your body. Most men find this very exciting, particularly if the light is on so that they can see what is happening. Quite a lot will want to climax in your face, which doubtless seems a bit strange to you! But I gather that there is a large section of the Scandinavian film industry which is completely devoted to producing rude movies at whose high point the Nordic gentleman hits the Nordic lady in the eye with his love fluid. (If this strikes you as daft, think how much dafter it looks when played backwards.)

CHAPTER TEN

Secret Erotic Arousal Techniques For Men To Use

Don't run before you can walk ● *If you've got problems* ● *Women aren't machines* ● *Nice things to do with her pubic hair* ● *Oiling her body, and her vulva* ● *Soaping her in the bath or shower* ● *Wine on the vulva* ● *Skilled use of your thumb* ● *Two-finger techniques inside her vagina* ● *Moving her cervix and womb* ● *Stroking her ovaries* ● *Massaging the 'G-spot'* ● *Bimanual love play* ● Postillionage ● *A horse in each stable* ● *Putting your whole hand (or other objects) in* ● *Using ice* ● *Using feathers* ● *Only do it if she likes it!*

Don't run before you can walk

Let me stress at the start that there's absolutely no point in your beginning to read this rather exotic chapter unless you've studied all the earlier ones – and not only made yourself very familiar with the basic methods of love play, but also practised them again and again and again and *again* (and preferably again). The trouble with men is that instead of concentrating on building a good relationship with a woman, they'd mostly far rather hear about some sexy trick that could turn her into an orgasmic volcano. But it really is no good my teaching you how to caress your lady's ovaries or to stimulate her magic 'G-spot' if, for example:

★You've got a lousy relationship anyway;
★You yourself know very little about the emotional factors that make women tick;
★You haven't got much idea about the basics of sex – but you just think that if you learn one or two clever techniques, everything will be OK.

It won't – as you'll assuredly find out. So if you're starting to read the book at this chapter – *don't*. Go back to the foreword *Don't Forget Romance and Laughter – and Love*, and begin there.

If you've got problems

Similarly, if you've got problems in your relationship, it's unlikely that this chapter of exotica is going to provide you with a solution. Sure: it's a chapter full of little tricks which a skilled man can use to give his loved one extra enjoyment, and to add spice to their relationship. And I must admit that some of the techniques I'm going to mention could help a lady who's having trouble in reaching a climax to get there. But in general, when people have problems in bed, learning some new and saucy trick isn't the way to solve them. Usually what's necessary is to re-examine their relationships, talk to each other – and perhaps seek professional help. So if you have difficulties in your relationship, don't begin by trying to find the answer in this chapter. I suggest you read the whole book – and particularly the sections on sexual problems (Chapters 6 and 17 to 21).

Women aren't machines

Don't make the all-too-common male mistake of regarding a woman as a sort of Space Invaders machine (twiddle the right knobs and you'll get a great score . . .). I can't repeat enough times that women are tender, sensitive, emotional, sometimes fragile and often lovely *people*, and are not machines – any more than men are. But in general, they're far more interested in atmosphere, *ambience* (good word that – means almost the same as atmosphere too), tenderness, warmth, friendship and love than in whether you've mastered trick No. 63 from Dr Delvin's Book of Practical Hints on How to Do It. If your relationship with a woman is good, then almost certainly she'll be intrigued and pleased by some of the exotic techniques described in this chapter – but only by *some* of them. Certain of them – which might be agreeable to some other ladies – may be of no interest to her (or indeed may be a real turn-off). You must accept this. As I said at the beginning of this section *women are not machines*.

(**Note:** incidentally, talking about machines, I'd like to make clear that the subject of vibrators and other sex aids is not dealt with in this chapter – as they're scarcely very secret these days. You'll find them in Chapter 16.)

Nice things to do with her pubic hair

A woman's pubic hair is nice, and it is sexy. But bear in mind that a lot of ladies are embarrassed about it – especially if it is wispy (which it often is in maturer women), or if it grows outside of the neat 'eternal triangle' which pin-up photographers have tried to tell us is normal (it isn't, necessarily). So, compliment her on her pubic hair. Take it between your fingers, twist it gently, stroke it and even tug it a little. Nuzzle it and take a little of it between your teeth. Another nice thing to do with it is to massage it with *oil* – see below. And don't forget the lovely idea described in D. H. Lawrence's *Lady Chatterley's Lover* – decorating the pubic hair with flowers. I well remember that at the time of the celebrated Lady Chatterley trial in Britain, it seemed to be only the filthiest-minded people I knew who thought that this bit of the book was 'obscene' and 'revolting'. If people like that think that such a practice is disgusting, then it must be worth trying!

Oiling her body, and her vulva

One of the more interesting discoveries in recent years has been to find that massaging your lady with oils or similar potions can be very nice for her. Of course it's more of a re-discovery, since it used to be done in ancient times. In fact both 'serious' masseurs (such as physiotherapists) and massage parlour *artistes* have been using oils for decades. And back in the 1960s and 1970s, Masters and Johnson found at their clinic in St Louis, Missouri, that use of a massage oil or cream could greatly help a couple's love play. (Indeed, they discovered that if a couple with sex problems rejected the idea of such a sex aid, the outlook for them wasn't so good.) It's certainly worth buying some unguent to apply to your partner's whole body, from her neck and shoulders to her feet. Massage it in gently and soothingly, using the pads of your fingers and thumbs. Begin with her muscles – especially those which are tired and painful – and gradually move on to her breasts and, lastly, to her vulva. (Incidentally, this will ease your entry later on.)

What should you use? In Britain, Canada and the US, people usually buy baby oil – which is very cheap, available from all pharmacies, obtainable without embarrassment – and hardly stains the sheets at all. In any Western country, you can also buy perfumed oils and creams in pharmacies and (rather more expensively) in sex shops.

Soaping her in the bath or shower

An alternative is to soap your partner gently (with lots of lather) in the bath or shower. Massage with soapy water is *very* sexy – and you can progress from a general lather of her whole body to massage of her breasts – and then later to her vulva. For some reason, gentle rubbing of soapy water on the vulva (and especially round the clitoris) is a fantastic turn-on for most women. Naturally, a few women don't like it – but most will happily enjoy delightful climaxes if you skilfully rub their clitorises with foam. (An occasional person is allergic to certain brands of soap or foam, but this is not very common.)

Incidentally, if you and your loved one choose to go on and actually make love in the shower or bath, this can be very good too. Having intercourse in the shower is decidedly pleasant, with the warm drops of water beating down upon the pair of you as your bodies fuse together.

Making love in a soapy bath is also really delicious. Some people have the mistaken idea that it's dangerous, but this isn't true – provided that you don't actually get yourself drowned under some large and voluptuous lady. (What a way to go!) The common belief that having sex under water could be harmful stems from the notion that the act of love could force water into the woman's womb. I can only say that I've never heard of such a thing happening, nor has any doctor I've asked. Indeed, in tropical countries it's quite common for couples actually to make love under the sea – if necessary with the aid of snorkels or aqualungs (see Chapter 14). This is a super experience and no harm seems likely to come of it, provided you aren't interrupted by a shark or a horny octopus.

Wine (and other things) on the vulva

It's commonplace for exotically minded lovers to put various edible or drinkable things on their sex organs – and then let their partners 'lap them up'. (This combination of food and sexuality seems to infuriate certain moralists, but that's no concern of mine, I'm glad to say.) The kind of things people put on each other's sex organs and then lick include cream, ice cream (brr-rrr!), jam, honey and – of course – wine.

I think the position about wine is best summed up by a question-and-answer which appeared some years ago in my column in the British national women's magazine, *SHE*:

> Q *My husband and I have a super sex life and we both particularly enjoy finding new and exciting ways of love play. I like being kissed 'down below' but I'm wondering if my husband's latest variation on this is OK? He is keen on wine, and the other night decided to try what he called 'combining two great pleasures' by kissing my most intimate area after first pouring on about half a glass of 1968 Burgundy. Do you approve of this?*

A No, I don't. After all there *are* certain
standards to be maintained in this age of
fast-slipping values, aren't there? The correct year would be a '64, '66 or '67 – or
indeed (dare I say it?) a '69.

On the other hand, while this kind of wine-bibbing is delight-
fully Bacchanalian, it can:

★stain the sheets;
★waste a lot of wine;
★more important, *sting the lady's vulva*.

If you find that the vintage you've chosen for the evening stings
your loved one's most tender spot, then do something else with it.
For instance, one agreeable thing to do when you're in love and
slightly tipsy is to take a mouthful of wine – and then transfer it to
your loved one's mouth in a kiss. (Do warn her first, won't you –
otherwise this can lead to a deplorable waste of Chateau Mouton-
Rothschild '76!) It's very nice *vice versa*, too.

Skilled use of your thumb

In Chapter 8, I've stressed that no man can be a skilled lover
unless he masters two digital arts:

★stimulating her clitoris, usually with your forefinger;
★popping the middle finger inside, and 'vibrating' it in and out
  (at, say, 200 inward movements a minute).

But there's another useful and little-known digital skill – using the
thumb. Once you've got your loved one well-lubricated and
receptive, try the effect of gently slipping your thumb into her.
The great advantage of this is that it produces sensations quite
different from those provoked by the other fingers. Also, it seems
to be easier to rotate the thumb without causing discomfort to
your lady. Once your thumb is comfortably inside, do just that:
rotate it. Press on all the structures within your reach:

★At the sides, there are various very receptive sensory (and
  sensuous) nerve endings;
★At the back, there is the rectum: some women go half-mad
  when a man's thumb strokes it *via* the vagina. (Others are

112

very embarrassed by the feeling, but you can't win 'em all);

★At the front, there's the bladder, the urethra (or urinary pipe), and the amazing and recently-discovered 'G-spot' which I've mentioned elsewhere in this book. All of these can be very effectively and gently stimulated by the pad of a loving thumb.

Two-finger techniques inside her vagina

Once you've mastered the basic techniques of:

(a) stimulating your loved one's clitoris;
(b) digitally stimulating her vagina with very rapid 'in-and-out' movements of your middle finger (see Chapter 8); and
(c) thumb stimulation (see above), then you're ready to move on to two finger techniques.

No rude remarks, please, though I've little doubt that the 'two finger' sign – the reverse of Churchill's 'V for Victory' – has its origin in sexual antics of this nature.

Follow this technique. Once the ring of muscles round the opening of the lady's vagina has relaxed, then slip two fingers in instead of one. If she's well-relaxed, this alone should produce a satisfying sigh! Next, gently move those two fingers in and out. I stress the word 'gently' because there is now double the chance of damaging her with your nails. Now practise pushing the two fingers together up the front wall of her vagina – and then spread them gently apart. Do this again, and again, and again, and it should produce a nice sensation for her. (As perspicacious readers will have noted, this subtle manoeuvre also stimulates the 'G-spot' – see Chapter 2, and also the later part of this chapter.)

Moving her cervix and womb

The cervix (neck of the womb – see Figures 5 and 6 on p. 18 and 21) is a very sexy area in some women, though others feel relatively little sensation from it. Once you've found out how to feel your lady's cervix (if in doubt, consult Figure 6 which shows a penis touching it), then by all means gently push it and move it around with your finger tips. But – and it's another of my big BUTs – take it easy. Some women – particularly those who have disorders of the cervix – do not like it being prodded. Obviously, your partner will tell you if moving her cervix causes discomfort.

113

More extensive movement of the cervix with your two finger tips will actually move the womb too. (This happens because the cervix is of course just the apex, or neck, of the womb.)

Gently moving the womb to and fro drives some women mad – especially if you do it while the womb is contracting in the ecstasy of a climax. But again, you must do this *very* gently. I have heard of one case in which a man did serious damage to the ligaments supporting his partner's womb – simply because of the violence with which he was shifting the unfortunate organ around.

And on a final note of caution, manipulation of the cervix and womb is definitely *not* a good idea if the woman is pregnant. There's a risk of infection, and, especially in the first sixteen weeks, of provoking a miscarriage.

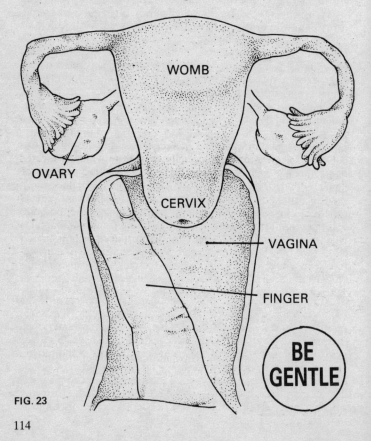

WOMB

OVARY

CERVIX

VAGINA

FINGER

BE GENTLE

FIG. 23

Stroking her ovaries

Only a few very skilled men ever master the technique of stroking a woman's ovaries. Look back at Figure 6 on p. 21 and you'll see where they lie. You'll note that they're not very accessible. Nonetheless, in the same way as men like the feeling of having their testicles stroked by a woman, some ladies do derive pleasure from skilled and gentle stimulation of their ovaries. But in the same way that 'balls' are tender organs, so too are the ovaries – very much so! Therefore, unless you have delicate and sensitive fingers, *don't* try this technique.

If you do have delicate and sensitive fingers, then here's what to do. (Incidentally, they have to be long fingers too: otherwise you'll never get anywhere near the ovaries.) Just gently press the soft pads of the tips of your middle and first fingers into one or other of the recesses that lie on either side of the cervix. You can see what I mean from Figure 23. If those finger-pads are really finely-tuned, you'll be able to feel the ovaries – each of which feels like a large, ripe cherry. Just stroke each one smoothly and lovingly – no more is necessary.

Massaging the 'G-spot'

As I've explained in Chapter 2, it became clear in the early 1980s that many women have a specially sexy zone which is located somewhere about half way up the front wall of the vagina (see Figure 7, on p. 22). This area is called the 'G-spot', and stimulation of it causes a rather unusual, and very pleasant, sexual sensation. This sensation may lead on to a vaginal – as opposed to an ordinary clitoral – climax. And, as pointed out in Chapter 4 (which is all about climaxes), an orgasm produced by pressure on the G-spot may be accompanied by a sudden release of a mysterious sexual fluid by the woman. Latest research indicates that this liquid is similar in nature to the fluid produced by a man's prostate gland. And it may be that the newly-discovered G-spot is actually the female equivalent of a man's prostate.

Be that as it may, if you want to stimulate the G-spot, then just slip a well-lubricated finger into her vagina, with the pad of the finger tip uppermost. Now rub that finger pad up and down the midline of the front wall. This will put pressure on her urethra – or waterworks pipe – and may make her feel she wants to pee. (It doesn't matter if she does.) More importantly, if she's one of those women who have a sensitive G-spot, then she'll enjoy the feeling very much.

I'd recommend trying this technique with a woman who has trouble reaching a climax – for the additional G-spot stimulation (which, in such cases, should be carried out at the same time as clitoral stimulation with your fingers or tongue) may well be enough to send her 'over the top'. If it does, then remember that she might possibly squirt quite a jet of love fluid, so be prepared to get an eyeful.

Bimanual love play

Another very advanced technique this – and one which few men have mastered. 'Bimanual', as you probably know, means 'with two hands' – and in bimanual love play you simply have:

★the fingers of one hand in your loved one's vagina;
★the fingers of the other hand on the lower part of her tummy, just above her pubic hair, so that the two sets of finger tips feel as if they're almost meeting through her skin.

This rather jolly arrangement helps you to exert all sorts of gentle (repeat *gentle*) pressure on her various sexual organs between your two hands. With practice, this can be a very nice way of giving her pleasure.

Postillionage

Postillionage, as I've explained earlier in this book, is the term applied to the now widespread practice of caressing your loved one's bottom with a finger. Indeed, it's so widespread that it's scarcely justifiable to put it in a chapter of 'secret' techniques! For many women (probably most, once they've got over the initial surprise) this is certainly a very sexually-stimulating thing to experience. This is because – however much moralists may disapprove – the bottom *is* an area of the body which is richly supplied with sensuous nerve endings.

However, as I've pointed out at the rear end of Chapter 2 the bottom is *not* a clean area of the body. Therefore, there are undoubtedly certain health risks to this practice. So even if all your friends say they do it, you should think carefully before you go in for it.

If you decide to do it to your partner, then the vital thing to remember is that your finger will almost certainly be contaminated with germs after touching her anus. Therefore in order to protect her, *don't put the same finger anywhere near her vagina till you've washed your hands*. If you do touch her vagina with a finger that's been on (or up) her bottom, then you may give her:

★a vaginal discharge;
★cystitis – a painful urinary infection.

In practice, many lovers get round the hygiene problem by only using the left hand for *postillionage* – keeping the right one for stimulating the lady's vagina and clitoris. Fair enough: but in any case don't forget to wash your hands when you get up.

Another problem with *postillionage* is that people's bottoms do have a tendency to be rather sore for one reason or another (for instance, piles). So don't press your partner into *postillionage* if she says she's got a tender rear end – you'll only turn her off, rather than on.

An unsubtle technique of *postillionage* can be very painful. You'll probably remember that in *Last Tango in Paris* Marlon Brando (and the sexy French lady who together with him popularised this technique throughout the world) eased things by using rather a lot of butter, much to the joy of the ailing dairy industry. This is not a bad idea: indeed, I don't think you should attempt any kind of penetration without a lubricant – for fear of hurting your partner. Vaseline, baby oil or cold cream will do.

Also, bear in mind that fingernails are sharp. So if you're going to go in for 'bottom play', make specially sure that the nail of your forefinger is cut short. Equally important (and strangely little-known) is the fact that you should approach the anus with the pad of your finger – not the nail. If you go in with the fingernail foremost, don't blame me if she leaps indignantly out of bed and departs!

More seriously, the practice of *postillionage* can have a health risk if you don't follow the hygiene rules I've given. (The fact that many male gays develop certain serious infections, for instance, the terrifying auto-immune deficiency syndrome (AIDS) which has caused such panic in the USA since early 1983, is almost certainly due to the fact that they go in so much for 'bottom play' of various sorts.) Be particularly wary of an increasingly popular variant of *postillionage* called 'anilingus'. This means actually kissing your lady's bottom. Though many women find it enjoyable, it exposes the man who's doing it to the very real danger of infection *via* his mouth. In view of the health dangers of anal-oral contact, I'm decidedly perturbed by the fact that the 1983 *Playboy* Sex Survey of 100,000 readers showed that 36 per cent of men and 39 per cent of women had engaged in this.

Since there's no way of preventing this risk, I think that this is one sexual practice which is probably best avoided. If you're going to kiss your loved one's backside, stick to her buttocks and Penetrate No Further.

A horse in each stable

This phrase just means having one finger in the lady's vagina – and the other carrying out *postillionage*. I've spent most of the previous section warning about the possible hygienic risks of *postillionage*. However, if you remember the hygiene precautions I've mentioned, then there is little risk from stimulating both her orifices in this way. But take great care not to let the 'bottom' finger touch the 'vaginal' one, as you could easily transfer germs from the former to the latter – and hence to the woman's vagina or to her urinary pipe.

Stimulation of both orifices can certainly be wildly successful, as long as the lady is relaxed and well lubricated. But you'll find that the partition which lies between her vagina and her rectum is very thin (you can probably feel one fingertip with the other). So take care not to damage it. As with so many other love play techniques, the secret of success lies in being very, very gentle.

Putting your whole hand (or other objects) in

Younger women often tend to be rather tense, and where this is so it's not advisable to attempt to put more than one, or perhaps two, fingers into the vagina. But when your loved one knows you well, really relaxes and produces lots of vaginal lubricant – then she may well enjoy it if you put three fingers or even more inside her. Naturally, you should be guided by what *she* wants: if she likes having most of your hand inside her vagina, then that's fine. But if she doesn't like it, then don't do it.

Many men – believing in the myth that women like having large things jammed up them – are keen on the idea of pushing phallic-shaped objects into their ladies' vaginas. These practices are encouraged by porno magazines – much bought by young men – which show women doing *very* strange things to themselves with cucumbers, bananas and so on. In practice, most women are *not* interested in having anything but the male organ (or masculine tongues or fingers) in their vaginas. Indeed, they're often revolted by the very notion!

In addition, some objects which gentleman push up ladies may either:

118

★cause damage – which may be serious; or

★get stuck – which may be highly embarrassing when you go along to hospital to have the 'foreign body' removed. ('She just tripped over this courgette, doctor. . . .')

In short, with the possible exception of certain properly-designed sex-aids (see Chapter 16), it's best not to push *anything* up the vagina except what Nature intended you to push up it. . . .

P.S. If you were turned on by the famous Champagne bottle episode in Erica Jong's recent best-seller *How To Save Your Own Life*, then forget it! Wine bottles are *dangerous* – and I can think of a decidedly better use for Dom Perignon.

Using ice

My advice column in *SHE* has opened my eyes to the fact that some couples use little cubes of ice as an aid to love play. Amazing as it may seem, what the man does is to insert a small cube into the upper reaches of the lady's vagina. He may then follow it in with his penis – and apparently the melting ice gives them both a pleasant tingle! Frankly, as long as the ice isn't actually cold enough to hurt the lady, I can't think of any reason why this particular frolic should be harmful. If she likes the idea, then try it.

Using feathers

A fairly recent development in the USA has been the introduction of feathers into love play. They're soft and tickly, and you can use them to produce very agreeable sensations in a woman by drawing them gently across her breasts, buttocks and vulva. No need to go to a sex shop – just buy a feather duster without embarrassment at your local hardware store! Similar nice sensations can be produced – particularly round the vaginal area – by such materials as fur, velvet and cotton wool.

Only do it if she likes it!

Some of the love play techniques described in this chapter are pretty outrageous. So if you're a man, remember that your lady won't *necessarily* like each and every one of them. Women are individuals who think for themselves – and your partner's wishes about what you want to do to her *must* be respected. If she doesn't fancy some technique I've described in this chapter, then don't pursue it. But if she *does* fancy it, then I hope you have a good time together.

CHAPTER ELEVEN

Secret Erotic Arousal Techniques For Women To Use

Not a cure for sexual problems, but they may help ● Skills that are worth learning ● Learn the basic facts first ● Some sexy things to do with creams and oils ● Rubbing yourself against him ● Kissing his nipples ● Kissing his perineum ● Kissing his testicles ● Bottom smacking ● Postillionage ● Massaging his prostate gland ● Feathers and fur ● Pheromones and perfumes.

Not a cure for sexual problems – but they may help

Can I get one thing clear at the start of this chapter? If your man has sex problems (for instance, if he's got trouble with getting an erection, or with reaching a climax – or if he's just generally lacking in interest), then I don't claim that the exotic techniques described in this chapter will actually cure him. On the other hand, it's true that they may help a bit, because very often a man's problems tend to start getting better if he's given intensive stimulation. This, of course, is just plain common sense. After all, if a man's virility is a bit down (perhaps because he's tired, or overstressed, or depressed) then he may well improve if his partner dresses up in a sexy nightie, puts on lots of perfume, and sets about seducing him.

Similarly, the intensely erotic love play techniques described in this chapter may help galvanise some poor man who's been performing a bit below par. Nonetheless, if your man has *persistent* sex problems (such as impotence or premature ejaculation), the best thing to do is for both of you to read the 'problem' sections of this book – and then if things still aren't improving – to seek medical help.

Skills that are worth learning

It will be well worth it for most women to learn the exotic skills detailed in this chapter because they'll enrich any relationship. Your man may not be turned on by all of them – but it's a fair bet that quite a few will drive him wild.

Incidentally, you yourself may feel doubtful about one or two of the love play techniques I'm going to describe. I must admit that certain of them may seem pretty way out. But most of them are worth trying. After all, they're mostly techniques which have a long and honourable history. And – if you'll forgive a bluntly practical point – you must remember that men very often seek the help of 'professionals' because – unlike their wives – these ladies offer the sort of exotic 'services' described in this chapter. It seems a shame when they could have them at home.

Learn the basic facts first

However, if you don't know a lot about love play, please don't begin with this chapter and hope it'll turn you into some super-charged sexual siren. You really need to learn the more basic facts about sexuality and love play first, which means starting at the beginning of this book, and not forgetting to take in Chapter 9 (which covers the more straightforward 'foreplay' methods). What follows is for the woman who is really an Advanced Student. . . .

Some sexy things to do with creams and oils

One technique which has been used for years by girls in the topless massage parlours is to enhance what you do to men with the aid of a suitable cream or oil. The reason for this is partly because creams and oils lubricate the contact between skin and skin (that's why physiotherapists use them for 'straight' massage). Also, there's something very sensuous about being rubbed with a nice, warm, pleasantly-scented unguent – after all, isn't it lovely to have your skin massaged with suntan oil?

What the 'topless' girls usually do is to work all over a man's body with their oil or cream, finally getting round to his penis. This is a good idea for you too – but don't delay too long in getting to your man's organ (remember: men like a much more rapid approach to the genitals than women do!)

It doesn't really matter what potion you use. As I've said in the previous chapter, baby oil (very cheap and obtainable without embarrassment at any pharmacy) is highly popular for sexy massage purposes in Britain, the US and Australasia. I wouldn't waste your time and money going to sex shops for far more expensive preparations.

Once you've worked round your man's body with the oil, cup a little more in your right hand to warm it for a few seconds. Meanwhile, a good ploy is to take the *base* of his penis between the forefinger and thumb of your other hand: this little 'courte-san's trick' is particularly helpful for promoting an erection –

which is pleasant for many people (male or female). A similar effect can be achieved by putting a moderately warm hot water bottle on your loved one's behind – perhaps holding it there during intercourse.

Postillionage

If you've read the earlier parts of this book you'll know that this means the practice so widely popularised in *Last Tango in Paris* and in many modern novels: putting your finger on, or even in, his bottom. In Chapters 2, 3 and 10, I've stressed that there are very real hygiene dangers from this practice, which seems to have become almost universal in some strata of Western society. I've also stressed that sticking your finger in someone's anus may be painful to them – and indeed may cause little cracks or cuts if you're not careful.

Having said all that, I have to accept that 'ass massage' (as it's sometimes known in America) is extremely popular with a very high proportion of men – and also with many women. Again, this is simply because there are a lot of sexual nerve endings in that area of the body. (Don't complain to me – it's not my fault if there's something amiss with the design.)

In the previous chapter I've described the precautions a man really must take if he wants to go in for *postillionage* on a woman. And if your bloke wants you to do it to *him*, then you should follow the same precautions. Briefly, these are:

★Once you've touched your partner's anus, your finger is probably contaminated with germs: so keep it away from your vagina (and his penis) till you've had a chance to wash it.
★Keep your fingernails neat, don't attack your bloke with the tip of them (use the pads of the fingers instead) and, whenever possible, use a lubricant like hand cream, face cream, or Vaseline.

I think it would be pig-headed of me to deny that *postillionage* gives a lot of pleasure to a lot of people. Also, it has undoubtedly helped many a man who's been having trouble keeping his erection going – for it's amazing what a strategically-placed female finger can do at a critical moment. But unless you want to wind up with a vaginal discharge or cystitis, please be careful how you use this technique.

Massaging his prostate gland

I'm afraid that this next technique-popularised in the novels of Harold Robbins – takes us one step beyond postillionage, as it involves putting your whole finger into your partner's bottom and massaging his prostate gland. The prostate is certainly a fantastically sexy gland, and makes a big contribution to the seminal fluid. So it's unfortunate that the only access to it is *via* the rectum. Look back to Figure 11, p. 34, and you'll see what I mean.

Rubbing a man's prostate with the pad of your forefinger will heighten his sexual pleasure, and probably intensify his climax. An odd 'side-effect' is that it may sometimes make his fluid shoot far further when he 'comes'. (If he's not careful, it may hit him in the eye.) The *good* thing about prostate massage is that it can greatly help flagging virility, particularly when carried out by a skilled woman on a middle-aged or elderly man. The *bad* thing is that it carries the above-mentioned risks which are inevitable when you put your finger in somebody's bottom. If you're going to do it, lubricate your finger carefully beforehand – and wash it carefully afterwards.

Feathers and fur

As I mentioned in the previous chapter, a lot of men now use feathers to tickle their ladies. You can do the same thing to your man – and in fact the practice of tickling a chap's penis and testicles with feathers has become quite widespread in the USA. (You may have seen Bette Midler leaping around on TV with what she archly describes as 'cock feathers'.)

You can use other soft materials to massage your man's body – and specifically his genitals, of course. Puzzling as it may be to the rest of us, leather gloves are considered very desirable for penis massage in some circles. And perhaps more immediately understandable are the sexy fur gloves which have been featured in one of the James Bond movies. Mink mittens on the penis are supposed to be extremely popular among the very rich – though *not* so popular with the poor old minks.

Pheromones and perfumes

Pheromones are special sexual scents produced naturally by human beings, but which are usually almost undetectable at a conscious level. However, they operate powerfully at an *unconscious* level – and there's some evidence that women who produce pheromones in good quantities tend to exert a strange attraction over men! You can now buy spray-on aerosol cans of female pheromone in the US, and they'll soon be available in the UK, Australia and elsewhere for women to spray on themselves at bedtime, or whenever.

(Incidentally, a *male* pheromone spray has been available in the UK for several years. I did a brief and very unscientific trial of it for BBC-TV and *World Medicine*, and was not greatly impressed by the results. It had no effect on my wife, and the main outcome of using it was that Dr Richard Gordon's dog became possessed of an intense desire to attack my private parts. Such is life.)

Perhaps more useful as an adjunct to love play is the liberal use of perfume. Far too many women – outside the knowledgeable circle of expensive courtesans – realise that a few dabs of perfume in their sexy places (under the breasts, in the pubic hair, and on the perineum) can do wonders towards driving a man wild! True, there's a very tiny risk that some ingredient in the perfume might cause a sensitivity reaction in delicate tissues. But it's a very small chance to take – especially when you realise that a few spots of Chanel or *Je Reviens* can help you create your very own Perfumed Garden.

CHAPTER TWELVE

A Guide To Intercourse Techniques For Men

Do men need advice on how to do it? ● Don't rush the entry ● What if you can't get it in? ● Will your thrusts bring her to a climax? ● Pressure on her clitoris ● Good positions for creating clitoral pressure ● Other ways of stimulating her clitoris during intercourse ● Stimulating her other sexy areas during intercourse ● Varying the angles, and the movement ● Don't come too soon ● But if you do . . . ● Don't forget contraception!

Do men need advice on how to do it?

The answer to this question is an emphatic 'YES'! Lots of folk believe that sexual intercourse is so completely natural that everybody knows how to do it by instinct. Would it were true! Sadly, many men are absolutely hopeless at intercourse – which is one reason why there are so many frustrated women around. A lot more men are not bad at it, but are a bit thoughtless or selfish – and so fail to give their loved ones all the pleasure which is possible. Unfortunately, few men are willing to admit their deficiencies at screwing: just as there is scarcely a man who'll admit that he's not a very good car driver, it's also very difficult to find one who recognises that he could improve his intercourse technique a bit.

The thing to remember is that intercourse is like golf (no jokes about getting your balls near the hole, please); what I mean is that no matter how good you think you are, you can always improve your game. For most couples, it's a good idea if he does, for as we'll see in a moment, most women are not entirely satisfied by their partners' intercourse techniques.

If any man reading this believes that his partner is totally and utterly happy with the way that he performs, then that's fine. But don't blame me if she decides to see if the milkman can make a better job of it.

Don't rush the entry

One of the great pleasures of sexual intercourse (for both parties) is the moment of entry. Ah, that delicious moment when the tip of the penis presses its way between the labia and pops gently through the encircling ring of muscle into the warm, welcoming vagina itself!

But don't *rush* that entry. Far too many men make the mistake of crashing in before their poor partners are ready – so that they are caused discomfort or even severe pain instead of immense pleasure. So, before you even attempt to go in, do use the love play techniques described in Chapter 8 – and (if you like) the more saucy and advanced ones described in Chapter 10 as well. This is particularly important with a woman who's never been pregnant, since the opening of her vulva is likely to be tighter.

It's also very important with a virgin, because she may well be tense and afraid of being hurt. She may have heard all those silly myths to the effect that first intercourse has to be dreadfully painful. (In fact, it shouldn't be, if the lady is properly relaxed. Severe pain on intercourse – or attempted intercourse – is most often due to the common emotional problem of vaginismus: see Chapter 18.) If you use the love play techniques properly, you will achieve two things:

★You'll make your lady's vaginal muscles relax nicely so that entry is easier.
★You'll make the love juices flow from her vagina, so that your entry is beautifully lubricated.

Incidentally, if you have persistent trouble in getting your lady love to lubricate, despite using all your best romantic efforts (and all the love play techniques mentioned earlier in the book), then it's often a help to use some artificial lubricant just before entry.

In the UK, vast quantities of KY Jelly and Durol are sold at pharmacies or prescribed at Family Planning Clinics for this purpose, and similar lubricants are available from pharmacists in the US and other countries. (At a pinch, Vaseline will do, but it's a bit messy, and tends to leave a woman feeling rather gummed up afterwards!)

One final point about the pleasures of entry. There's a widespread belief (particularly in the USA) that the man must somehow 'hit' the woman's clitoris as he goes in. Some blokes even believe that you're supposed to come out *with every stroke* and hit it again! Well, there's no need for these crazy pole-vaulting experiments. Certainly, it's very nice for the lady if your penis brushes against her clitoris on the way in, but it's certainly not a necessity, for the stimulation of the clitoris during intercourse is achieved in quite a different way, as we'll see in a moment.

What if you can't get it in?

Don't worry: it happens to every man at some time! Don't be embarrassed, but just tell your partner frankly that you've lost your erection – and try to treat it with a sense of humour rather than getting uptight about it. (The tenser you become, the less likely you are to get your erection back.) She will be able to help you if she's sexually knowledgeable – not only by rubbing your penis, but by using two techniques described in the next chapter.

Of course, if you're having severe and persistent problems with erection, you should read the later chapters devoted to sex problems.

Note: bear in mind that difficulty in getting it in may be due to the woman suffering from the 'tensing up' condition called 'vaginismus' – discussed later in the book. If she cannot relax her vaginal muscles, it's difficult to get a stiff penis in: to get a slightly floppy one in may be downright impossible. See the advice given later in this chapter.

Will your thrusts bring her to a climax?

Sadly, the answer is probably 'no' – unless you're in a lucky minority. This may come as a surprise to you if you've learnt most of your sexual knowledge from the novels of Harold Robbins (a man who is the world's largest-selling novelist – and also one of the world's biggest sources of sexual mis-information). It doesn't matter how big you think your penis is, or how deeply and powerfully you think you can thrust. Just thrusting alone will probably not be enough, as the work of Shere Hite in America has shown so clearly.

It's true that many women do derive enormous pleasure from deep, driving thrusts, far inside their bodies. But especially for the two-thirds (yes, *two-thirds*) of all women who don't usually reach a climax during intercourse, something else is needed: namely, pressure on her clitoris.

Pressure on her clitoris

As you'll know if you've read the earlier part of this book, the clitoris is really the main 'seat' of a woman's sexual desire. If it's not stimulated, then her chances of having a climax are not all that good. If you don't know where the clitoris is, then look back at the illustration on p. 14. *That's* what you've got to stimulate during intercourse.

(Incidentally, the story that the clitoris can turn up in other parts of the body is all nonsense: this myth seems to have originated with the famous sexploitation movie *Deep Throat*, in which Linda Lovelace played a lady whose clitoris was supposed to be located somewhere south of her tonsils.)

How are you going to stimulate your loved one's clitoris during intercourse itself? Since the mid-1960s doctors have tended to believe the teaching of famous US sexologists Masters and Johnson – who were of the opinion that the thrusting of the penis inside the vagina sort of 'tugs' on the clitoris, and thereby stimulates it.

However, Ms Shere Hite's more recent research has cast serious doubt on that theory. She tells me that from the vast number of completed sex questionnaires she has received from American women, it does now appear that really *direct* pressure on the woman's clitoris is usually necessary for full sexual satisfaction. That direct pressure usually comes from the man's pubis – that is, the hard, bony area just above the base of his penis, below the pubic hair.

Good positions for creating clitoral pressure

Whenever possible, try and press your 'pubes' hard against your lady's. This will compress, and so stimulate, her clitoris. And that'll be particularly useful if she's one of the large majority of women who don't usually have an orgasm during intercourse itself.

You may find it difficult to get *enough* clitoral pressure in the 'standard' or 'missionary' position, in which the woman lies flat on her back with the man on top. If this is so, then it's a good idea to switch to (for instance) positions in which you are able to get your legs further *between* your lady's thighs, so that you approach her more from underneath: in this way, your pubis may grind more effectively on hers, though this varies a bit from couple to couple.

Let me explain one or two of these positions:

★You can lie on your back with the lady sitting astride you. This gives you a more vertical entry, and lets you get the base of your 'pubes' right against her clitoris so that you seem almost locked together.

★You can put her on the edge of the bed with her legs raised, and stand or kneel in between her thighs. Once again, the 'clash' of pubic hair on pubic hair will stimulate her clitoris beautifully.

★You can make love to her in the 'missionary' position – but

131

with several pillows under her bottom. This tilts her pelvis up quite a lot, and once again helps you to get your pubis (and the very base of your penis) up against her clitoris.

There's more about positions of love-making in Chapter 14, and from the various exotic postures described there, you should be able to find several which enable you to really get *underneath* your partner so that you can drive up into her clitoris. But another useful technique is to enter her in the 'missionary' position and then to turn your whole body sideways so that your head is sort of pointing to 2 o'clock (or 10 o'clock), as in Figure 24. Curiously, the mere fact of having turned sideways like this will tend to bring your pubic bone into better contact with her clitoral area, and so increase her satisfaction. Above all, do remember that successful intercourse is not just a question of thrusting. The most important movement is grinding against the lady's clitoris!

FIG. 24

132

In Britain, Australia and New Zealand, it's common for gentle-man to refer to the act of love as 'a grind'. That's an expression which at first seems rather tasteless – but I think that Shere Hite would agree that 'grinding' is exactly what so many men forget to do!

Other ways of stimulating her clitoris during intercourse

There are other ways of stimulating a lady's clitoris during inter-course. You could, for instance, wear a 'clitoral stimulator' – though personally I haven't very much faith in these sex aids (which are discussed further in Chapter 16). More practical is the simple procedure of reaching down with your hand and rubbing her clitoris with your finger pads. This is often startlingly effective – especially in helping the woman who can't quite reach an orgasm during actual 'screwing'.

The problem, of course, is that your hand tends to get squashed between the two of you. This can sometimes be quite painful! You can get round this by using one of the 'non-face-to-face' positions described in Chapter 14. For instance, many couples achieve greater success by making love with the gent *behind* the lady, so that he can reach round with one hand (or even both) and stimulate her clitoris.

As a variant, some women actually prefer to stimulate their own clitorises during intercourse. Men occasionally take this as some sort of insult, but there's no need to feel that way. After all, any woman who has regularly masturbated – and many women have – will know exactly what feels best on her own clitoris. So if your loved one wants to rub her own 'clit' while you're making love to her, then why not?

Stimulating her other sexy areas during intercourse

Many men forget that while you're going in for all that thrusting, grinding, etc, etc, it's also a good idea to stimulate the rest of the lady's body. (Incidentally, she is a *person*, so why not begin by stimulating her brain by telling her nice things about how good she feels while you make love?)

A frequent complaint from women is that some men don't touch their breasts during intercourse. Admittedly, this is a bit difficult in the traditional face-to-face positions, because your hands get squashed – but do your best! Obviously, stimulating her breasts is easier if you're making love to her from behind or from the side – for instance in one of the positions shown in Chapter 14.

In fact, stroking almost any part of her body during sexual intercourse is good, and so is gently patting or slapping her bottom – a procedure which will often take a woman over the top into a climax.

Love bites are good too, but don't overdo them. If you bite too hard at the critical moment of intercourse you may actually *hurt* the lady – and so stop her climax rather than helping her to reach it.

In the chapters on love play, I've spent some time in discussing the advantages and dangers of *postillionage* – which means putting a finger in her bottom. Many men actually do this to their ladies *during intercourse itself* (which is easiest if the lady is on top), and I must admit that this can be a very considerable additional stimulus to the woman who likes that sort of thing (not all do).

If you do it properly (and it must *only* be done with a well-lubricated finger), you can feel your own penis inside her vagina with your fingertip. But *do* bear in mind the dangers detailed in earlier chapters – and when you remove the 'rectal' finger, *don't* put it anywhere near her vagina.

A safer – and more hygienic – technique is to slip your finger inside her vagina while your penis is already inside. This is easier in a very well-relaxed lady (especially one who's had children), and it'll give both of you various pleasant and unusual sensations.

Varying the angles – and the movement

Just a brief note to stress the fact that a skilled lover will take considerable care to vary the angles at which he inserts his penis – for instance, by changing to one or other of the positions shown in Chapter 14.

Inexperienced men don't usually realise what a difference a slight change of angle during intercourse can make. It can alter the pressure on the clitoris – or it can put pressure on the now-famous G-spot described in earlier chapters. It creates variety, and it's nice both for your lady and for you.

Also don't forget to vary the speed and type of your movements. Doing it slowly, then more quickly, and then 'teasing' her by slowing up again is all part of the game of intercourse.

So is changing the type of movement: don't just be satisfied with the dreaded thrusting and grinding: try moving your penis from side to side inside her, then turning it in a circular fashion – and then perhaps 'twitching' it in her vagina by sudden contractions of the muscles near its base. Variety is the spice of love!

Don't come too soon

Perhaps the most important rule for a man to remember during intercourse is this. Don't 'come' too soon! Again and again, women feel unsatisfied after sex, just because their partners have reached a climax too early – and then probably turned over and gone to sleep! A recent survey in France showed that about 50 per cent of French wives complained of this habit. And *zut alors*, who shall blame them?

So, a safe rule is to keep going until you're sure that the lady is really satisfied (and remember, many women aren't just satisfied with one climax these days . . .).

But if you *do* come too soon

If – as happens to almost every man sometimes – you do accidentally come too soon, then please don't leave your loved one high and dry. (Scarcely the appropriate phrase, but never mind.) Instead, bring your partner to a climax with your fingers or your tongue in one of the ways described in Chapter 8.

If you *keep* coming too soon then you probably have a touch of the common condition called 'hairtrigger trouble' or 'premature ejaculation'. This isn't your fault, so don't be embarrassed about it. If the trouble is very mild, Chapter 6 may help you sort it out. But if you're in real trouble, read Chapters 17 to 21, which are about more serious sex difficulties. You'll almost certainly need medical help – but you *can* be cured.

Don't forget contraception!

Finally: don't forget the basic fact which seems to slip the minds of so many men when they have intercourse. *It tends to lead to babies.*

Far too many males seem to think that this aspect of intercourse just isn't their responsibility: as the boys so often say in England, 'It's up to the bird, innit?' No, it's NOT just up to the 'bird' – it's the responsibility of both of you. So before you put your penis into that warm, throbbing vagina [*calm down, please – Editor*], do make sure that one or other of you has taken the appropriate precautions. Full details in Chapter 22.

CHAPTER THIRTEEN

A Guide To Intercourse Techniques For Women

Relaxing ● *If you're tense* ● *Lubrication* ● *Contraception* ● *Helping him in* ● *Wriggling and squirming and squealing* ● *Trying various positions* ● *Getting good stimulation to your clitoris* ● *Helping him with 'Florentine intercourse'* ● *'Milking' techniques* ● *Toning up your vaginal muscles* ● *Doing other nice things to him during intercourse.*

Relaxing

The most important thing for a woman to do in order to enjoy intercourse is just to relax. That may sound very obvious, but you'd be surprised at the tens of thousands of people who regard intercourse as some sort of sexual Olympic Games, in which they must achieve gold medals, or world records or whatever.

Be particularly careful to avoid the common habit of 'observing yourself' during intercourse – in other words, constantly keeping an eye on your performance and thinking 'How am I doing? How does he rate me?' To hell with how he rates you – just lie back and enjoy yourself!

If you're tense

If you're tensed up (as many women are, particularly when they're inexperienced – and also when it's the first time with a new man), then try one of the relaxation techniques taught by psychologists.

Personally, I think the easiest one is just to concentrate on breathing deeply. There is a curious mechanism of the human body whereby concentration on breathing can help relieve tension. Oddly enough, doctors aren't usually taught about this – but the trick is well-known to actors, to Indian yoga experts, to behaviourist psychologists *and* to some women in labour (a curiously assorted group, you may think).

Indeed, it was an actor friend who taught me the technique of regular breathing (in order to relax before going on TV). In just the same way, you can use breathing techniques to help you relax if you're the least bit tense about intercourse. Try them out just beforehand – or indeed during intercourse if you want to.

Just lie there on the bed and *think about breathing*. Concentrate on breathing in through your nose – and as the air flows in, think in a nice, relaxed way about your diaphragm (the sheet of muscle which lies under your lungs, separating your chest from your stomach). Imagine as you breathe in that it's going right down into your abdomen. . . . Then, as you breathe out, just concentrate in your mind on the one word 'relax . . .'. This technique can work wonders if you're not too uptight.

Another useful relaxation technique which you can use just before intercourse is this. While lying there, tighten up your vaginal muscles as tautly as you possibly can. Then after about twenty seconds, let go. Go on – just let everything go! You'll be surprised at how much those tight muscles will relax.

But if you're having more severe problems with tension, so that you're getting quite a bit of pain on intercourse (or even find it impossible), then obviously I'd like you to read the chapters devoted to sex problems – and particularly the section on the condition called 'vaginismus' (Chapter 18). This trouble *can* be put right, but you'll almost certainly need help from a doctor or psychologist in order to overcome it.

Lubrication

Successful intercourse depends very largely on good lubrication of your vagina. The lubrication comes of course from the 'love juices' which we now know flow mainly from the walls of the vagina. There probably are certain other sources of the 'love juices' – but from your point of view, the important thing is that they should start flowing a bit when you begin to think about sex. (If they haven't flowed just a little while you've been reading this book, then I've failed badly.)

They should flow a great deal more when your man starts saying romantic things to you, and caressing your body and – most of all – your clitoris. Since they provide the basic lubrication of love, he shouldn't (if he's got any sense) attempt to put his penis inside you till they're really flowing well.

If they don't really flow, then intercourse is difficult, painful, or even impossible. This can be due to tension on your part – which is usually also associated with an inability to relax the vaginal muscles (see above). If the relaxation exercises I've described earlier in this chapter don't help, then you should read the chapter of this book dealing with sexual difficulties – and in particular, the section on the common condition of vaginismus.

But very often, a woman's 'dry vagina' is just due to the fact that her husband/lover isn't preparing her adequately with skilled love play. If this is the case with you, make your man read the chapters on love play – and insist that he does it (love play, I mean) for as long as you need in order to make yourself nice and moist and welcoming!

Special note for mature ladies: in the years after the menopause, intercourse is quite often difficult because a drop in hormone levels tends to make the vagina short of lubrication. A course of vaginal female hormone cream prescribed by your doctor will almost always put this right.

Don't use the cream for longer than your physician says is necessary, as it can have side-effects. In one remarkable case, a woman's husband absorbed so much of the stuff during years of intercourse that he actually developed breasts!

Contraception

Just before we get into actual intercourse (so to speak) let's just remember one vital thing. Lots of women get uptight about sex because they're not adequately protected against its well-known side-effect: *babies*.

And they're quite right to be worried. With 150,000 abortions a year in Britain, 1¼ million in the USA, about 60,000 in Australia, and countless millions of unwanted babies being born worldwide each year, any woman who has sex with any man has a right to be scared – *unless* she's adequately protected.

So, before you allow that penis into your vagina, do make sure that either one of you (knowing men, it'll probably be *you*) has taken adequate contraceptive precautions.

Frankly, unless you're addicted to living dangerously, it's almost impossible really to enjoy sex when the thought of pregnancy is in the back of your mind. (Except, of course, when you're actually *trying* for a baby.) So, if you're not entirely sure about methods of protecting yourself against pregnancy please read Chapter 22 *before* you actually let him in!

Helping him in

Now that you're not only nicely relaxed and lubricated but also protected – your man is ready to enter you. This is certainly one of the most delicious moments in the whole wonderful catalogue of love: as I've said in the previous chapter (which was intended for men) the second when he actually puts himself inside you can be so beautiful that some couples actually 'disengage' and 're-engage' again and again in order to savour repeatedly that splendid moment when the tip of his penis pops between your labia.

But remember that even if you are totally relaxed, the moment of entry can often be a moment of considerable tension for your poor partner, because one of the saddest facts about sex is that so many men tend to lose their erections *just when the moment arrives to put it in.*

As a woman, you may not have realised this till now. But virtually every male has a secret fear that his penis will collapse just as he's trying to insert it into the vagina. Such fears are very common – and very justifiable in middle-aged and elderly men – and in those who are nervous about their performance.

This is where you can help your man. For a start, if he *does* have problems with his erection, for Heaven's sake don't laugh at him or (as some women – quite incredibly – do) get scornful or indignant or insulted. I'm sure you can see that such a reaction would be quite unfair to a man, who can't help losing his erection. (Also, making fun of a man because of his loss of potency can have rather disastrous results – the more sensational British Sunday papers regularly report cases in which a man who has been mocked in this way goes berserk and kills the unfortunate woman in question.)

Mind you, I'm not suggesting that such violent outcomes are likely between you and your man. Nonetheless, if your bloke has this sort of trouble just as you try to start intercourse together, do be sympathetic – and if possible help him to see the funny side of it, without hurting his feelings!

If he *does* 'fold', then you can rapidly help him get going again by skilled use of your hands and mouth (plus a few sexy whispers and so on) along the lines described in Chapter 9. And when he attempts re-entry (as the astronauts put it), it may be easier for him if you swing your body over so that you're *above* him, and then lower yourself onto the penis that you have gently rubbed up into erection.

But prevention is better than cure, so let me close this section by making one vital point. The agonies of worry which so many men face over the 'moment of entry' need never occur, if a woman gets in the habit of taking her loved one's penis in her hand *and guiding it in herself.* In these circumstances, it's most unlikely to collapse. This simple technique – if more widely known – would help millions of couples, especially those who are past the first flush of youth.

Note: another useful technique for helping your man maintain his potency *during* intercourse is described later in this chapter, under the heading 'Florentine intercourse'.

Wriggling and squirming and squealing

I scarcely have to say this, but if you're in any doubt whatever, most men absolutely love it if, during intercourse, you wriggle and squirm and squeal as much as possible!

Wriggling and squirming increases the direct sexual stimulation for both of you – and squealing is a real 'turn-on' for a man. Also, it's of great practical help if you can use the pitch and intensity of your squeals to help him realise when you're reaching a climax.

Trying various positions

In general, most women (not all, by any means) tend to be less adventurous than most men about trying varied positions for love-making. But don't let yourself get stuck with only 'screwing' in one position. Not only is this rather boring for him: it can get very dull for you too.

As Milton might have remarked: 'Tomorrow to fresh woods and postures new.' (Sorry, Milton.) Seriously, you may be quite surprised at how satisfying it is to try all sorts of different positions, which create many different sensations in your vagina as your loved one's penis goes in at various angles – and which also help greatly to increase the sheer fun of bedtime.

Some of these positions will increase the pressure on your clitoris (which is good); others increase the pressure on your 'magic G-spot' (which is also good); others leave your husband's or lover's hands free to reach round and stimulate your clitoris with his fingers (which should be very good indeed . . .).

Anyway, in a moment I'll be discussing how certain basic intercourse positions can increase the stimulation on your clitoris. And you'll find a full description of more exotic sexual postures in Chapter 14.

Getting good stimulation to your clitoris

If you've read the earlier part of this book, you'll know that

★The clitoris is the basic seat of women's sexual enjoyment – and the usual source of climaxes
★The majority of women do not reach a climax during actual intercourse (as opposed to love play)
★The main reason why so many women don't have an orgasm during intercourse itself is lack of clitoris stimulation.

In the previous chapter (Chapter 12), I've already pointed these facts out to the men, so if you feel that your partner isn't giving you enough clitoral stimulation during intercourse, I suggest you get him to read that chapter.

But you yourself can help him to increase your clitoris stimulation, in the following ways:

★Choose a position in which your 'pubes' really *grind* against your man's pubic bone – and insist that he does this if you feel you're not getting enough pressure on your clitoris.

★If that isn't enough, sexily draw him into one of the positions (see Chapter 14) in which he has a hand free to reach down and rub your clitoral area.

★If all else fails, rub your clitoris yourself.

If – like most women – you've masturbated at some time, you'll know exactly what to do to give yourself pleasure. You might possibly find that your man feels threatened at the idea of you stimulating your own clitoris. Too bad!

In fact, most men will simply feel excited at the idea that you're so 'horny' that you want to rub yourself while they're making love to you. (They'll probably want to take the credit for making you feel this way, so let them preserve their illusions. Tread softly, as W. B. Yeats said, for you tread on their dreams.)

Helping him with 'Florentine intercourse'

As I've already tried to make clear to female readers, a large proportion of men – particularly those over thirty-five – spend a good deal of time worrying about their erections, and how long they'll be able to maintain them. Indeed, a journalist in one of the British Sunday newspapers recently interviewed a man whose hobby was kite-flying – and who said with startling perspicacity that the male sexual symbolism of the sport was obvious: 'It's a question of "Can you get it up?" and "How long can you keep it there?" ' Another symbol of this constant male fear was the recent popular movie called *Can You Keep It Up for a Week?*

Anyway, to cut a long story short, lots of men do tend to lose their erections in the middle of intercourse – which is frustrating for both of you. But you can prevent this if you use the technique known as 'Florentine intercourse' – which was presumably a practice once much employed in the city of Florence. (Where they've got some very shaky erections . . .)

Florentine intercourse is also very good to use even if your partner hasn't got any troubles with his erection, since it's highly stimulating for both of you. All you do is this:

Reach round behind your bottom and put your hand between your thighs at the back. Then grasp his penis as it goes in and out of your vagina – and rub it!

It's a delightful manoeuvre which I can thoroughly recommend. The only thing you have to be careful of is that you don't make it so exciting that your man 'comes' there and then.

'Milking' techniques

One of the great 'intercourse arts' which is said to have been known to naughty ladies for thousands of years is that of 'milking' the penis during intercourse. This isn't as difficult as it sounds. You have certain quite powerful muscles in the region of your vagina, and it's quite easy to twitch them. Just give a few twitches during intercourse and you'll be surprised at the effect on your man; it's as if someone has suddenly taken hold of his penis and given it a warm, encouraging squeeze!

In fact, ladies who want to be Advanced Lovers may like to know that there are really two sets of vaginal muscles – and if you're *really* skilled, you can use the two sets (one after the other) actually to 'milk' your man's penis.

The *outer* set are the ones which you use when you want to stop yourself peeing. The *inner* set are the ones you use when you want to stop a bowel motion. If you use first the outer set and then the inner set, you'll produce a delightful 'milking' action on your lover.

In practice, true co-ordination of the two sets of muscles is only achieved by a few really determined (and really sexy) ladies. But if you just give a quick twitch of either of these pelvic muscle groups from time to time during intercourse, both you and your man will enjoy it very much.

Toning up your vaginal muscles

Lots of women find that these 'love muscles' have been weakened by childbirth. Not only is this a bad thing sexually (since it makes the vagina slack, and prevents them from carrying out the sexy techniques mentioned in the last section) – but it can also be a health problem. Slack muscles can lead to prolapse, or descent of the womb, in middle or later life.

Happily, you can do something about this. You can protect yourself against prolapse *and* improve your sex life by regularly doing what are called 'Kegel exercises', which are described at the end of Part (ii) of Chapter 6.

If you do these regularly, you'll soon have a vagina that would coax a climax out of any man.

Doing other things to him during intercourse

While flexing your vagina and all that kind of thing, don't forget that you can enthuse your bloke by doing all sorts of other nice activities.

By 'all sorts of other nice activities', I mean all the things we've already discussed in the chapters on 'foreplay' or love play. In particular:

★ Stick your tongue in his mouth
★ Love-bite him – bearing in mind that if your relationship is an illicit one, you'd better be careful where you make those marks (or 'hickies', as they call them in Scotland).
★ Urge him on vocally: if you're stuck for something to say, then 'I love you' (if you mean it) or 'Fuck me' (which presumably you *do* mean) are both pretty appropriate and very, very erotic.
★ Caress his nipples
★ Hold his testicles (gently)
★ Stroke and pat his bottom
★ If you want to (and if he wants to) go in for *postillionage* – bearing in mind the health risks I've spelt out in earlier chapters.

One final thought: watch out that none of these exciting activities sends him blasting into a climax before *you* are good and ready for him!

CHAPTER FOURTEEN

More Exotic Ways Of Having Intercourse

The positions of love-making ● *Is it all worth trying?* ● *Position changes can help the handicapped* ● *Basic positions* ● *Variations of face-to-face positions* ● *Face-to-face with the woman above* ● *Face-to-face with both standing* ● *Face-to-face lying on the side* ● *Rear entry positions* ● *Rear entry with man beneath* ● *Rear entry standing* ● *Rear entry, both on side* ● *Doing it sideways on* ● *Cuissade positions* ● *Flanquette positions* ● *Doing it in unusual places* ● *In the open air* ● *In cars* ● *In the bath tub or the shower* ● *In Jacuzzis and swimming pools* ● *Underwater* ● *In planes* ● *In space* ● *Making love in front of mirrors* ● *Fantasies with intercourse.*

The positions of love-making

There's an awful lot of rhubarb talked about the various positions of love-making. As you probably know, books (and even videotapes) have been published which purport to show about 793 different postures. But when you come to examine these compilations carefully, you tend to find that position 424 differs from position 423 only by the fact that in the latter posture the lady flexes her left big toe!

So there's no real answer to the oft-asked question 'How many positions are there?' – because it all depends how you define a position. Personally, I'd say that there are about nine basic 'postures', and I'll be detailing them in this chapter. But obviously, you can vary any of these postures by some slight alteration of the position of the limbs, and you may find that doing this produces mild but agreeable changes in sensation.

Is it all worth trying?

Yes, it is. Of course, if you're both happy with just sticking to the

basic position which you've used all your lives, then that's fine. But for most people (and especially for men) variety, as I've said before, is the spice of love. So trying a few other positions can give quite a distinct fillip to your love life, and generally make it more exciting. Experimenting with new positions is especially well worth trying if your desire has been flagging a bit recently – and I'd particularly recommend a change of position to middle-aged lovers who find that things have been getting in a rut (if you'll forgive the phrase).

Position changes can help the handicapped

One other point which I'd like to stress is that there are a lot of couples whose sex lives are impaired because one or other of them is handicapped – so they can't manage the 'ordinary' positions.

I must say that my eyes have been opened by some of the advice columns letters which I've received on this subject. For instance, there are clearly many middle-aged and elderly ladies who have the all-too-common condition of arthritis of the hip – and who suffer such pain from the disorder that they cannot part their thighs enough to have sex with their husbands in the 'classical' or 'missionary' position.

I've been very surprised to find that many of these ladies don't actually know what other positions are available. And I do believe that telling them about these other positions – and indeed about the '69' position of love play described earlier in the book – has helped them.

Basic positions

As nearly everybody knows, the basic position of love-making is the one shown in Figure 25, and it's often called the 'traditional' or

FIG. 25

145

'missionary' position – because missionaries are supposed to have told their converts that it was the only *respectable* posture. It's a very good position, actually (as a Scots doctor friend of mine remarked: 'Aye, they knew a thing or two, those lady missionaries . . .').

But it doesn't give quite as much penetration as many other positions do. And, as I've explained in previous chapters, it doesn't always give the really intense pressure on the clitoris which is essential for many women if they're going to reach a climax during intercourse itself.

Variations of face-to-face positions

So for this and other reasons, it's well worth trying these variations for a start:

VARIATION 1   The first and simplest variation is for the woman just to straighten her legs and to spread them wide on the bed. Entry is just a little more difficult with the legs like this, but the sensation produced is slightly different from that felt in the basic position.

FIG. 27

FIG. 26

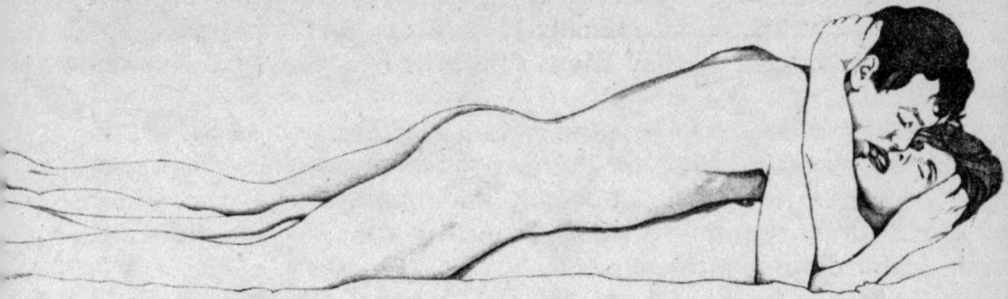

VARIATION 2   The man lies with his legs *outside* the woman's (as in Figure 26). His thighs squeeze hers together, and her thighs compress his penis. For that reason, this technique is useful if the woman's vagina has been slackened a bit by childbirth.

VARIATION 3   The woman brings her legs up over the man's hips or waist (as in Figure 27). This alters the tilt of her pelvis and so gives very good penetration of her vagina. She can, if she wishes, cross her legs round his middle, so increasing the sense of closeness.

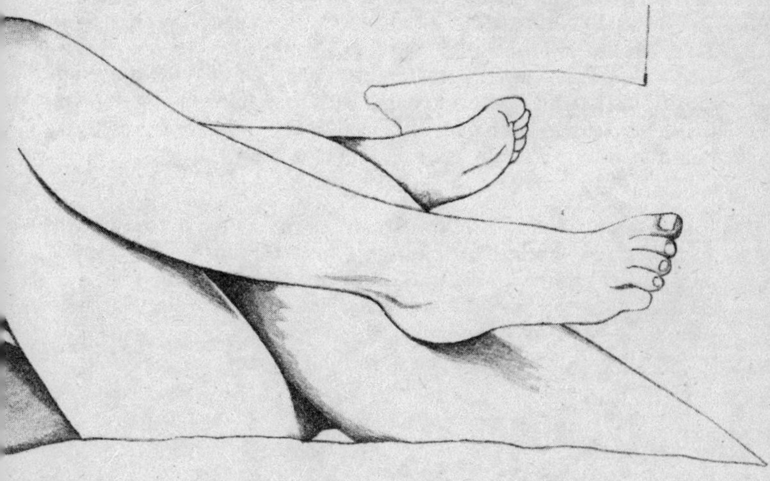

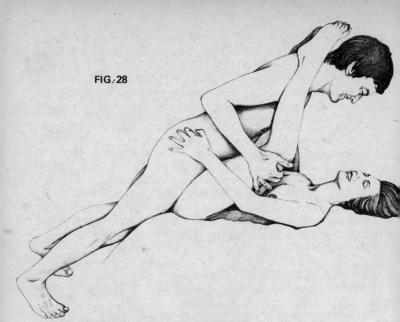

FIG. 28

VARIATION 4   This variation is merely an extension of the last one, but you need to be more supple. The woman draws her legs even further up so that she can hook them over her partner's shoulders (as shown in Figure 28). This gives very deep penetration indeed, so it's important that entry should be gentle.

You shouldn't usually start intercourse with this rather athletic position. It's much better to begin with something else and, if you wish, work up to deep penetration after ten, twenty or even thirty minutes when the vagina has had time to really relax.

VARIATION 5   Using a pillow. In any of the above positions, you can produce subtle alterations in the depth and angle of penetration by simply putting a pillow or two under the lady's bottom. This usually works best when she has her legs in the air, as in Variation 3 above.

148

VARIATION 6   Split levels. The last three techniques we have mentioned also work very well if the two partners are on different levels, e.g. if the woman is lying back on the edge of the bed while the man kneels on the floor (as shown in Figure 29). An inventive couple can think of several such situations – for example, with the woman sitting in a chair, or perhaps lying back on a snooker or pool table, while the man stands between her legs.

Face-to-face with the woman above

This range of positions is very useful, particularly when (as is so often the case) there's a big difference in the weights of man and woman. Let's face it, no matter how enthusiastic one is about the missionary position and its variations, they're not always a lot of fun for a 100lb woman who's gasping for breath beneath a 200lb man.

FIG. 29

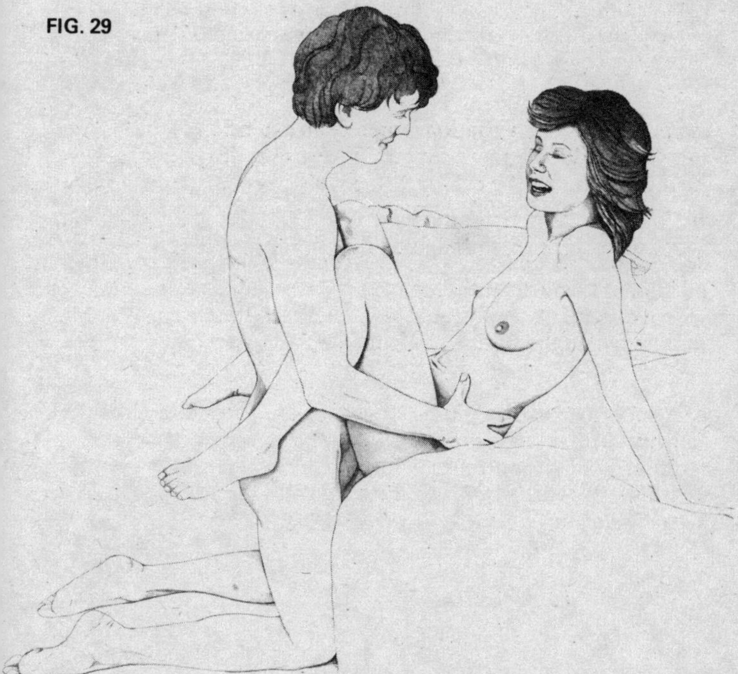

FIG. 30

So, many couples quite often make love with the man lying flat on his back and the woman lying on top of him, as in Figure 30. Her legs can be inside or outside his – the former position gives her an opportunity to exert pressure on his penis with her thighs.

VARIATION 1   The woman simply raises the top part of her body on outstretched arms so that her partner can see and feel her breasts, which is nice for him.

VARIATION 2   The 'frog position'. The woman places the soles of her feet on the upper surfaces of the man's feet and both of them spread their legs wide apart with knees bent (in much the same attitude as that of a frog's legs). Their lower limbs are now in close and intimate contact all the way down, and this enables them to 'work together' in a most agreeable way during intercourse.

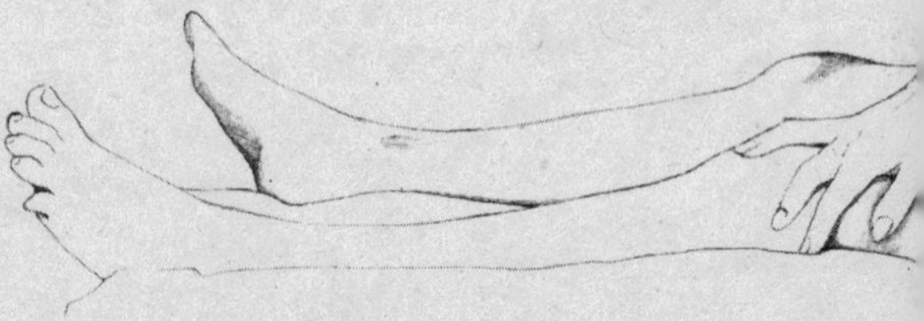

VARIATION 3   The woman kneels astride the man's hips as shown in Figure 31. This position is very useful when a man is having trouble with his potency or his control. For the reasons why, see the sections on Problems with Sex. Like the next variation, it's also very good in pregnancy.

VARIATION 4   Very similar to No. 3 except that the woman sits on her partner's penis with her legs stretched out on either side of his chest or over his shoulders. She can then bump up and down in the movement that the French so aptly describe as 'the Lyon stagecoach'. Or, if she likes, she can turn a complete circle while still sitting on her man, so that naturally his penis also rotates through 360 degrees inside her vagina.

151

FIG. 32

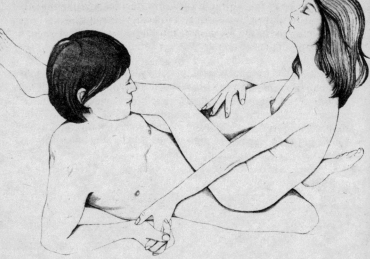

VARIATION 5   The 'X-position'. While sitting on her partner as in
Variation 4, the woman leans completely backwards until she is
flat on the bed. Because considerable pressure is put on the penis,
it tends to pop out unless the couple take things very gently. Once
the position is achieved, the penis presses on the woman's celebrated G-spot, which she may well enjoy. It may also make her
want to pee if her bladder is full.

In practice, this variation is often more comfortable and satisfying if the man puts one of his legs across the woman's thigh as in
Figure 32. Note that the couple are holding hands, which is not
only romantic but which helps them to pull his penis more deeply
into her.
(Note for advanced lovers: this is really a *flanquette* position –
details later in this chapter.)

VARIATION 6   This starts off rather like Variation 3, with the
woman kneeling astride the man's penis – but now he has his legs
outside hers and wraps them round her body. He then uses his legs
to tug himself up repeatedly into her vagina, a rather exotic
procedure which can give both partners a pleasantly wild and
abandoned feeling. Frankly, he has to be reasonably athletic to try
this.

VARIATION 7   Lying on top of her partner, the woman slowly turns her whole body first through forty-five degrees and then ninety degrees (more than this is difficult to achieve) so that she is lying across him with his penis pressing into the side wall of her vagina. If the penis comes out while you are rotating, go back and start again.

This position is quite nice for long, lazy love. It enables the man to stimulate his loved one's breasts with one hand and her bottom (by love slaps, etc) with the other.

VARIATION 8   Just like Variation 3, except that the husband sits on a chair (as shown in Figure 33) with his wife astride him.

FIG. 33

Face-to-face with both standing

Face-to-face love-making in a standing position is very common, because unmarried people sometimes have nowhere to make love except up against a wall. Intercourse in these inauspicious circumstances is usually hurried, awkward and unsatisfactory, partly because most men are a good deal taller than most women. Only the Napoleon and Josephine couples of this world can achieve a reasonably comfortable entry in a face-to-face standing position. Some people in this unfortunate situation try to get round the problem by standing the lady on a couple of bricks – but there is the ever-present danger that she may fall off half-way through and thus shatter what little romantic atmosphere there is about this way of having intercourse.

But making love standing face-to-face in the bedroom without the encumbrance of clothes is a quite different matter and can be great fun. The woman will often need a firm stool (a footstool is ideal) to stand on, unless she is taller than her partner, and she should lean against a wall for support, bracing herself against the man's thrusts.

VARIATION 1   This is only for young, lusty men with strong backs! The man picks up his partner, around the waist or by the buttocks, and lifts her into the air. She wraps her arms round his neck and her legs round his body and rocks vigorously to-and-fro.

VARIATION 2   Much the same but even more acrobatic. The woman leans right back until her head and hands are on the floor, while her legs remain wrapped round her partner's body. Few men have the strength to manage this for more than a minute or so but the position certainly provides quite an amusing variety of love-making for prospective Olympic athletes.

VARIATION 3   Making love on the stairs can be a very good way of getting round the problem of difference in height between man and woman.

Face-to-face, lying on side.

Often known in Britain and Australia as 'having a bit on the side', this is the final face-to-face position. It makes entry a bit difficult, but once in, it's pleasant and agreeable for long slow love-making interspersed with conversation. It's nice for couples who want to go to sleep afterwards with their sex organs still joined together.

But advanced lovers will usually prefer one of the *flanquette* positions described in a moment.

Rear entry positions

These positions used to shock 'moralists' in years gone by, mainly because they associated the idea of rear entry with the way that 'brute beasts of the field' (to quote the marriage service) have intercourse. These methods were also supposed to be favoured by allegedly 'inferior' races and were therefore deemed not suitable for 'civilised Europeans'. Even today, the first position we are about to describe is sometimes known as coitus *à la négresse*, though in fact black girls do not seem to have any special interest in this position.

VARIATION 1   What happens here is that the woman kneels on the bed with her head well down, as in Figure 34. Her man kneels behind her and gently enters her vagina, with one or other of them using a hand in front of the vulva to steer the penis in (you may

FIG. 34

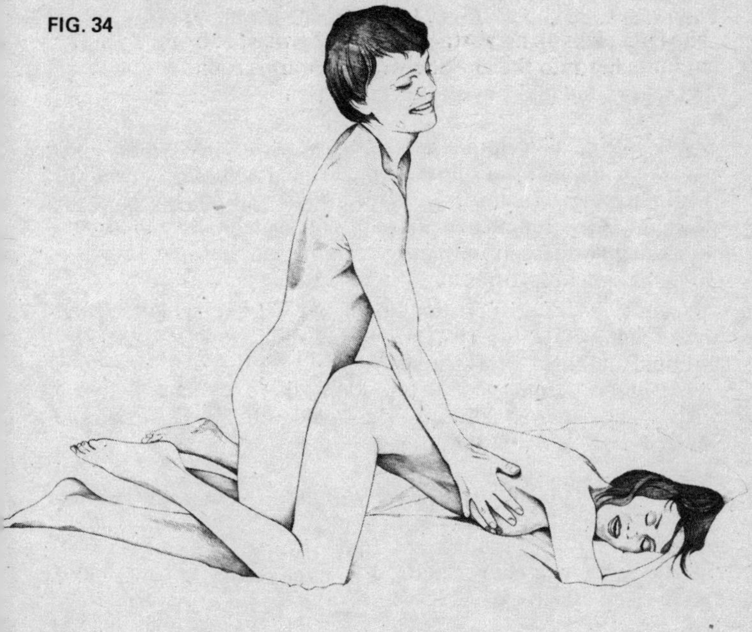

have to keep it there throughout). As with all the other rear entry positions this position gives the man an ideal opportunity to stimulate the woman's breasts and, of course, her clitoris with his finger tips.

VARIATION 2   Instead of kneeling, the woman lies flat on her face on the bed with legs apart. This makes entry a bit difficult, but the woman can help the penis in with her hand.

VARIATION 3   Instead of kneeling *between* the woman's legs, the man places his knees on either side of her. Then he slowly and gradually eases forward until he is virtually sitting astride her back and 'riding' her. This is an advanced technique and should not be rushed; it may be uncomfortable and completely unsuccessful if the woman has not been prepared and stimulated by careful love play.

VARIATION 4   Split levels. The woman lies face down with legs apart on the edge of the bed while her partner kneels behind her.

VARIATION 5   Very similar, but the man grasps his lady's thighs and then stands up, so that he is holding her rather as in a child's wheelbarrow game.

Rear entry, with man beneath

Many men do like to lie flat on their backs with their partners (also face upwards) on top of them. Almost invariably one or other of them has to place a hand in front of the vulva to keep the penis from popping out. Some women achieve quite an unusually intense climax as a result.

VARIATION 1   It's very pleasant if the man lies flat on his back and the woman just sits on his penis while facing away from him. By altering the angle to which she leans forward she can produce agreeable variations in the sensations she experiences. If she wishes, she can gradually lower her head until her face is on the sheets between her partner's legs.

VARIATION 2   Much the same as Variation 1, but with the man sitting up as well.

VARIATION 3   The same thing, but with the man sitting on a chair instead of on the bed.

Rear entry standing

This is a very nice way of making love, and easier than face-to-face standing intercourse. The woman bends over so as to reveal the exciting sight of her vulva between her thighs. She can, if she wishes, lean against a chair or, preferably, a more solid structure such as a chest of drawers as chairs tend to get knocked over as things become more hectic towards the end.

VARIATION 1   The woman stands upright instead of bending over. Entry is not to easy this way, but the man can more readily caress his loved one's breasts, kiss her neck and murmur sweet nothings in her ear.

VARIATION 2   The woman bends forward until her hands are on the floor, and then her partner helps her to wrap her legs around his body. This position again is really for athletes only, and the man should bear in mind that his partner will *not* enjoy having her face rammed repeatedly into the carpet! A very large feather cushion under her arms may be helpful.

Rear entry, both on side

Intercourse with both partners lying on their sides (her bottom tucked cosily up against the lower part of his stomach) can be very satisfying. As with the corresponding face-to-face love-making position, it's possible for both partners to fall asleep after orgasm with their genitals still in contact – an advantage which many couples value.

VARIATION 1   The woman leans forward so that the top half of her body is at right angles to the man's. This produces an interesting change in sensation in the vagina and in the penis. If he wants to, the man can increase the effect by gently leaning backwards. This does, however, make communication between the lovers rather difficult!

VARIATION 2   As for Variation 1, but the woman moves one of her legs back (either between the man's legs or above them) until it is in a straight line with the top half of her body. By subtle alterations in leg position she can produce all sorts of interesting effects for both partners.

Doing it sideways on

The basic way of doing this is for the woman to lie flat on her back with the knees bent or (if she prefers it) her legs in the air. Her man lies on his side, with the lower part of his body curled under her bottom so that her legs are across his thighs. This very comfortable position, shown in Figure 35, is useful during pregnancy.

FIG. 35

VARIATION 1   The man lies flat on his back on the bed while his wife sits across his thighs. This is not so comfortable, but may be chosen as a change.

VARIATION 2   This is virtually the same thing but with *both* partners sitting. The man is usually settled on a comfortable chair with his partner seated across his lap so that his penis comes up between her thighs and enters her vulva. Some couples take pleasure in doing this with their clothes on (apart, perhaps, from the lady's panties), thereby adding spice to the procedure.

'Cuissade' positions

This French term simply means that the man takes his lover from a half-rear and half-sideways angle – in other words, he enters her from behind, but with one of his legs through hers. This is easier to explain with a picture than to describe, so look at Figure 36.

   Cuissade positions allow the penis to enter the vagina at all sorts of interesting angles and (if the man lies back at right angles to the woman) to a remarkable depth.

FIG. 36

'Flanquette' positions

This is another French term which simply describes the side positions in which the entry is 'half-facing', rather than 'half-rear'. In other words, the man is face-to-face with his partner but with his leg thrust between hers. Look at Figure 37 which makes this clear.

There are many *flanquette* positions for you to discover for yourselves, but they're all nice and they all allow very good penetration, usually combined with pressure on the clitoris by the man's thigh. One word of warning – the fact that the woman's leg is between the man's thighs renders him vulnerable to a very obvious injury. So whatever happens, a woman *must* be careful not to bring her knee up suddenly!

Doing it in unusual places

Now, having got all those jolly positions out of the way, let's turn to the question of doing it in unusual places. This is a good idea too – especially if one or other of you has become a bit bored or a bit jaded with sex in the same old bedroom.

For a start, you can make love in other rooms of the house. The slight 'naughtiness' of this (plus the thrill of knowing that there's a faint chance of being discovered) often adds great spice to this kind of love-making – particularly for a woman.

Good places to try are:

★Sitting rooms: obviously, settees
 and *chaises-longues* are ideal for love-
 making. So too is a comfortable rug in
 front of a warm fire.

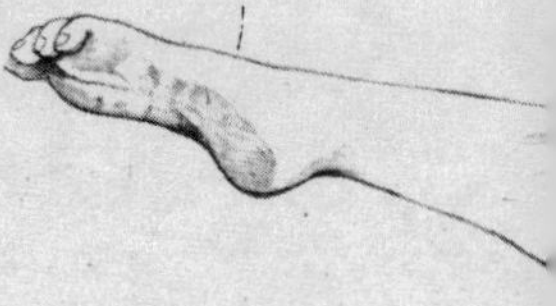

FIG. 37

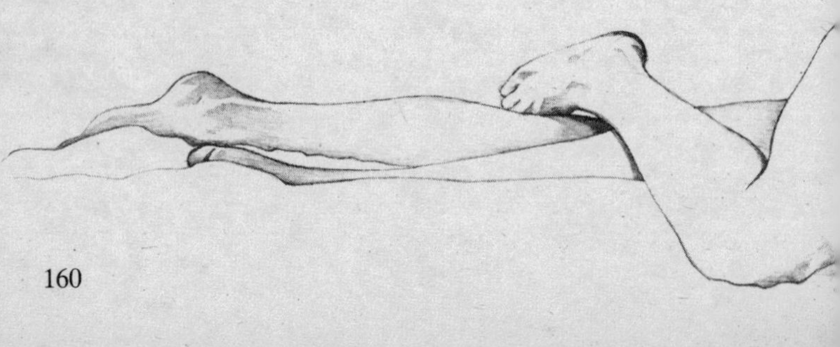

FIG. 38

★Stairs: oddly enough, a staircase is a very good place to make love standing up – because (as you can see from Figure 38) the man can stand on the step *below* the woman. This avoids the great problem with standing intercourse: that it's so difficult for the man to get under his partner.

★Kitchens: certainly, there's a spice of the piquant and unusual in making love in the kitchen – though you have to be careful not to knock the saucepans off the cooker! Probably the easiest thing is for the woman to hitch up her skirt at the rear, turn her back on her lover and lean forward over the kitchen counter or worktop while he enters her from behind. In this position, she can even wave to the neighbours through the window without their knowing what's going on. (See Figure 39.)

FIG. 39

★Dining rooms: if the carpet's warm and you put a couple of cushions down, then this is another good place to try. If you want something a little different, why not 'make it' under the table? I wouldn't try it *on* the table unless you're very sure that the legs are strong enough.

Mind you, there is the famous story of the woman who asked her doctor for aphrodisiac tablets to give to her husband – and then came back next morning to complain.

'I gave him one of these tablets, doctor,' she said. 'And he immediately grabbed me, pinned me down on the table, and made wild, passionate love to me among all the knives and forks.'

'Well,' said the doctor, rather bewildered. 'Wasn't that what you wanted?'

'Certainly not,' said the woman indignantly. 'We'll never be able to go to that restaurant again.'

In the open air

If the climate permits it, there's nothing like a bit of open-air love-making to pep up your relationship. This is partly because having sex in the Great Outdoors somehow seems extremely natural and healthy – and partly too there's once again the slight 'naughty' thrill of knowing that you just might be discovered. Even if you live in a town, it's quite surprising what you and your loved one can discreetly get up to in the shrubbery or the ferns of your local park.

And if you can get out into the countryside or onto a beach – well, I can assure you that there are few things nicer than making love under a blue sky with someone you adore – while the sun beats down on a bare bottom. . . .

P.S. Watch out for ants – and sunburned buttocks. . . .

In cars

There's a long tradition of making love in parked cars (making love in moving ones is slightly more difficult). Naturally, this tradition has grown up because most of the couples involved have had nowhere else to go. In practice, making love in an automobile is generally uncomfortable, cramped, and fraught with the risk of damaging your more tender parts on protruding bits of the vehicle. In cars the size of Minis, it's all too easy to prang yourself on the gearstick, or to set off the horn at the moment of orgasm. However, automatics are easier – and I'm told that making love on the back seat of a Rolls-Royce can be very civilised.

More seriously, some married couples do actually like going out to make love in the car – so as to recapture the thrill of those illicit days when they first met. Hence the success of Billy-Jo Spears' famous record *'57 Chevrolet*.

Note: In most countries the police can nick you for doing it in cars – even if you're married to each other. So watch it.

In the bathtub or the shower

As I've briefly indicated earlier in the book, the shower and the bathtub are great places to make love. Unfortunately, the average tub is a bit small for two, but it *can* be managed – though whoever's underneath might be well advised to bring a snorkel.

When I've mentioned it in correspondence columns, readers have often written in to ask if sex in the tub could lead to water being forced into the womb and causing harm. But I've never heard of such a case, and I don't believe this is a risk. You're in far more danger from slipping on the soap.

In Jacuzzis and swimming pools

Readers in chilly Britain or Ireland may not all know that a Jacuzzi is a delightful sort of bathtub in which jets of water squirt at you under the surface, soothing and massaging you. (They're very good for bad backs!) Invented in the US by the Jacuzzi family, they're often situated outdoors, and have become very popular in North America and Australia and many sunny countries. But if you can afford it, you could have one fitted indoors.

The makers of Jacuzzis have very sensibly realised that people would want to get up to all kinds of hanky-panky in these nice, warm tubs – therefore, they make them big enough for two people (or more, if your tastes run to that sort of thing).

So, if you want to make love in a Jacuzzi, have a good time. My experience with them has been that they can be ferociously hot – hot enough to make you feel faint. Unless you want to pass out during sex (*not* a good idea when you're in 500 gallons of whirling water) it may be best to keep the temperature control down.

What about swimming pools? If you're one of the fortunate few who have access to a private one, then this too is a good place to make love. (If you try it in the Glasgow Municipal Baths, you'll get banned for weeks.)

Non-swimmers should only make love in the shallow end but in deeper water – as Graham Greene points out in his splendid novel

The Comedians – it's possible for a lady just to hang onto the side while the man gently takes her from behind.

Underwater

This brings us to the subject of making love *underwater* – either in pools or in the sea. For good swimmers this is absolutely delightful, since the water buoys you both up so that you're virtually weightless. (Also, if you wear face masks, the water's natural magnifying effect produces some very interesting appearances. . . .)

Seriously, those who live in warm countries will find underwater love-making with a face-mask and snorkel is great fun. If you're a trained diver and want to 'do it deeper' with an aqualung, you'll know that (what with all those straps and whatnot) it's *not* as easy as it appeared in the James Bond film *Thunderball*. But it can be done. . . .

Watch out for the bends.

In planes

There's an organisation called 'The Mile-High Club' which consists entirely of people who've 'made it' at altitude in a plane. As far as I can make out, most of the members are air-hostesses and cabin staff who have nipped into the toilet together at 40,000 feet. Frankly, I think this must be *very* uncomfortable, but if you want to try it, good luck to you.

In space

At the time of writing no-one has 'done it' in space (at least, as far as I know). But a number of people have written poems about making love in orbit – because they've realised that weightlessness will give lovers a complete freedom of movement which they can never achieve on Earth.

So, one day you may be able to score in space. And that day may not be as far away as you think. The Russians have announced their intention of arranging for a woman *to have a baby in space* – and there are already rumours that they may be planning for a pair of male and female cosmonauts to achieve the actual impregnation in orbit!

I'm sure Neil Armstrong wouldn't have got involved in that sort of thing.

Making love in front of mirrors

Finally, back to Earth and more prosaic things. Lots of couples find that using mirrors is a great way of pepping up their sex lives. Men in particular do tend to enjoy watching themselves making love – and also getting unusual views of their loved ones' bottoms! In fact, once they get used to the idea, a lot of women like it too.

As you probably know, *bordellos* through the ages have featured enormous mirrors fixed to the ceiling directly above the bed so that the frolicking couples can look directly up at themselves. Nowadays, some people are bold enough to fix up such mirrors above their own double beds at home.

However, that sort of fixture does tend to attract comment from one's more strait-laced neighbours and relatives! So, if you don't want to make your 'mirror-gazing' too obvious, then it may be best to settle for one of these alternatives:

★Have a long dressing table mirror (preferably body length) beside the bed – then the two of you can watch each other sideways, so to speak, when you want to.
★Fix up a tilted mirror on the wall: with a little cunning, you can angle it so as to see whatever it is that you want to see. . . .
★Get a cheval mirror – that is, one of those long looking-glasses which you can wheel around on a stand. If you wheel it up to the foot of the bed, you can then tilt it horizontally so that whoever's underneath gets some highly original views of whoever's on top. (Mind out that you don't kick the cheval mirror, or it'll flip over and clonk you one!)

Fantasies with intercourse

Finally, let's deal with the use of fantasies during intercourse. Lots of men and women do use them to make sex more exciting – and a jolly good thing too, particularly if you've been having a bit of trouble with lack of sexual desire recently, and find that a spot of fantasy peps you up a bit and makes you a better lover, and so better able to make your partner happy.

It's widely believed that only men go in much for fantasies, but that isn't true at all. There are many books about the extra-ordinary diversity and richness of female fantasies. In brief, the main male fantasies include

★Making love to a favourite film or TV star
★Making love to some other attractive women who the man

fancies (say, a friend or a colleague at the office)
★Being in bed with more than one girl
★Being involved in group sex
★Lesbianism (women may find this odd, but men are very often 'turned on' by it: hence the popularity of lesbian acts in sex shows)
★Having someone else make love to their partners (again, this fantasy may seem odd – but a lot of men are turned on by it).

Common *female* fantasies are rather similar and include:

★Being made love to by a handsome screen star
★Being made love to by a friend or acquaintance whom the woman fancies
★Being made love to by a succession of men
★Being raped (personally I find this almost incomprehensible – since as a doctor I know how appalling the results of rape are)
★Being involved in group sex

As you can see, some of these fantasies would be highly dangerous if they were really acted out. But if they remain just as sexy dreams in the mind, then that's OK.

There is, I must admit, one slight danger. Behaviourist psychologists have discovered that the fantasies which people indulge in at the moment of climax tend to influence their subsequent sexual behaviour. These psychologists use this remarkable discovery to help people with problems of sexual orientation. (For instance, if a man has abnormal sexual desires, they'll encourage him to masturbate to 'straight' heterosexual fantasies.)

You can probably see the danger here: if you keep thinking about the same fantasy just as you reach a climax, then you may well find yourself getting keener and keener on actually *acting out* that fantasy in real life. At the very least, this might mean that you go and start an affair with the man/lady next door instead of just fantasising about it!

Should you tell your partner about the fantasies which you have during intercourse? Obviously, it's more honest to do so – but if you think he or she might be jealous, then it could be best to keep them to yourself.

However, it's undeniably true that lots of couples really do make intercourse much more exciting for each other by exchanging fantasies in bed, and by pretending to be Roman gladiators, Vestal Virgins, TV newsreaders, all-in wrestlers, or whatever turns them on. A little of what you fantasy does you good.

CHAPTER FIFTEEN

Way-Out Antics – And Their Dangers

What is a 'way-out' activity? ● *Bondage* ● *Leather, rubber, plastic, high heels and so on* ● *Videotaping your sex life* ● *Blue movies and videos* ● *Wife-swapping and 'swinging'* ● *Group sex* ● *Sado-masochism* ● *Drugs and sex* ● *Pornography* ● *Rectal intercourse.*

What's a 'way-out' activity?

Everyone has their own ideas about sex, and you'd be surprised at how many people there are who think that anything except intercourse in the traditional 'missionary' position is 'abnormal' or 'kinky'. (Dr Kinsey's research in the USA showed that such views are specially common in people who haven't had a lot of education.) Similarly, you may well think that some of the antics described earlier in this book – specially the love-play chapters – are 'way out'. Alternatively, you may possibly feel that much of what I'm going to include in *this* chapter is pretty normal!

All I can say is that sex is a very subjective business. And in this chapter, I'm just going to include all the common activities which I personally think tend to be a bit bizarre – *mainly because they have, in some cases, certain dangers or may indicate psychological problems*. Please don't assume that I'm condemning you if you go in for these practices: but I think it's only reasonable to point out the risks.

Bondage

Bondage means being tied up (or in some other way restricted) while you're having sex. It's very popular – as anyone who wanders into a sex shop and sees the handcuffs and whatnot on sale can testify. *Why* should it be popular? I tend to agree with the orthodox psychoanalysts' view that it's because the sexual part of many people's minds likes being reminded of the time when they were tightly strapped up as tiny children.

Anyway, it's pointless to argue about the possible causes of the widespread interest in bondage. What is important is to point out that every now and again some poor soul gets killed because bondage has been taken too far – usually because he or she has been gagged and has choked to death. Personally, I think it's utter lunacy to go in for *any* form of bondage which involves gags or constriction on the neck.

Even if you just try 'milder' forms of bondage, you should always have some pre-agreed signal which will let your partner know that you've had enough; that you're not kidding; and that you want to be released NOW.

Having said all that, I must say that I know of quite a few people who seem to get a bit of harmless fun by *gently* tying each other to the bedposts. The attraction of this lies partly in the fact that it's quite nice to be pinned down helplessly while somebody you love does sexy things to you.

If you're inclined toward this sort of thing, I'd suggest you confine it to tying the wrists and ankles very, very gently – for instance with soft material like dressing gown belts. Do *not* use harsh ropes, which can hurt skin very badly.

Leather, rubber, plastic, high heels and so on

Lots of people seem to have 'fetishes' for certain materials and objects. This is utterly incomprehensible to those of us who *don't* have such interests – but in fact most fetishes do become more or less understandable if you think about them in the psychoanalytic terms I've mentioned above.

In other words, though it may sound a bit 'pseud' to say so, it could well be true that people with fetishes have had their libidos 'fixed' in early infant life – fixed on something they took pleasure in coming into contact with as babies. Thus:

★Rubber and plastic freaks may well be emotionally 'harking back' to the time when they rolled around on rubber or plastic sheets as infants

★High-heel shoe freaks (who are so astonishingly common in the USA and Canada – but not so frequently encountered elsewhere) may be harking back to the time when they rolled about on the floor being gently poked by Mummy's shoe.

But I can't explain leather fetishism in this way – unless leather addicts are emotionally hung up on Mummy's leather shoes or the leather straps of early childhood. (Certainly, bondage and leather fancying often go together.)

Now, I can't say that there are really any dangers in this fancying of rubber, leather, plastic and boots. Indeed, I think it was most unfair that some years ago the British police closed down what seems to have been a pretty harmless magazine called

Rubber News – especially as the 'respectable' British newspapers today continue to publish ads for strange rubber garments. ('Keep warm this winter with latex bloomers!')

But if you're 'into' these things, do for Heaven's sake tell anybody you're thinking of getting married to! Many a bride has had a nasty shock when she found that she was expected to wear a rubber apron on her wedding night. And one lady member of the English aristocracy – who had only ever had sex with her plastic-fetishist husband and assumed that his antics were quite normal – briefed *all* her five daughters on sex with the simple words: 'Men expect you to wear plastic mackintoshes in bed, gels . . .'

Videotaping your sex life

With the sudden boom in video equipment (including cameras), a lot of couples have discovered that they can tape themselves making love – and then watch the 'action replay'! Frankly, I have a feeling that in a few years' time this will be considered quite normal, run-of-the-mill behaviour. But for the time being, if you do it then you should obviously remember to keep the tape somewhere safe. It would, to say the least, be embarrassing if the kids got it mixed up with their Space Invaders game. . . .

Blue moves and videos

Again, many people – some of them, I may say, purporting to be paragons of sexual virtue – have got involved in blue movies in recent years. The explosion of interest in video has greatly increased this trend, and a very senior figure in the British videotape industry recently told me rather sadly that one of the main reasons why families are buying video players is that so many Dads want to look at rude programmes.

Still, if you and your missus want to look at a slightly naughty movie or videogram, I can't see that it's going to do you any harm. Indeed, it may well do you some *good* – for many sex problem clinics in the USA (and a few which operate more discreetly in Britain, Europe, Australia and elsewhere) actually use rude movies or videos in the treatment of men and women who are lacking in libido, in order to pep up their desire.

The only thing that worries me about all this is that there are blue movies and blue movies – if you see what I mean. And with the explosion in the videotape industry, it'll be impossible for the police – or anybody else – to control the really nasty and vicious ones.

Personally, I've only ever seen two more-or-less blue movies under perfectly legal circumstances and in the cause of research (what a wonderful excuse!). One was really rather nice and – as far as I recall – showed a young couple making love in a way that would be a pleasant 'turn-on' for most couples.

The other was absolutely *awful* and, in effect, glorified gang-bang rape – perpetuating the really pernicious myth that that was what most women really wanted.

So, if you want to turn your loved one and yourself on with a slightly rude movie or video in the bedroom, then fair enough. But I suggest you stay clear of some of the nastier products being churned out by the film and video industry.

Wife-swapping and 'swinging'

Two more activities which have increased greatly in recent years are wife-swapping and 'swinging' (which really just means a more promiscuous form of wife-swapping – with contacts being made through magazines, newspapers or parties).

Now that virtually 100 per cent effective contraception is here (see Chapter 22), I suppose it's inevitable that more and more people will go in for wife-swapping. (Incidentally, why doesn't anyone ever call it 'husband-swapping'?)

Superficially, the idea is very attractive – particularly to men. After all, there's a lot of truth in the old verse:

> Higamus, hogamus:
> Woman monogamous.
> Hogamus, higamus:
> Man is polygamous.

And in fact, it's usually the man who takes the lead in wife-swapping – trying to persuade his spouse to join in and have sex with somebody else. Rather surprisingly, she sometimes becomes the more enthusiastic participant after a while.

It's certainly true that wife-swapping can pep up a couple's sex drive. But it has really colossal dangers – which are:

★If you're not using adequate contraception, the wife may get pregnant by somebody else's husband.
★If one of you has an 'outside' relationship, this may introduce VD into the foursome.
★With rather alarming regularity, people who go in for wife-swapping tend to fall in love with the new partner. . . .

In addition to all this, there's the great danger of jealousy. Yes –
jealousy. It's incredible how strong sexual jealousy is in many
people's hearts – even when they've cheerfully said to their
husbands/wives: 'Yes, go ahead and have sex with so-and-so.'

If you don't read the more sensational newspapers, you probably don't know just how often jealousy rears its head in such
situations. But I assure you: it's not uncommon for (say) a man
who's encouraged his wife into 'swapping' suddenly to turn
jealous – and to plant a knife between his new rival's ribs.

I'd agree that there are some pairs of sophisticated couples who
greatly like each other's company, and who can cope with a spot of
discreet 'swapping' on holidays or at other times when it'll cause
no scandal. But as long as sexual jealousy still exists in the world,
most couples who go in for wife-swapping are entering into an
emotional minefield.

Note: a lot of people take up wife-swapping through clubs which
advertise in magazines, newspapers and elsewhere. This is really
crazy: not only do you have no idea who might turn up on your
front doorstep, but you may attract the attention of the more
scandalous newspapers – or the police.

Group sex

As with wife-swapping, the idea of group sex is highly attractive to
many people – especially men! But, leaving moral issues aside, it
has some terrible drawbacks. For example, my doctor colleagues
most often hear about group sex activities when the ninety-three
participants at the local orgy all make their way to the VD Clinic.

There are also all the problems which I've mentioned in connec-
tion with wife-swapping. In addition, there's the fact that while
sexual activity between two friendly couples can be kept discreet,
an orgy can't.

So, taking part in group sex can leave you open to blackmail.
And (as one or two doctors have discovered recently, I'm afraid)
anyone who has a respectable position to keep up on the community may find that indulging in group sex leads to himself/herself
being spread across the front page of the newspapers.

The other thing I can say about orgies (never having been to one
myself) is that a slightly tipsy doctor's wife once revealed to me
across a dinner table: 'Unfortunately, you're more or less obliged
to be ——ed by some *very* decrepit-looking people . . .'

Sado-masochism

It's very hard for most of us to understand either sadism or masochism. But it is true that, as Dr David Stafford-Clark, Consultant Psychiatrist at Guy's Hospital, London, remarked many years ago, 'The giving and taking of *small* amounts of pain during sex is normal.'

I've italicised that word 'small'. For while it's normal to enjoy love-bites, bottom-pinching, gentle slaps and so on, things are beginning to get out of hand when a man (it's usually the man) NEEDS to give or experience pain.

Frankly, I'd advise a woman who finds herself with such a man to get out *fast*, unless he's willing to seek psychiatric help. And any lady who encounters one of that appalling band of men who actually like inflicting severe physical pain on women should not only depart, but give his name to the police as well. That way, you just might save somebody's life.

Drugs and sex

Far too many people try to use drugs to 'improve' their sex lives these days. This is usually futile, stupid and dangerous. In the chapters on sex problems, I'll be dealing with the possible ill-effects of drugs which your doctor may *prescribe* for you. But here's a brief run-down of the drugs which so many men and women take of their own accord:

NICOTINE (IN TOBACCO)   Gives you lung cancer and greatly increases your chances of heart attacks and other diseases. It calms you down slightly: otherwise, no known effect on sex life – unless the bad breath which it causes turns your loved one off!

ALCOHOL   *Small* amounts tend to have a tranquillising effect – so the odd dry Martini (or whatever) certainly helps you relax. In these small amounts, grog can therefore be good for nervous gentleman who have a tendency to 'come' too soon – and nervous ladies who have vaginismus (see the chapters on sex problems).

However, *larger* amounts of booze – particularly on a regular basis – tend to have a disastrous effect on people's sex lives. Sadly, a vast number of men lose their sexual desire and/or become impotent because of their regular intake of alcohol: hence the deadly accurate phrase 'brewer's droop'.

In fact, old Shakespeare (who probably knew a thing or two about brewer's droop) summed it all up in *Macbeth* when he said of alcohol:

'Lechery, Sir, it provokes and unprovokes:
It provokes the desire, but it takes away the performance.'

CANNABIS (MARIJUANA, POT, DOPE, HASHISH)   It's a bit difficult to be specific about the effect of cannabis on sex (or, indeed, the effect of it on *anything*). Firstly because there are so many wildly different types of cannabis – something few people seem to realise. Secondly, the amount of medical research which has been done on this drug is amazingly small. Indeed, it's not long ago since doctors were asserting that it was (a) addictive, and (b) caused people to commit murder – statements which most young adults knew by experience to be nonsense.

Moderate amounts of *mild* cannabis preparations seem to have a modest tranquillising effect, and so might help sexual 'nerves'. Larger amounts probably depress sexual function. Heavy users may have a lowered sperm count.

Warning: In most countries, the penalties for cannabis use are still quite severe.

BARBITURATES   Vast numbers of young people experiment with barbiturates, because of the fact that these sleeping pills produce a drowsy, dreamy feeling – in which (obviously) one can feel very relaxed about sex.

But 'barbs' are very, very dangerous. Their long-term effect is to put a damper on your sex life. More importantly, they can – and often do – kill people.

HEROIN AND MORPHINE   Frankly, anybody who uses heroin or morphine (morphia) for sexual or any other purposes is out of his/her head. The 'drug culture' has popularised the use of heroin as a fast way of producing a pleasant state of euphoria in which, of course, it would be agreeable to enjoy any pleasure – including sex.

But heroin and morphine soon ABOLISH your sex drive altogether. Both are highly addictive – especially heroin. To *inject* heroin for sexual stimulation (or any other reason) is absolutely crazy. If you get hooked – as you probably will – there's every chance that you'll wind up *dead*.

LSD   Back in the 1960s, the gurus of the drug culture were busy claiming that LSD was great stuff for making sex more magical. Some of those gurus wound up in mental hospitals, while others killed themselves.

I have encountered one patient who claimed that her difficulty in reaching orgasm was helped by LSD – which, she said, let her have 'hundreds' of orgasms, one after another. But the enormous dangers of LSD are such that it is lunacy to use it to try to pep up your sex life. Men and women really *do* sometimes jump out of windows when they've taken LSD. And many people go completely mad on a 'bad trip' and have to be admitted to psychiatric hospitals. Also, the woman who claimed that LSD helped her to reach orgasm subsequently found that she couldn't reach it without the drug.

COCAINE   In the last few years, a second wave of cocaine use has spread from California, across the USA and thence to most other Western countries. I use the expression 'second wave' because the first wave of popularity was back in Sherlock Holmes' time (*circa* 1910) – it died out when people realised the danger of the drug.

Snorting 'coke' has become very fashionable among the affluent – you *have* to be pretty affluent to be able to afford it – and some of them use it to try to heighten sexual pleasure.

Frankly, I think this is crazy. Sidney Cohen, MD – who is Clinical Professor of Psychiatry at UCLA, and one of the world's greatest experts on cocaine – says that cocaine can cause death, paranoia, cocaine psychosis, and severe depression. He says that the drug stimulates the 'reward centres' in the brain to such an extent that 'Some people . . . will do anything for cocaine'.

He adds that monkeys who are given it become so hooked that they will give themselves electric shocks in order to get it. Addicted monkeys will work for it in preference to food, even though they are starving. And – you've guessed it – *they lose all interest in sex*. 'Nuff said.

AMYL NITRITE ('SNAPPERS' OR 'POPPERS')   This is another drug which is widely used in the US to try to enhance sexual pleasure – and whose use has spread elsewhere. (As this book went to press, I was horrified to learn that a related drug – butyl nitrite – is on open sale in British sex shops.)

It's inhaled from a little capsule which is 'snapped' under the nose just before a climax. The idea is that the drug will instantly do rather strange things to the blood vessels so that you feel a bizarre 'flush' during orgasm. *Note that the drug also affects the blood vessels of the heart*.

All I have to say about this kind of idiocy is that Peter Sellers sniffed amyl nitrite in an attempt to 'enhance' a climax with Britt Ekland – and promptly had a massive heart attack. Why anybody would need to 'enhance' a climax with Britt Ekland, I wouldn't know. You have been warned.

Also, as this book was being completed, US doctors published new research which suggested that the now-widespread use of amyl (and butyl) nitrite in the USA by gays was responsible for a new and serious illness in which the body's resistance to infection is severely impaired. A number of people are reported to have died from this condition, but I must stress that it may be due to a virus and *not* the drug.

In short, most drugs except possibly *small* amounts of alcohol (and perhaps small amounts of cannabis, if you can avoid clashing with the law) are BAD for you sexually. Not only that, they tend to be disastrous for your health. Steer clear of them.

Pornography

Now for pornography. Should you use it in your sex life? The trouble is that no-one (least of all the law-makers) agrees on what constitutes pornography! The name actually comes from two Greek words which together mean 'writing about harlots'. Clearly, that's *not* what most people mean by pornography today.

Lots of couples use such things as nude magazines and Japanese 'pillow books' in their love-making. Indeed, many sex clinics in the US (and a moderate number – more discreetly – in the UK and elsewhere) actually dish out nude magazines to their patients in order to help their sex drive. Curiously enough, this often works – even in women, who are traditionally said not to be interested in sexy pictures!

Personally, I can see nothing wrong in nude pictures of men and women. I'm sorry if you disagree – but I feel that the human body is one of the most beautiful things in Creation: to categorise it as 'obscene' is quite absurd.

On the other hand, there's no doubt that a good many of the books and magazines which are so widely on sale in almost every large city these days have a very vicious streak in them. Some glorify sadism or masochism or child abuse – and I suspect that they may even encourage people to go in for this sort of thing.

Furthermore, a great deal of the *written* pornography which is bought by many young men (*and* lots of older ones) contains the most extraordinary and misleading rubbish about sexuality – especially female sexuality. As a rule, it seems to be churned out by men whose ideas about women and their emotional needs belong to the Stone Age. Personally, I think any woman, whether a committed feminist or not, ought to picket the offices of the idiots who write this stuff!

So, if you and partner want to look at sexy pictures in bed, then that's fine. But be selective in what you buy – and steer clear of the misleading and dangerous rubbish which is peddled by the vice kings.

Rectal intercourse

Elsewhere in this book, I've gone on at some length about the hygiene risks which are involved in the common practice of anal love play. You run the same risks if you go in for actual rectal intercourse.

In other words, the rectum isn't a very clean place: it invariably contains germs, and these can cause BIG trouble – especially if they're transferred to the woman's vagina.

But the fact must be faced that people *do* go in for rectal intercourse, particularly when the woman has a period and doesn't particularly want to have vaginal sex. Some years ago, a British Medical Association booklet estimated that *one in five married couples had tried anal intercourse*. Rather alarmingly, the 1983 *Playboy* Sex Survey of over 100,000 US men and women showed that 47 per cent of males and 61 per cent of females had tried anal intercourse. So it's common in both the US and the UK.

This is quite surprising, in view of the fact that British law expressly forbids it – even between husband and wife. (It permits it between male gays.) Similar laws exist in most countries, following the tradition set by the Emperor Justinian – who banned rectal sex because it was a well-known cause of earthquakes.

Anyway, if you want to go in for this form of intercourse, *be careful*. Naturally, it's important for hygiene reasons that the lady should have an empty rectum. After withdrawal, the man must wash his penis, and on no account should he put it anywhere near the vagina until it *has* been washed.

To avoid causing the woman discomfort or pain (and to prevent little cracks or cuts) it's essential to use a lubricant, and to take things *very* gently.

'J' said in her bestseller *The Sensuous Woman* that this kind of intercourse can open up for a woman 'a whole new area of sensations to increase your personal sexual satisfaction'. True. But it can also make her very sore (and *very* windy). And it can upset some women quite a bit. In short, a lady should only do it if *she* wants to – and if she understands the risks involved.

CHAPTER SIXTEEN

Sex Aids – And Where To Get Them

Warning ● *Are there any* sensible *sex aids at all?* ● *Vibrators* ●
Clitoris stimulators ● *Creams and other potions* ● *Beware of tablets*
● *Geisha balls* ● *Artificial penises or dildoes* ● *Penis rings* ● *Other*
exotica ● *Those peculiar dolls.*

Warning

I said towards the end of the last chapter that a lot of erotic reading
material was rubbishy, dangerous, and produced by fairly sleazy
people. *You can say the same again about most sex aids.* In many
large cities, the sex shops are part of a multi-million dollar
industry which is in the hands of some very, very dubious people.
True, there are some sex shop proprietors who are honest and
who seem to see themselves as providing a sort of service to the
community – but mostly it's a tough commercial business!

So, let the buyer beware! Much of the stuff which is sold in sex
shops is useless and ludicrously over-priced junk. Most people
who have difficulties with sex don't need extortionately-priced sex
aids: they need someone to talk to (and preferably a bit of
information about where they're going wrong).

To be fair, there are a very few sex aids which are of some help
to people. And, of course, I accept the fact that many people go
into sex shops just to buy something *as a joke* – perhaps a 'Willy
Warmer' for the husband's birthday, a blow-up doll for the boss's
Christmas present, or a pair of crotchless knickers for a wife with a
sense of humour.

But don't let yourself be ripped off. If you go into a sex shop,
beware of seductive salesladies – or salesmen – who come up
alongside you and hint that '*This* is just the thing you require.'
(Nudge, nudge; wink, wink!)

If you don't want actually to *go* into a sex shop (though the
places are so crowded these days that you needn't feel embarrassed about it), then most of the larger chains of shops will gladly
send you a catalogue with mail order prices. But have a care, if
you're easily shocked! These full-colour catalogues tend to leave
nothing whatever to the imagination – and to deal with subjects
that may not be your cup of tea at all.

If you're a lady who only wants to buy a vibrator so she can get an orgasm, you may find it a bit shattering to be offered gay movie extravaganzas and artificial vaginas. . . .

Are there any *sensible* sex aids at all?

Yes – a few. When I saw the first sex aids on open display in shops about fifteen years ago, I found it almost impossible to believe that anybody could get any pleasure out of them – or that anybody's sexual difficulties could be improved by them.

Well, clearly some people *do* get pleasure out of sex aids: otherwise the industry wouldn't be booming. More importantly, over the years I've been very surprised to find that a small number of sex aids are genuinely helpful to certain people who have problems – particularly women who can't reach a climax. By far the most useful of these aids is the vibrator.

Vibrators

You may – like me – find vibrators almost totally uninteresting. But millions upon millions of them have been sold round the world since about 1970, when they first became popular. And, as I've indicated above, doctors do really encounter women who can be helped to reach orgasm with the aid of a vibrator.

First of all, what is a vibrator? It is an electrical device which jigs about at high speed – in order to produce a pleasant and stimulating sensation in whatever area it is placed on. (They're good for rheumatism, too.) It's important, of course, to ensure that 'vibes' which run off the mains, rather than a battery, are properly earthed. Otherwise, you may blow your fuses permanently.

When vibrators first appeared in the shops some years ago a lot of people were offended by them and thought them obscene. This is why they still tend to be advertised (in the most respectable journals) as being for general massage ('the revitalisation of those tired tissues' as one advertisement felicitously puts it).

There is nothing medically wrong with these devices, provided that a couple don't expect that a vibrator will be an instant and magic remedy for any sexual difficulties they may have. If a couple buys one just to add to their bedroom fun, that's fine.

The most commonly used type of vibrator, shown in Figure 40, is made of plastic and was quite obviously designed by a man. It is, as you can see, penis-shaped, hard, cold and unyielding. It also makes a devil of a racket, so that anyone who lives in a house or apartment with thin walls would be well advised to use it only when the neighbours are out.

179

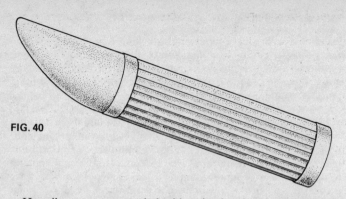

FIG. 40

Happily, more romantic-looking (and quieter) vibrators are slowly coming onto the market. They can be placed in the vagina, on the penis, or (most commonly) over the area of the clitoris, where of course they have the greatest effect. Some types can be strapped to the back of the husband's hand; if he then places the tips of his fingers on the wife's clitoris the transmitted vibration will give her quite an agreeable and unusual sensation.

I wouldn't for a moment claim that 'a touch of the vibes' is just the thing for *every* woman who has difficulty in having an orgasm. (Lots of ladies find the very sight of these devices a bit revolting.) But some feminist groups are very successfully using vibrators to help their 'patients' to achieve orgasm. And you can't get away from the fact that people do walk in and tell their doctors: 'I've managed it at last – with a vibrator.' OK, it's not the real thing – but for some women it works. And it's most likely to work in the following circumstances:

★ Where the woman has no current sexual partner
★ Where her partner is unwilling to use (or doesn't know how to use) basic love play techniques
★ Where he's handicapped – quite commonly by arthritis of the fingers – and so cannot really help her to reach that climax.

Incidentally, if you do get a vibrator be careful where you keep it – even today, such things can cause embarrassment! Recently an airline pilot told me that there had been a full-scale emergency drill on his aircraft when a strange buzzing sound was heard from a bag. After the airport bomb disposal squad had been called, it turned out (of course) that the cause of the trouble was a vibrator belonging to the blonde in seat 34C. . . .

180

Clitoral stimulators

These devices are just rubber rings which fit round the base of the penis. As you can see from the picture of a typical model (Figure 41) there's always a projection of some sort on the top surface, and this is supposed to rub against the wife's clitoris during intercourse and so excite her.

If you want to buy one of the stimulators for fun, go right ahead. But bear in mind that quite a lot of women do find them uncomfortable (if not actually painful) – so don't be disappointed if your purchase fails to do all that the saleslady claimed for it. (I bet *she* doesn't use one.)

FIG. 41

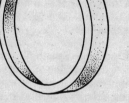

Creams and other potions

Sex shops sell various sorts of creams, ointments and drops which you're supposed to apply to yourself or your partner in order to produce sexy results. These potions are usually pretty expensive, and in most cases it's very doubtful if they're of much use.

★ Creams or oils for general massage of your partner's skin could be helpful in some cases. But you might just as well buy baby oil far more cheaply at a pharmacy.
★ Potions which are supposed to promote erection are unlikely to be much use. They tend to contain a mild 'skin-warming' ingredient of the kind which athletes rub into strained knees – and it's just possible that this sensation of warmth might help erection a bit.
★ Creams or jellies which are supposed to delay the male climax contain a local anaesthetic – and they might possibly be a bit of help to a bloke with very mild premature ejaculation. Anything *less* mild, however, needs proper treatment (see the chapters on sex problems).

Beware of tablets

Sex shops are very big on tablets – tablets which are supposed to increase a man's virility, or tablets which are supposed to turn a woman on. Most of those which have been analysed by doctors have turned out – so far as I'm aware – to contain nothing but grossly overpriced rubbish. Don't waste your money on them!

In fact, there is – sadly enough – no tablet as yet which will have either of the above desirable effects. So the sex shops usually just sell pills which contain a few vitamins and minerals.

If there were any more powerful ingredients in such tablets, they'd probably be dangerous. And if anybody ever tries to sell you pills which allegedly contain 'Spanish fly', steer clear of them. Spanish fly (cantharides) is *not* an aphrodisiac, despite its fame: it just produces an irritation of the female urinary passage. Unfortunately, this irritation can be so severe as to be *fatal*. And from time to time it happens that some stupid man slips a bit of Spanish fly into a woman's food or drink – and kills her.

Geisha balls (or 'duo-balls')

Geisha balls are so bizarre as to be quite amusing. They're little pairs of balls (each about the size of a large marble) which are designed to have a tendency to roll about. The idea is that women who want to experience more sexual stimulation during the ordinary course of the day can put these geisha balls into their vaginas. As they walk around, the balls move about and stimulate them. . . . Amazing!

I'm told by an American woman sex counsellor that quite a few US women wander around all day with these things inside them. The only problem is that they tend to make a loud 'clonking' noise – and if this happens at the office, you can hardly say to your colleagues: 'I'm sorry – it's just my balls banging together.' There is also a slight danger of your geisha balls getting stuck. Need I say more. . . .

Artificial penises or dildoes

Again, it may come as something of a surprise to you but there is a very big market in dildoes (which are penis-shaped objects) and actual artificial penises – which are carefully shaped and coloured to look exactly like the real thing.

Dildoes are nothing new: they've been used in the East for hundreds of years – and back in 1670 His Majesty's Customs were recorded as seizing a batch of several hundred which some optimist was trying to import into Britain.

It's a little difficult to say who's using all this vast number of artificial phalluses. But some are clearly employed by impotent men who can't otherwise satisfy their wives – which is fair enough.

Penis rings

Various rings which go round the base of the penis are claimed to help men who have problems with erection. (Some varieties go round the testicles as well.)

It's difficult to get any scientific evidence that these things really do help impotence – though they're probably worth a try, in the hope that their effect in preventing blood from flowing out of the male organ may enhance its erection.

Two well-known varieties are 'Dr Richards' ring' – a slim rubber loop which the man draws tight round the base of his male member – and 'The Blakoe Energising Ring' – a device which is said to produce an additional benefit in the shape of a small electric current generated by its little metal plates.

Other exotica

There are so many crazy and useless things in sex shops that there's no point in my discussing all of them.

However, I should make a brief mention of:

Condoms with rabbits' ears and other projections: these are supposed to give additional stimulation to the inside of the vagina. Maybe . . . but don't rely on them for contraception, as they may not be made to very high standards.

Goat's eye rings: these too are worn by the man on his penis and are supposed to give extra stimulation to the inside of the vagina. They are rings with what look like long eyelashes sticking out all round. (Whether they're really made from poor old goats I don't know, but I hope not. I don't think that the British Goat Society would like it.)

Bottom beads: these are strings of beads which you are supposed to insert into your partner's rear end – and then pull out suddenly at the moment of climax. Ye gods! Not to be recommended if he/she has piles. . . .

Rectal vibrators: the function of these is fairly obvious, but I wouldn't recommend them. Alas, objects pushed into the bottom have a nasty habit of *being carried upwards inside and getting lost.* This usually means a surgical operation to retrieve them. (You'd be surprised at what surgeons have to remove from people's abdomens. Would you believe *egg-cups*?)

Those peculiar dolls . . .

Finally, those strange inflatable ladies. Incredibly, these also sell in vast numbers and, though some are just bought as a joke, others are clearly purchased to be used.

My personal knowledge of this subject derives from the fact that a couple of years ago I was rung up by the Consumer Affairs Officer of the London Borough of Barnet (no less). He told me that a 'consumer' in Barnet had actually come into the municipal offices and made a complaint about the lack of satisfaction he'd achieved with a blow-up lady which he'd bought. (The Consumer Affairs Officer quoted him as saying plaintively: 'On the label it said I'd never be lonely again – but I still am.')

What Barnet Borough Council wanted me to do was to provide a medical report on this extraordinary lady. I found that she was constructed of hard, unyielding plastic (which could scarcely have given any consumer much warmth or tenderness). Also, her major problem was that she had a hole under her left armpit! This made her deflate so fast that I reckoned that it was doubtful if any but the most premature of prematurely-ejaculating consumers could have achieved 'satisfaction' with her. I'm glad to say that on the basis of my report, the consumer got his thirty-five pounds back.

Serious note: Although I've been sending up these dolls, it has been recently pointed out to me by the Chairwoman of the British National Association of Family Planning Doctors that apparently they do fulfil a useful function for the many poor, handicapped souls who have very strong sexual urges – but who have no real hope of ever gratifying them with a real woman. So there you are.

CHAPTER SEVENTEEN

Major Sex Difficulties And Why They Occur

*What are the major problems? ● Are they physical or emotional? ●
What physical disorders are there? ● The causes of emotional
problems ● There are few magic remedies, but there IS hope.*

What are the major sex problems?

As I said at the start of this book, the major sexual difficulties are
very, very common, and threaten countless marriages, which is no
joke when you look at the appalling divorce figures in every
Western country, from New Zealand to Scandinavia. Clinics
which offer help for this major problem are flooded with couples
who desperately need help. And perhaps the one bright spot in a
bleak situation is that these days help *is* available for the disorders
that cripple so many people's love-lives.

What are these 'major disorders'? Here's the list:

IN MEN

★Impotence (difficulty in achieving an erection – or just total
inability to do it at all).
★Premature ejaculation (in other words, 'hair trigger trouble' –
or coming far too soon).
★Ejaculatory incompetence (an awful mouthful of a name
which just means 'not being able to come at all').
★General loss of sexual desire – which (not surprisingly) is
often associated with impotence.

IN WOMEN

★Vaginismus (the incredibly common condition in which a
tightening up of the vaginal muscles – plus a lack of vaginal
lubrication – makes intercourse intensely painful or downright impossible).
★Inability to reach orgasm.
★General lack of sexual desire – indeed, in many cases complete absence of it.

Incidentally, these last two common female problems often go together – since clearly a woman who has lost her desire for sex is not very likely to be able to have an orgasm (though that's not always true . . .).

It used to be a widespread medical practice to refer to these two problems together as 'female frigidity' – but I think it's high time that *that* ridiculous expression was dropped. There's nothing 'frigid' about many of the women who can't reach a climax or who've suddenly and inexplicably lost interest in making love with their husbands. Indeed, they're often very warm and loving people who desperately want to be able to enjoy a rich and satisfying physical relationship with the man they love. Happily, there are now ways of helping them.

Are these disorders physical or emotional?

Nearly always emotional. That comes as a big surprise to many men and women, partly because most people like to have a good solid physical cause for anything they're suffering from. It's a natural human trait to believe that whatever problem you've got really ought to be due to some slight structural abnormality (which could perhaps be corrected by an operation) or to a 'hormone imbalance' (which could be cured by taking the right pills). *Unfortunately, this is rarely so.* In most cases of sexual difficulty, the basic problem lies in the person's emotions – not in his or her body.

But let me make two important points:

1. The fact that a sex problem is 'emotional', doesn't mean that it's the person's fault. Nor does it mean that he or she actually wants to have the problem – indeed, in most cases he or she would be happy beyond belief to get rid of it!

I get rather fed up with husbands or wives who become angry and bitter when they're told that their partners' sex problems are emotional. 'There you are,' they cry triumphantly. 'It's all in the mind.' So it is – but it's certainly nothing that the poor sufferer should be blamed for.

2. The other important point to grasp is this – and it's something many people find rather hard to understand. What we call 'emotional' disorders – arising in the brain – are in fact intimately connected with changes in brain chemistry. Very little is as yet known about the chemical changes which constantly take place in our brains. But it's slowly becoming clear that all our human moods (excitement, depression, fear, hunger, joy, lust or anything you like) are deeply dependent on those brain chemical changes.

Doctors are now realising that the line between 'physical' and 'psychological' disease is *not* sharp – as most non-medically trained people imagine – but very blurred indeed. For instance, let's say that a man has an immensely frightening experience, perhaps in wartime – and that he becomes impotent as a result. We'd call that an 'emotional' illness – but *it's actually due to the changes in brain biochemistry which the original terrifying experience has produced.*

Similarly, a woman who has been raped as a teenager – and who thereafter finds sex intensely frightening and painful – is said to have 'an emotional problem'. But once again, what has happened is that the shock of the dreadful experience she has been through has produced certain biochemical changes in her brain which have *made* her tense and nervous about sex.

So the boundaries between 'physical' and 'emotional' disorders are not as clear cut as we once thought. And what that means is that no-one who has a sexual problem should feel ashamed or embarrassed because of the fact that it's 'only' emotional.

What physical disorders are there?

Having said all that, I must admit that it's still useful to be able to separate off the sexual disorders which are generally regarded as 'physical' – in other words, the ones in which there is little or no 'emotional' cause for the symptoms.

In fact there aren't many purely physical disorders, as I said at the start of this chapter. Indeed, we can sum them up in a few pages:

SEX PROBLEMS DUE TO MEDICATION   Regrettably, quite a few of the pills and medicines which your doctor may prescribe for you can screw up your sex life. (This isn't your doctor's fault, incidentally – all drugs can have side-effects.)

The main agents which can interfere with your sexual desire are:

★Sedatives and sleeping pills
★Tranquillisers – though these can have a *good* effect on sex if you're very nervous
★Blood pressure drugs
★Diuretics (or 'water pills')
★The contraceptive Pill; though it's fairly uncommon for it to reduce a woman's sexual drive, this can happen.

187

But, in general, if you're on *any* tablets and you lose interest in sex or have trouble with reaching an erection or with having a climax – *then ask your doctor if the pills could be causing this effect*.

Drug side-effects of this sort are now very common (particularly with pills for high blood pressure). Such side-effects have mostly been described in men. But since the early 1980s, I have felt more and more certain that a lot of female tablet-takers – specially those women taking blood pressure pills – are getting symptoms such as loss of desire because of the treatment.

In fact, this is exactly what you'd expect since many of these drugs are intended to work through affecting the two great 'unconscious' (autonomic) nervous systems of the body – the sympathetic and the parasympathetic. As you may recall from Chapter 4, these two systems also control sexual functions like erection and climax. So, the message is clear: if you're having trouble with sex and you're on pills (especially blood pressure pills), then discuss the possibility of a change of tablet with your doctor.

SEX PROBLEMS DUE TO ALCOHOL OR OTHER DRUGS   I've already said in Chapter 15 that most of the drugs which are taken for kicks can really mess up your sex life. If you stop using them in time, your sex life will probably get better.

By far the biggest offender world wide is *alcohol*. Countless men have become impotent (or just lost their sexual desire) because of over-indulgence in booze. So, have a care, all you men who're keen on the beer or whisky. Alcohol depresses your output of male sex hormone and may abolish your sexual desire almost completely.

SEX PROBLEMS DUE TO GLANDULAR DISEASE   These are really much rarer than most people think. As I've said, lots of men and women who have difficulties with sex think that it's all because of a hormone problem. But that's not often so. Indeed, a simple examination of your genitals and body-hair distribution by your doctor will usually more or less rule out any hormone deficiency.

However, it is true that some recent research in the USA has suggested that male hormone deficiency is a commoner cause of impotence than was once thought. A group of researchers has found that a surprising number of impotent men have a low level of the male hormone testosterone. But it's possible that the low level is actually *due* to the sexual inactivity – and not the cause of it.

In cases of doubt, your doctor would probably suggest going to an endocrinologist (gland specialist) or having a hormone profile done at the nearest large hospital lab. But such hormone tests are expensive, so of course they shouldn't be undertaken lightly.

SEX PROBLEMS DUE TO OBESITY   It may surprise you to learn that US sex researchers Masters and Johnson found that in many men who are impotent, a major factor is *being overweight*. It's not yet clear why this should be so. Possibly the presence of excess fat has some unknown effect on the hormones, or perhaps it's just that the knowledge that he's fat makes a man lose confidence in himself as a virile male.

Either way, the encouraging thing is this. If the man loses weight and gets rid of his paunch, his impotence will often get better. My impression is that slimming can often have the same desirable effect on women.

SEX PROBLEMS DUE TO GYNAECOLOGICAL DISORDERS   Since so many physical disorders of the sex organs are painful, it's not surprising that they can screw up your sex life. Of major importance in this area are the common infections like thrush (also known as candida or monilia) and trichomonas ('TV'). These are described in Chapter 22, which is called 'Keeping Sex Safe'.

The point to grasp about them in relation to sex problems is this. They make the female sex organs sore and tender, and this not only makes love-making painful at the time, but may also trigger off a sort of 'fear cycle'. This leads to long-term muscle tension in the vagina – in other words to the common sex problem of 'vaginismus' – referred to earlier in this chapter – in which any approach to the vagina makes the woman tighten up. Vaginismus is dealt with more fully in Chapter 18.

Similarly, other painful physical disorders of the sex organs can set up a fear cycle – and thus a long-term sex problem associated with tension.

For instance:
★A newly-delivered mother who has a great deal of pain because of a tear (or an episiotomy cut) may develop a fear cycle – and hence long-term vaginismus.
★A man who has had a painfully tight or infected foreskin can develop a similar fear cycle – and the resultant tension may make him impotent or cause him to ejaculate prematurely.

Fortunately, the outlook is pretty good in such cases – once the counsellor or doctor has explained to the patient just *why* his/her tension symptoms developed in the first place.

The causes of emotional problems

So the majority of serious sex problems are emotional ones. But what causes them? We've already said that some emotional problems are due to fearsome experiences (like rape). Others are related to depression, tension, stress, tiredness and overwork.

But the sad fact is that most often the basic origin of the emotional difficulty lies in 'faulty programming' early in life. A person's childhood and early teenage years are of immense importance to his or her later sexual success – or failure! If a child has been given the impression that sex is 'dirty', or 'frightening' or 'painful' or 'violent', then there's every chance that she or he is going to have sexual problems after growing up. And unfortunately, lots of folk *are* still brought up to think that sex is something 'disgusting'. More than eighty years after the end of the Victorian era, its hangovers (and hang-ups) remain with us. Countless men and women reach adulthood with their sexuality maimed by their parents' attitudes. (Yet it's *not* the poor old parents' fault – for they only got that way because *their* Mums and Dads brought them up with restrictive attitudes too!)

It is not necessary for a parent actually to tell you that sex is 'dirty'. In practice, it would often be quite sufficient to cause problems *if your mother or father never told you anything at all about sex*. In many families, this deliberate (and often tension-charged) avoidance of the subject often gives the unfortunate boy or girl the feeling that sex is 'unmentionable'.

I'd say that even in this so-called 'permissive' age, at least one in four Western families fall into this category. The kids are told nothing about sex, and pick up what little they can from wildly-misinformed and very lavatorial playground gossip – plus perhaps some *very* sketchy sex advice provided by the school. (Alas, as Kinsey showed, sometimes that sex advice is given by teachers whose own hang-ups are so great that they just make things worse for the children.)

As a result, vast numbers of people in the West grow up with only the vaguest ideas about sex – except that it's something pretty 'filthy' and 'nasty'. (How could anybody *reasonably* apply such words to this beautiful activity?) If you grow up thinking sex is filthy, of course you're going to be loaded with guilt about it, and you're therefore highly likely to be hit by conditions like impotence (if you're a man) or vaginismus (if you're a woman).

Not everyone with a major sex problem has had the kind of restrictive, puritanical background I've described. But many patients *have* – and it's not until all children are given reasonably well-informed advice about sex and its beauties – and its dangers, of course – that the terrifyingly high incidence of sex problems will diminish.

(Incidentally, it's not until all kids understand about sex and its dangers that we'll reduce today's appalling total of unwanted pregnancies, abortions and VD. But that's another story.)

There are few magic remedies – but there IS hope

From what I've said above, you'll appreciate that in the minority of sex problems in which the cause is physical, then there is a good chance of an almost instant cure. A classic case was that of Nancy and George – who'd both had intense pain on intercourse ever since she'd had a baby. Examination revealed that the medical student who had stitched up her torn vagina had left behind a non-absorbable stitch – which was stretched across her 'tunnel of love' like a taut piano-wire. One snip of the scissors removed the thread and solved *that* problem.

But for most people, there is no magic or instant remedy. It's perfectly natural for people to want a magic pill or a wonderful operation that will put everything right; but life just isn't like that, and usually a good deal of hard work, on the part of both the couple and the therapist, is needed before things can be got straight.

Occasionally one comes across patients who say that their sexual troubles have been instantly corrected by some aphrodisiac (love potion) or sex aid bought in a shop. That's fine for them, but I think the rest of us should realise that this is a 'placebo effect' – in other words, they got better because they *believed* that whatever it was that they spent their money on would cure them.

For most people, however, eliminating any kind of serious sexual problem is likely to be a slow business, even in the care of a skilled counsellor or doctor. Probably the most effective therapy for sexual difficulties is that carried out at the American Reproductive Biology Research Foundation in St Louis under the direction of Masters and Johnson. This involves a period of residential treatment for both husband and wife under the care of two highly skilled psychotherapists, who go very fully into the emotional background of both partners and try to 're-train' them sexually.

Naturally, this kind of intensive therapy is expensive (particularly for those who have to pay their air fares to the USA) and for this reason it is never going to be universally available to everyone with a marriage problem. But happily, the St Louis team's researchers have so revolutionised the treatment of sexual difficulties that many doctors and counsellors all over the world are finding that they can get quite good results with modifications of Masters and Johnson's methods, and without the need for the husband and wife to have 'in-patient' treatment.

These results are *not* obtained overnight, however; they're only likely to be achieved where the husband and wife are willing to co-operate with the therapist (and with each other) over a period of many weeks or months in unravelling the tensions that have caused their difficulties.

There are numerous other effective methods of treatment – all of which I'll be detailing in Chapter 20. Some of them are immensely successful, particularly the behaviourist psychological techniques and (in Britain and the Commonwealth) the 'Seminar' method based on the work of the late Dr Michael Balint.

So, whatever your sexual hang-up, don't give up hope. Today there is at last a good chance that you can be cured. And if that cure saves your marriage – and perhaps your sanity – then by Heaven it's worth searching for.

CHAPTER EIGHTEEN

The Main Female Difficulties

*A note about causes • Being treated together • Vaginismus •
Inability to reach orgasm at all • Inability to reach a climax during
intercourse • General lack of sexual desire.*

A note about causes

As I've indicated in the previous chapter, it's not a woman's *fault*
if she has sexual difficulties. Most of the millions of ladies who
have sexual troubles would be only too glad to be free of them. So
it's no use a husband or lover blaming a woman because she's
unresponsive or because she complains of pain during intercourse. (As we'll see in a moment, part of the problem may well
lie with *him*!)

If you've read the previous chapter – and if you're in sexual
difficulties, you should certainly do so – you'll know by now that
most of the time, women's sexual problems (like men's) originate
in the emotions, rather than being physical. That's why a girl
who's been brought up to regard sex as 'nasty', 'dirty' or 'painful'
is very likely to have psychosexual problems when she grows up.
But as I've said, there is a minority of cases in which the problem is
actually sparked off by a *physical* condition – for instance some
painful infection of the vagina.

Being treated together

Whether the cause is emotional or physical, it's usually best if the
couple are counselled together – not the woman by herself. It's
often difficult for the man to realise this because (since most of us
men have a large streak of the old Male Chauvinist Pig) we tend to
assume that 'It's all the woman's fault'. This is not true; so, as a
rule, there isn't a lot of point in advising one partner and not the
other. So often, it's not just the husband (or just the wife) who
needs help, it's the relationship. So the 'marital unit' (to use the
fashionable phrase) must be given therapy as a whole.

A lot of people find this very hard to understand, but – to take
one common example – the man whose wife can't relax her vagina
to let him in must realise that if *he* were to learn more about the
techniques of love play (see Chapters 8 and 10) *she* would

probably find it easier to become less tense. Furthermore, it's a fairly basic rule in sexual medicine that if one partner has a problem, the other quite often has one too. Indeed it's quite fantastic how frequently the woman with so-called 'frigidity' or vaginismus marries a man who is impotent! Sometimes the 'healthy' partner will indignantly deny that he or she has any difficulty at all, in the face of overwhelming evidence to the contrary.

For instance, Annie was brought along to a clinic by her husband Richard to get her 'fixed up'. What apparently needed 'fixing up' was Annie's alleged 'frigidity'. In fact, it transpired that although Annie did have some problem with her libido, her *real* difficulty was that her husband climaxed far too soon. (In other words, he was a 'premature ejaculator'.)

Annie and Richard were taught by the doctor how to overcome this difficulty (using techniques described in the next chapter), and Richard's 'staying time' was rapidly increased by about twenty minutes.

This in turn rapidly helped to put Annie's problem right (for the poor girl had no adequate stimulation from intercourse till now). But it was noteworthy that when Richard attended the clinic for the last time he said rather arrogantly to the doctor: 'Thanks for putting my wife right. She was in a lot of trouble till she saw you.'

The counsellor gently reminded him: 'And you're better too. . . .'

'Me?' said Richard, gazing out of the window. 'Oh no – *I* never had a problem.'

Male chauvinist piggery is not dead!

Vaginismus

(**Note:** a few causes of vaginismus are caused by *physical* disorders of the vagina, such as infection or a painful childbirth tear: see Chapter 17.)

As I've indicated earlier in this book, what the word 'vaginismus' means is that whenever an approach is made to the affected woman, the muscles round the opening of her vagina close down like a mouth saying 'No!' She doesn't mean this to happen, but she can't help it. Indeed, she probably doesn't know it's occurring at all. To her, it seems as though her vagina is very narrow, or as if there's some obstruction (like the hymen, or virgin's veil, which is described in Chapter 2) preventing the penis from getting in.

Of course, there *isn't* a physical barrier and the whole problem is caused by muscular spasm. This is aggravated by dryness of the vagina, because only when a woman is both relaxed and sexually excited will the love juices flow. (For techniques of making them flow, see Chapters 8 and 10.)

Let's look at a typical story. Jane had grown up without being told much about sex, and her only experience of sexuality was the unpleasant one of being exposed to a 'flasher' as a young teenager. The result was that Jane was secretly terrified of her own vagina. She thought of it as a tight, narrow passage up which one day some rapist of a man would force his penis.

Typically of women who have vaginismus, she was scared stiff of having an internal examination by a doctor – and also quite terrified of using tampons, lest they hurt her. A history of never being able to insert a Tampax is so absolutely typical of vaginismus that I call it 'the Tampax test'.

She practically doubled up every time any boyfriend tried to touch her anywhere between her neck and her knees. So, not surprisingly, she got married as a virgin – and remained a virgin for quite a while *after* marriage. Her husband Arthur was quite unable to penetrate her.

Some men become impotent when faced with a wife as vaginismal as this. But Arthur, a kindly and sympathetic man, didn't. Eventually, he and Jane went to the local Family Planning Clinic. Though the doctor there was a woman, it was some time before Jane would let herself be examined by her.

However, at last the doctor managed to persuade her to relax enough for a gloved finger to be inserted into her vagina. Once this was done, the understanding doctor was able to sit (still with one finger in Jane's vagina) and talk to her about her deepest fears. And as Jane talked, her vaginal muscles at last began to relax. Most doctors who work in Family Planning Clinics see this kind of reaction time and again each week!

The doctor then got Jane to pop her own finger into the vagina. Like most girls in this situation, she was pleasurably surprised at how roomy and wide her love passage was. The doctor advised daily self-exploration of her vagina – and after a few months she was able to let her husband slip a finger inside her. He had to be taught how to arouse her in order to make her vaginal muscles relax and her love juices flow, because up till now he hadn't had a clue! From then on things improved fast and eventually the two of them were able to enjoy a happy sex life.

Jane's disorder is probably commoner than measles. In the old days, it couldn't be cured (and you can imagine what misery and frustration that caused). But today, most women with vaginismus *can* 'get straight' – with the help of an understanding partner and the type of counselling described above – or other types of treatment discussed in Chapter 20. As these methods of treatment become more widely available, the number of marriages in which sex is uncomfortable, painful or downright impossible will rapidly diminish.

Inability to reach orgasm at all

This is sometimes described as 'frigidity' – an unpleasant term which I deplore – since most so-called 'frigid' women *aren't* cold and unloving: they're often very warm, cuddly ladies who would like nothing better than to reach a climax!

Can I make it absolutely clear that a woman who can't 'come' does *not* have a problem with her clitoris or vagina. Many ladies who can't reach a climax think it must be because they don't have the right nerve connections in these sex organs which is all nonsense – and I must repeat that the problem arises *not* in the sexy parts, but in the emotions.

What can be done about 'anorgasmia', as it is called? Let's look at a typical case history of a woman who was successful in overcoming her inhibitions and therefore her inability to 'come'.

Margaret was thirty-five and had been married for twelve years. Her problem distressed her to such an extent that even when trying to explain what was wrong with her, she burst into tears.

'It's dreadful,' she sobbed, 'because I try desperately hard, but whenever I think I'm about to come, my husband reaches his climax and that's that.'

For a start, Margaret was *trying too much*. She was so tensed up about her performance before she started that there wasn't the remotest chance of success. Her family doctor listened to her fears, spent some time in reassuring her that she was physically quite normal, and then prescribed a mild tranquilliser to help her relax at bedtime. (Some patients prefer a dry Martini.)

Then he turned his attention to Margaret's husband, Frank. It became clear that Frank – like Richard – was a sufferer from premature ejaculation who could scarcely have maintained his erection long enough to satisfy *any* woman. Furthermore, he simply hadn't the faintest idea of how to caress his wife's body.

So Frank was taught the basic love play techniques, as outlined in Chapter 9, of stimulating the breasts, clitoris and vagina with his fingers, lips and tongue, while Margaret was taught methods of prolonging his erection and delaying his climax. (See Chapter 19.) The results were remarkable. Within a few weeks Margaret became much less tensed up in bed, and was able to reach her first ever climax, as a result of tongue stimulation.

Before very long, Frank could prolong intercourse for up to fifteen or twenty minutes, which turned out to be quite sufficient for Margaret to reach her climax. Nowadays, on the odd occasions when she doesn't quite get there in time, her husband is almost always able to bring her to orgasm by finger caresses within a matter of ten seconds or so.

There are many other women who remain unable to 'come' despite the fact that their husbands are perfectly competent lovers. Often, they are strictly brought-up people who are so afraid of losing control of their emotions that they simply can't let themselves go in bed. 'It seems as if I'm terrified to let the fuses blow,' as a number of women express it.

In practice, a lot of these ladies can be helped by frank discussions of their problems with a counsellor – preferably with their husbands/lovers present as well. What I find particularly fascinating is that they often begin to get better as soon as they have the reassurance of a woman doctor that it's OK for a 'respectable' woman to have an orgasm! It's fairly obvious that in such cases the previously hung-up lady is seeing the woman doctor as a 'mother substitute' who's telling her: 'Yes, dear – it's all right for you to enjoy the pleasure of your own vagina.'

Apart from simple reassurance, various types of treatment can be effective and help 'anorgasmic' women reach a climax – see Chapters 20 and 21.

Inability to reach a climax during intercourse

As I hope I've made clear in the early part of this book, most people simply do not realise that at the present time a woman who reaches a climax through love play, but not through intercourse itself, is *statistically normal*.

This startling finding – which overturns all previously-held concepts of normal sexuality – was made by sex researcher Shere Hite in the late 1970s. Shere – a lady for whom I have a lot of respect – found that ROUGHLY TWO-THIRDS OF ALL WOMEN DON'T REACH A CLIMAX DURING INTERCOURSE ITSELF. Two very large surveys conducted by British women's magazines have recently confirmed that what she said was true.

Now you may say that in an ideal world, *all* women would reach a climax during intercourse – preferably at the same time as their husbands or lovers. Of course, I agree; and I think that when the world finally throws off its sexual inhibitions, that day will finally come (if you'll forgive the phrase). But at the moment, the important thing is that the vast majority of women who don't reach a climax during intercourse itself but only during love play shouldn't regard themselves as 'abnormal'.

For the woman (or rather the *couple*) in this situation, here are a few basic tips:

1. Remember that you're NORMAL.

2. Try to avoid the common trap of 'observing yourself' – in other words concentrating on your own performance. Just lie back and enjoy it!

3. Make sure your contraception is adequate. The reason why many women can't reach a climax during intercourse itself may be that they are too worried about getting pregnant.

4. Make sure that you go in for really adequate foreplay (love play) before intercourse – twenty minutes or more if necessary, so that the lady is really worked up by the time the man enters her with his penis.

5. Once the man is in, ensure that he makes a real effort to grind his pubic bone against the woman's own 'pubes'. (If you don't know where the pubic bone is, see Chapters 2 and 3.) This grinding action provides intense stimulation of the woman's clitoris, and it can be achieved:

(a) By using one of the positions in which the husband is able to get more 'under' the wife (see Chapter 14). Doing this tends to bring the part of the pubic bone which lies just above the base of his penis into firm contact with her clitoris.

For instance, a good position which achieves this effect is the one in which the woman kneels above and astride the man (with her knees on either side of his hips). She can then grind her 'pubes' against his as hard as she wants to.

(b) By using *flanquette* positions – again, see Chapter 14 – in which the man's upper thigh and groin tend to press against the clitoris, with pleasant results.

(c) By making love with the man lying across the woman: this too can create a lot of pressure on the clitoris and help her to a climax.

6. Remember that it's a great help if the man uses his fingers over the woman's clitoral area during intercourse. This isn't all that easy, I must admit, since a man's hand tends to get rather painfully squashed between those two pulsating bodies. But here are some ways round the problem:

(a) Make love using one of the 'rear-entry' positions (see Chapter 14). This makes it very easy for the man to reach round and give really intensive stimulation to the woman's clitoris with his finger-tips – just as he would during love-play, in fact.

(b) Choose a face-to-face position in which the man's lower body isn't so tightly jammed against the woman's that it's impossible for him to get his fingers in between them!

A suitable position is the one in which the man is lying on top of the woman, but with his legs *outside* her thighs. The fact that his body is lifted a little (because part of his weight is on his knees) gives him just that extra little bit of room to use his hand – which may be enough to let him bring his lady to that much-desired climax.

(c) Pick a position in which the woman can stimulate her own clitoris with her fingertips during intercourse.

At first that particular suggestion comes as a great surprise to many couples – but in fact a spot of 'do-it-yourself' can be a great help in getting a lady to a climax.

Also, it's often easier for the woman to slip her hand in between their two bodies – simply because of the fact that the pads of her fingers are already facing towards her clitoris. It can really be very awkward for the man to slip his hand between the two clashing pubic bones and at the same time to turn the hand round so that his finger-pads are facing the clitoris.

7. Because the newly-discovered 'magic G-spot' (see Chapter 2) is so sensitive in some women, try using positions in which the 'G-spot' is stimulated by the penis. As the 'G-spot' is usually about half way up the front wall of the vagina, you can (for example) put pressure on it with the penis simply by having the woman sitting astride the man – and then leaning right back so that his organ presses hard along the front vaginal wall.

8. If all else fails, use a vibrator during intercourse. Again, you may have to adopt slightly adventurous positions in order to be able to get the vibrator onto the clitoral region while the penis is in the vagina.

9. I must add that it'll probably help if your man keeps telling you during intercourse that he loves you. . . . Gentlemen, please take note!

But don't forget what I said at the beginning of this section: if a woman only has an orgasm during love play (not during actual intercourse), she's *not* abnormal. Enjoy what you've got – after all, it's better to 'come unscrewed' than not to 'come' at all.

General lack of sexual desire

It's incredibly common these days for a woman to walk into a doctor's consulting room and say unhappily: 'I've just lost interest in my husband, doctor. . . .' For reasons which aren't yet understood, this is specially frequent after a woman's just had a baby – and sometimes also when she's pregnant.

At other times, the symptom starts after a woman's just been through some major crisis in her life. And you probably won't be surprised to know that it can also happen when she's been very tired or overworked. Interestingly, it can also occur when a woman has recently moved house. Perhaps this is to do with all the trauma that house-moving involves.

But Freudian psychiatrists point out that old Sigmund called the house a 'vaginal symbol' for a woman – and they maintain that if a woman isn't too happy about the new house she's living in, she may express it as lack of interest in her own vagina. All this sounds very complicated to me, but perhaps there's something in it.

MEDICATION AS A CAUSE OF LACK OF DESIRE   What about medication? Well, the type of medication which most people tend to associate with 'lack of interest' is the Pill. Any number of women (and men) are keen to assert that 'the Pill can turn you off sex'. Frankly, I think that this whole idea has been greatly exaggerated. Many women are *sexier* on the Pill (probably because they're happy about knowing that sex is safe).

When a woman says that the Pill has 'turned her off', it often transpires that she really had psychosexual problems before she ever started on the Pill. In such cases, it's not surprising that stopping the Pill doesn't cure the lack of libido.

But – and it's a big 'BUT' – I must admit that there are a small number of women who genuinely *do* seem to be turned off sex by the Pill – and who do get better when the brand of Pill is changed, or when they come off the Pill altogether. (If you try this cure, do make sure you use some other form of contraception instead.)

What other kinds of medication could interfere with a woman's desire? In her outstanding medical textbook *Disorders of Sexual Desire*, the distinguished US researcher Dr Helen Singer Kaplan lists many drugs which may possibly damp down people's sexual desire. (A good deal of attention has been paid recently to the effect which such drugs can have on *men's* sexual desire – but in the last few years I've become increasingly convinced that this kind of medication can lower desire in women too.)

Here's an abridged version of Dr Kaplan's list:

★Alcohol, except in low doses.
★Tranquillisers, in high doses.
★Narcotics.
★Steroids (cortisone-like drugs) in high doses.

★Some drugs for high blood pressure.
★Some diuretics (anti-water retention tablets).
★Some drugs for angina.

So clearly, if you're suffering from general lack of sexual desire and you're taking any of the above drugs, check with your doc to see if this could be the cause of the problem.

TREATMENT Unfortunately, it's only in a minority of cases that drugs are the cause of lack of desire.

Much more often, the woman has a deep seated hang-up which isn't easy to put right. As Dr Helen Singer Kaplan says, the disorder of 'lack of sexual desire' is generally more difficult to cure than other female sex problems.

However, one good thing is that quite often *the problem gets better by itself*. Heaven knows why – but it does! Secondly, just as with other female sex problems, it's often the case that the woman starts to improve after she's talked to a female doctor and (in effect) been 'given permission' to get horny about sex, because, once again, she sees the lady doctor as a kindly mother-figure. Thirdly, other treatments – described in Chapter 20 – can work. Let's finish by looking at a trio of case histories:

★Penelope was thirty-one, had been married for eight years, and gradually lost all interest in sex. On the rare occasions when her husband could persuade her to do it, she seemed to wake out of her lethargy and actually enjoyed it. But by next day, she'd invariably lost all her natural desire again. In addition, she felt constantly tired and worn out, and was sleeping badly.

Penelope went to her family doctor, who rapidly diagnosed that she was actually suffering from depression. He put her on a short course of anti-depressants (which, incidentally, are *not* the same thing as tranquillisers), and these rapidly lifted her mood.

He also arranged a couple of visits to a psychiatrist who specialised in treating sexual problems, and who tried out some therapy (described in Chapter 20) which involves exposure to erotic material. This, coupled with the lifting of the depression, had the desired effect – and Penelope was soon enthusiastically demanding sex from her delighted husband.

★Ruby was twenty-seven and complained that she couldn't summon up any interest at all in any of the boyfriends she'd had. In fact, she seemed always to have been rather lacking in sexual desire for men.

She went to a psychologist who had a special interest in sex problems – and after a few discussion sessions the main cause of the problem became clear. Ruby was basically lesbian in orientation. This isn't really very surprising. Roughly one woman in twenty is lesbian (and many more are AC/DC), and it's not surprising if a basically gay woman feels little desire for men.

Once Ruby had come to terms with the fact that she was gay, she was able to form a good relationship with another woman – a relationship in which (for the first time in her life) she felt plenty of desire.

★Linda was thirty-five and had been sleeping with a married man for about five years. She went to a doctor complaining that for over twelve months she'd had little or no sexual desire – though she could reach a climax if her lover insisted on having sex.

After a number of counselling sessions, it became obvious that although Linda had some minor hang-ups (connected with her rather puritanical upbringing), there were two main factors causing her lack of desire:

(i) she felt guilty about sleeping with someone else's husband;

(ii) she wasn't actually in love with him any more.

Once Linda faced up to the fact that she was no longer in love with her married lover, life became clearer for her. She brought the affair to an end – and soon afterwards met someone else whom she really liked. Not surprisingly, her sexual desire was perfectly normal with him.

These three cases illustrate the fact that the causes of lack of desire (like the causes of other sexual problems) can be very complex – and can take quite a bit of unravelling. But unravelled they *can* be – as we'll see in Chapter 20.

CHAPTER NINETEEN

The Main Male Difficulties

Causes • Mutual treatment • Premature ejaculation ('Hair trigger trouble') • Impotence • 'Ejaculatory incompetence' (inability to come) • General lack of desire.

Causes

As a rule, the more severe male sex disorders which I'm going to deal with in this chapter are due to emotional causes – not physical ones. In other words, these problems are nearly always 'hang-ups' – caused by emotional stresses deep within the brain. As I explained in Chapter 4 (which is about 'How Everything Works') the brain and the central nervous system send out unconscious signals through two nerve networks which are called the sympathetic and the parasympathetic nervous systems – plus a third one about which relatively little is yet known (see below).

The *sympathetic* is the one which releases adrenalin and related chemicals into the bloodstream – the chemicals which make you het up, excited and anxious. It also tends to make you 'come' – and tends to take away your erection. So, if deep-seated tensions cause the sympathetic nervous system of your body to release too much adrenalin and similar chemicals, you may either:

★Come too soon (that is, suffer from *premature ejaculation*); or
★Be unable to get a good erection (that is, suffer from *impotence*).

These two disorders – premature ejaculation and impotence – are by far the most common sexual problems seen in men. Literally millions of men suffer from them. Unfortunately, there is as yet no magic chemical remedy for them. It would be nice if we could give some pill that could put these disorders right, perhaps by blocking the sympathetic nervous system. But at the moment, we can't.

Tranquillisers can sometimes help a little bit (by taking the edge off a man's nervousness). But taking male hormones will scarcely ever help – because it's not usually a hormone deficiency that's the cause of the problem. (Admittedly, if a man has great faith in male hormone pills, the simple fact that he *believes* in them may help –

simply by restoring his confidence.) However, at the moment, we just don't have an 'instant' remedy for male sex disorders. Yet happily, they can now very often be cured.

Cure depends largely on trying to 're-train' the brain – for, as I've explained, it's deep within the brain that the basic causes of these disorders usually lie. The pioneering work of Masters and Johnson in the USA has shown that such 're-training' can be enormously successful. For instance, 'M & J' cured no less than 98 per cent of their patients with premature ejaculation. The results of re-training men with impotence are not as good – but again, cure *is* possible. So if you (or your man) has one of these difficulties, read on.

Mutual treatment

Just as with female sex problems, it's usually best if the couple are treated *together* – in other words, they should both go along to the therapist or counsellor. There are several reasons for this. In the first place, the man will very often need the woman's practical help in bed in order to overcome his difficulty. This is especially true with premature ejaculation, as we'll see in a moment.

Unfortunately, in cases where the wife/fiancée/girlfriend *won't* help the man with his treatment (and perhaps won't even come along and see the doctor), the success rate is pretty low. Virtually every man with problems needs a woman's help if he's going to overcome them.

Secondly, it's often the case that when a man has some sexual difficulty, his partner has problems too. For example, it's astonishing how often a man who is impotent turns out to be married to a woman who has vaginismus (and *that's* a combination that makes successful intercourse pretty unlikely). So most doctors and counsellors who specialise in this field like to talk to the couple together. There's usually little point in the man going along for treatment by himself.

Premature ejaculation ('Hair trigger trouble')

Premature ejaculation is one of the commonest of all sexual problems. Very mild cases will respond to simple distraction techniques – in other words, if the man thinks about other things (say, work, golf or football) when he's starting to make love. And it can be a help if he pinches himself or bites the pillows whenever he feels an unwanted climax coming on.

Mild cases may also be helped with local anaesthetic ointment –

available without prescription from sex shops – which is applied to the penis before intercourse, thereby dulling the sensation. Quite a few people obtain benefit from either a stiff drink or (preferably) taking a medically prescribed tranquilliser shortly before bedtime. If these measures fail, the doctor may suggest a course of anti-depressant pills, which sometimes work.

But really, far and away the best therapy (which is necessary in *all* severe cases) is the re-training programme which was developed in St Louis by Masters and Johnson – and which has given such wonderful results, even in what used to be virtually incurable cases.

First, I must stress that ideally the technique should be used under the guidance of a doctor or psychologist who is experienced in counselling people with sexual problems. If you don't have somebody like this to advise you, then you will almost certainly get the finer points wrong – and so you won't achieve the desired result.

The therapist usually advises an initial period of sexual abstinence, during which the couple only cuddle each other. This is the famous 'sensate focus' method which Masters and Johnson use for all sexual difficulties. It's discussed further in the section on 'M & J's' work in the next chapter. After the period of 'sensate focus' comes the 'anti-ejaculation technique' which they invented.

The technique basically involves a special grip which enables the wife to turn her man off whenever he feels he is close to reaching a climax. What the woman does is this: sit on the bed with your back against the headboard. Spread your legs wide apart. Your partner lies on his back the other way up, with his head towards the foot of the bed, and his bottom up between your thighs; his feet are on either side of your hips, as in Figure 42.

Doubtless that sounds a bit bizarre, but you'll find that it all works out quite nicely so that your hands are in just the right position to stimulate his penis by rubbing. Doing this shouldn't bring him to a climax, *provided that both of you have agreed that there is absolutely no attempt at intercourse*. (As I've said, it's deep anxiety about intercourse which makes the premature ejaculator 'come' too quickly.)

As soon as your man has got a really good erection (or sooner, if he feels that there is any danger of a climax) you apply the 'squeeze grip' shown in the same drawing. It is vitally important to get the position of the grip right: your thumb should be on the side of his penis which is nearest to you when he is erect, and your index and middle fingers should be on the far side. Remember that the index finger must rest just *above* the ridge which runs round the head of the penis, and that the middle finger rests just below it.

When you apply the grip, squeeze the man's penis firmly for about four seconds between the thumb and the other two fingers. I know that this sounds painful but I assure you it isn't! In fact, if properly done it will completely remove any urge to reach a climax, and will make your husband's penis lose some of its stiffness.

You then go on rubbing as before, until your husband once again has a good erection (or feels that he is in danger of 'coming') – at which point you use the 'squeeze grip' technique again.

Repeated sessions of this teach a man good ejaculatory control, and restore confidence in himself. After a few weeks, it is usually possible for the woman to move forward and 'mount' him – which will normally mean having her thighs *outside* her partner's – see Figure 31, p. 151. *She withdraws momentarily and applies the 'squeeze grip' whenever he feels that an unwanted ejaculation is about to occur.*

FIG. 42

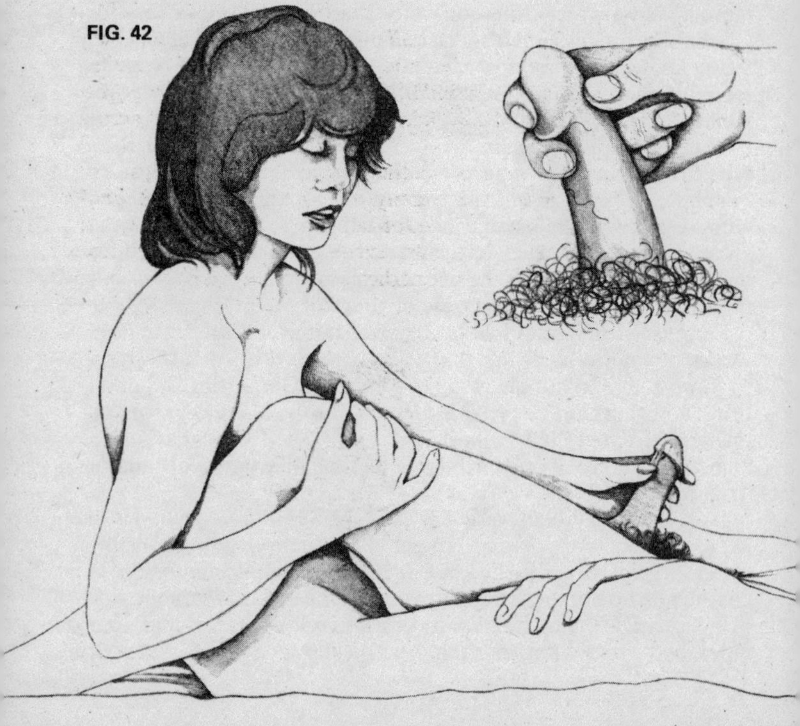

Masters and Johnson's treatment – which was based on work by Dr James Semans in Florida back in the 1950s – represents one of the greatest steps forward ever in the history of marriage guidance and sex therapy – for it has saved countless marriages which were threatened by this miserable and frustrating problem of 'hair trigger trouble'.

Impotence

Impotence is certainly one of the major marital problems of all time – which is why men are always exchanging nervous jokes about it. (Remember the recent James Bond movie in which 007 made love to the girl deep underwater in a mini-submarine, and somebody expressed the hope that he wouldn't get 'a touch of the bends'?)

But first let's define our terms. A lot of people don't understand what impotence means, and think it means infertility, or something like that. It doesn't. As I've indicated at the start of this chapter it means partial or complete inability to get the penis stiff enough for intercourse.

Let me make quite clear that *all* men have this trouble at some time or another – usually when they're tired out, or have had too much to drink. But regular and repeated difficulty in obtaining an erection affects tens of thousands of men, and for obvious reasons threatens their marriages.

Why does it happen? Let's get the *physical* causes out of the way – though there aren't very many of them. Indeed, the only common known physical causes of failure to get an erection are: diabetes, use of narcotic drugs, excess intake of alcohol, and treatment with certain pills or medicines.

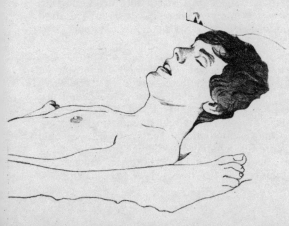

Your doctor may – with the best of intentions – prescribe pills or medicines which affect the ability to achieve an erection. These include: certain anti-depressants; certain tranquillisers and sedatives; many drugs for the treatment of high blood pressure and fluid retention; and possibly certain new drugs for the treatment of ulcers.

One *rare* physical cause is over production of a hormone called 'prolactin' by the pituitary gland. This can be treated with a drug called bromocryptine.

It's generally thought, however, that most male problems with erection are due to emotional causes. This isn't surprising when you consider that a man is under such pressure to 'perform' – while at the same time, many men are besieged by doubts and guilts about their sex lives. (No wonder too that some men are impotent with one woman, while they're perfectly okay with another.)

As I've said above, orthodox medical thinking has concluded that a man's erections are largely connected with his parasympathetic nervous system but his actual climax is due to his sympathetic nervous system (the one which releases adrenalin). This neatly explains the well-known fact that when a man is unusually het-up, anxious or guilty (in other words, when his sympathetic nervous system is releasing vast quantities of adrenalin), two consequences follow: firstly, he tends to have trouble getting an erection, and secondly he tends to reach his climax far too soon.

All very neat and tidy. But recently I've been surprised to discover that medical science has not actually *proved* that the nerve endings of the parasympathetic nervous system really do what they're theoretically supposed to do to a man's penis. That's why it's exciting that new research at the Hammersmith Hospital in London seems to have shown that a *third* unconscious nervous network may play a part in producing penile erection. This third autonomic nervous system is called the 'peptidergic system' – look back to Figure 14, p. 38.

Dr Julia Polak and her colleagues at the Hammersmith say that this peptidergic nervous system has many nerve endings in the erectile tissue of the penis – where they are thought to release an erection-producing chemical called 'vaso-active intestinal polypeptide' or (appropriately enough) VIP for short.

The implications of this work are really fascinating; for if we could find a drug that would mimic the action of VIP, we would probably have a cure for impotence – whether from physical *or* emotional causes. And that would be one of the real medical breakthroughs of this century in terms of relieving human misery.

But for the moment, we haven't got one, so what's to be done if it affects *your* marriage?

Well, the important thing is to get counselling as soon as possible, before things get worse. Too often the husband becomes desperately embarrassed about what he regards as his failure, and he doesn't want to tell anybody about it. So he avoids sex altogether, hoping against hope that the trouble will go away.

The result may well be that his wife decides she is being scorned, and so needless bitterness arises between them. Alternatively, some women are cruel enough to sneer or laugh outright at an impotent man, which of course makes things much worse for him.

What about remedies? As with other sexual problems, the basic idea of therapy is to let both parties talk about their problems with the doctor or counsellor and so come to realise why the trouble is happening. Many men improve as soon as they can be persuaded that they are not suffering from some dreadful physical disease – or turning into women!

Therapies vary, but usually the wife is taught that when her husband fails to get an erection she shouldn't just roll away in disgust, frustration or self-pity but that this is the time for her to (metaphorically) roll up her sleeves and get down to work on stimulating his penis (see Chapter 9). This is usually best done with the husband lying flat on his back and the wife sitting facing him.

In this position, there is far less demand on the man, and he can just lie back and enjoy being stimulated. When an impotent man tries to make love in the 'missionary' position, it is usually at the anxiety-provoking moment of climbing onto his wife that he loses his erection.

As the man gets more confidence (and as his erection gets firmer) the wife can learn to move forward and 'mount' him, but as a rule this should *not* be attempted until the couple have been under treatment for several weeks. When the time comes to insert the penis, *it's important that the woman should use her hand to steady it; by gently supporting it at the moment of entry, she can help to prevent it from folding in the middle.*

Indeed, if only more women knew that simple fact, countless cases of impotence would be cured right away! Every woman should be aware that many men – especially those in their middle years – need a little helping hand to direct the penis into the vagina at the moment of entry. That reassuring hand will often prevent the collapse which is so demoralising to a man who's trying to get inside.

Incidentally, a very useful trick for keeping things going once the man is in is for his partner to reach round behind her bottom, and gently stimulate his penis with her fingers as it goes in and out. This excellent technique for overcoming partial impotence is called 'Florentine intercourse' (see Chapter 13).

There are other ways of helping men with impotence, and these are briefly discussed in the next chapter (Chapter 20), which is about the various schools of sex therapy.

'Ejaculatory incompetence' (inability to come)

This is nowhere near as common as the other two male problems we've just discussed. But there are quite a few men around who are reasonably interested in sex, and who can get a good erection – but who just can't reach a climax. Naturally, this is very frustrating for both them and their wives – and it does make having children rather difficult.

In some cases, the problem is due to some drug being pre-scribed by the man's physician – a drug which is interfering with the balance of the two nervous systems we've mentioned already, (the sympathetic and the parasympathetic).

But some healthy young men who are taking no tablets at all have this problem of 'ejaculatory incompetence'. It seems to me that they're often males of relatively moderate sexual desire, and some of them have scarcely, if ever, masturbated during their teenage years (something which is most uncommon in men).

Although there are various schools of treatment of sex prob-lems (see the next chapter) many therapists base their treatment for this one on the scheme developed by Masters and Johnson. After a brief initial period prescribed by the therapist – say, a few days – of sexual abstinence and 'cuddling up' (described by Masters and Johnson as 'sensate focus'), the couple move on to the basic technique for overcoming inability to 'come'.

It may surprise you that all that this involves is for the man to lie flat on his back with the woman kneeling beside him (or – more conveniently – between his thighs), *rubbing his penis like mad*, for up to two hours at a time if necessary!

Obviously, she has to be skilful at stimulating his male organ, and it's a help if she studies the techniques described in the earlier chapters of this book. Inevitably, the man's penis tends to get rather sore, so it's helpful if his partner uses Baby Oil or some other gentle lubricant on his organ.

Crazy though this treatment sounds, it usually works. A typical case was that of Bill, a twenty year old sailor who'd been married for a year and who'd *never* reached a climax in all that time. (He thought he'd had one or two as a teenager, but was a bit vague about it.)

He and his wife Samantha went to see a specialist, who listened sympathetically to their story, and then told Samantha what to do. Samantha was a girl who was more than keen on sex, though she didn't know very much about it. It had never occurred to her that a woman could set about rubbing a man's penis with her fingers – but once the physician had suggested this idea to her, she took to it with a will.

Very sensibly, while doing it she murmured all sorts of sexy endearments to Bill, brushed the tip of his penis with her breasts, kissed it, and generally made the whole experience as delightful as possible for him.

Not altogether surprisingly, at the end of his third two-hour session Bill amazed himself by suddenly reaching a climax. For some months afterwards, Samantha had to keep giving him what she called 'my little rub-ups', but eventually Bill became conditioned to responding far faster – so that they were able to have a very good sex life together.

Samantha reckoned that by that time she'd developed arm muscles like an Olympic weight-lifter's, but she didn't mind one little bit. . . .

General lack of desire

General lack of desire is a bit different from impotence (in which there is just inability to achieve a good erection). Loss of desire is much less common in men than it is in women, and in fact it's way down the league table of disorders seen at psychosexual clinics.

However, quite a few men do go to see their doctors complaining of 'loss of interest'. They're not actually impotent – in other words, they can do it if they really want to, and if the sexual stimulation is sufficient – but most of the time they just don't seem to be interested.

Commoner causes of this lack of desire are:

★Depression
★Overwork
★Stress
★Plain, ordinary 'falling out of love' with the partner
★The fact that the partner has let herself go, and become (say) fat or otherwise unattractive

211

★Alcohol – which decreases the output of male sex hormone
★Medication prescribed by doctors

Although this last group – medication prescribed by doctors – is very far from being the most frequent cause of general lack of desire in men, it's worth bearing in mind. The list of potential desire-inhibiting drugs which US expert Dr Helen Singer Kaplan lays down is this:

★Sedatives
★Tranquillisers (in high doses)
★Some anti-high blood pressure drugs
★Some diuretic (i.e. anti-water retention) pills
★Female hormones (which are sometimes given to men with serious disease of the prostate gland and – very, very rarely – for other purposes: for instance, in experimental contraceptive Pills for men).

But many, if not most, men who are lacking in general desire are simply tired out or depressed. Depression can be treated with anti-depressant tablets (not the same as tranquillisers), while tiredness and overwork are best treated by resting more, by avoiding overwork, and by getting adequate sleep.

Regrettably, far too many men find it very hard to *stop* themselves overworking (for the most understandable of reasons). But it's desperately important for the man whose overwork and tiredness are affecting his sex life to say to himself: 'Which is more important – my work or my love-life? Working hard – or satisfying the woman who loves me?' In most cases, there's only one answer to these questions. . . .

In this chapter and the previous one, while discussing the various common female and male disorders, I've briefly mentioned some of the more common forms of sex therapy (especially 'Masters and Johnson' treatment). In the next chapter, we're going to look at *all* of the commonly available treatments in more detail.

CHAPTER TWENTY

Going To A Sex Clinic – The Types Of Treatment Available

A warning about bogus sex clinics ● Don't be embarrassed about going ● The various schools of sex therapy ● Sex therapy from your own doctor ● Masters–Johnson treatment ● Behaviourist treatment ● Psychoanalysis and other Freudian treatments ● The 'Balint' or 'Seminar' method ● Marriage guidance counselling ● Hormone therapy ● Hypnotism ● Treatment by a urologist ● Treatment by a gynaecologist ● Treatment by the 'SAR' method ● Surrogate partner treatment ● Self-help treatment.

A warning about bogus sex clinics

A doctor friend of mine recently went to the USA, where he'd been invited to meet the head of a new 'school' of sex therapy. 'Hi, doc!' said the leader as they shook hands. 'Wanna go to a fuck-in tonight?' Clearly, the 'school' wasn't all it purported to be!

I think that that particular story illustrates the possible dangers of the new boom in sex treatment. If you'd wanted to go to a 'fuck-in' (whatever that may be), then doubtless that particular organisation's 'therapy' would have been great fun for you. But of course, most men and women who suffer marital and sexual difficulties aren't looking for the sort of clinic that charges you money to attend an orgy!

Most people who have worries about their sex lives are primarily in need of a sympathetic ear (the ear preferably being attached to a doctor, psychologist or counsellor), plus commonsense personal advice – and, very often, one of the kinds of therapy discussed in this chapter. So, be a little wary, especially if a clinic wants you to spend a lot of money on treatment. It may be a rip-off.

I'm afraid there are also occasional instances of so-called 'therapists' establishing sex clinics only in order to gratify their own sexual whims on clients. This isn't common, but I'm sorry to say that I have come across rare cases of doctors offering lady patients what has been termed 'penile therapy'. (The patients were getting screwed, in both senses of the word.)

Therefore, be a bit careful about choosing a sex clinic. If you approach one which is recommended by or run by one of the highly-respectable organisations listed in Chapter 21, you're most unlikely to go wrong.

Don't be embarrassed about going

I hope that all that hasn't put you off the idea of going to a sex therapist if you and your partner need help. I must admit that lots of people are really scared of attending a sexual medicine clinic. It's often particularly difficult for the man, partly because of the fact that in our crazy culture all men are supposed to be highly virile and tough and *macho* – and it's a great humiliation for them to have to admit that there's something amiss with their sex lives.

In Britain and in many other English-speaking countries sex therapy has tended to develop inside Family Planning Clinics. So it's relatively easy for a woman with a sex problem to sit in the waiting area without embarrassment: people will just think she's come to get a prescription for the Pill, or whatever. For a *man* to turn up in one of the female-dominated Family Planning Clinics isn't so easy – especially if he's the male among fifty waiting women. The best thing, gentlemen, is to look as though you've come for advice about a vasectomy (or you could wear the self-satisfied smirk of a man who's so far burst every size of sheath the Family Planning Clinic can offer him. . . .)

The various schools of sex therapy

One thing which is very bewildering for your average consumer is that, whereas there was once virtually no sex therapy available, there are now all kinds of different varieties or schools of thought, at least in the developed countries of the world.

Which one is best? Well, there *isn't* a best, as a rule. If you've got problems, you'd do best to look at what varieties of treatment are available in your area, and then (perhaps with your family doctor's advice) choose the one which most appeals to your type of personality.

Unhappily, some of the various schools of sex therapy don't seem to get along very well with each other – and some of them prefer to ignore the existence of the others totally! For example, behaviourist psychologists appear to enjoy absolutely appalling relationships with therapists who are Freudian (or psychoanalytically-orientated) – which is a pity, since it'd be better if they were allies rather than enemies.

However, the dislike (or just sheer mutual ignorance) that exists between certain 'sects' of sex therapy is likely to continue for years to come. What this means for *you* is this: if you're not getting on well with one school of therapy, don't expect them to refer you to another one. Sadly, they may dislike the alternative method of treatment – or just be unaware that it exists.

This is where your family doctor may be able to help. With luck, he'll know about all the various methods of treatment which are available in your area – and will be able to advise you on which ones might suit you.

One final comment about the various 'schools' of sex therapy: alas, some of them take themselves a little too seriously. For instance, I've found that certain therapists get extremely upset if a writer (i.e. me) tells the public what these therapists actually *do*, in reasonably clear English. Perhaps they feel that if people get to know what their techniques are, those techniques will somehow lose their mystique. . . .

Anyway, try and keep a sense of humour if you have to seek advice about a sexual difficulty. In sex (as in many other areas), laughter really is quite often the best medicine.[1]

Sex therapy from your own doctor

If you live in a part of the world where the tradition of having a family doctor is still strong, then you're lucky. I've already indicated that a good general practitioner can be a great help in referring you to a clinic where you can get sensible advice. In addition, your family doctor can himself (or herself) be extremely valuable in giving you reassurance and commonsense advice about sex problems. It's no longer true that GPs aren't interested in this area of medicine: many of them are, and are only too keen to give whatever help they can. A few have had extensive training in sexual medicine.

However, it is a fact that in the UK and some other countries a family doctor has only about *five minutes* for each patient seen in his surgery and it can be a bit difficult for him to spare a lot more time than this on a regular basis. Most doctors will do their level best to *make* time for this sort of problem, but naturally there is bound to be a minority who are not interested. Obviously, if this is so, you should try and find yourself a new doctor.

In summary, your GP should be able to do vaginal examinations with a speculum; he can also advise on contraception and prescribe contraceptives; treat depression (often a potent factor in sex problems); and investigate and treat common infections of the sex organs. As I've said, he should also have a good idea of what facilities (if any) are available for treating sexual disorders at nearby hospitals. Altogether, not a bad person to have on your side.

[1]Readers' Digest, 1953.

Masters–Johnson treatment

Developed by the famous US sex researchers, Virginia Johnson and Dr William Masters, this system of treatment has revolutionised sexual medicine. Unfortunately, the *full* Masters–Johnson treatment involves a period of residential therapy for couples at St Louis, Missouri – obviously outside most people's financial reach. (However, if you're well-off by all means go and see them.)

But Masters' and Johnson's ideas have nevertheless had an immense influence on the way sex disorders are treated throughout the world, and a number of doctors and psychologists are using modified versions of Masters–Johnson therapy, particularly for impotence (i.e. failure of erection), premature ejaculation (where the 'squeeze technique' has now cured many men), ejaculatory incompetence, vaginismus and female loss of desire.

In general, Masters–Johnson therapy depends on careful exploration of the couple's problems (ideally using both a male and female therapist), followed by a period of time during which they abstain from what for them are the rather stressful demands of intercourse. During this time, they are asked to engage in what's called sensate focus – which basically just means cuddling up together, naked and warm, *but with no actual sexual activity*. The general idea is to produce a tender and loving atmosphere – and perhaps to re-create the early days of the couple's courtship.

Only after at the very least some days of sensate focus do the couple move on to sexual pleasuring and petting – with no attempt at intercourse, or indeed at *any* sexual goals at all. The whole objective of this period is just for the couple to enjoy warm, loving and relaxed caresses together.

This period of adjustment helps them to recover their self-confidence – or perhaps gain it for the first time. Only after this has been done do they move on to the specific technical manoeuvres prescribed by the therapists, such as the 'squeeze technique'. And only after that do they return to having intercourse.

Masters–Johnson type therapy in modified form is provided by some GPs and by quite a lot of Family Planning Clinics. In the UK, the National Marriage Guidance Council is training a number of male and female therapists in the method. It's also available from a handful of hospitals.

'Non-residential' Masters–Johnson therapy of this sort is now spreading through the world and can give very good results. For instance, in cases of premature ejaculation ('hair-trigger trouble'), a well-motivated couple have something like a 90 per cent chance of cure.

Behaviourist treatment

One of the major schools of modern psychological medicine is behaviourism. Psychiatrists and psychologists who follow this school believe that there's no point in digging around too deeply in a patient's subconscious: they hold that what matters is the symptom – and that if you treat and cure the symptom itself, all will be well. (Freudians and psychoanalysts disagree violently with this idea, because they believe that if you only cure a patient's symptom, then his inner conflicts will make him produce another one.)

Behaviour therapy relies on using straightforward 'no-nonsense' techniques to abolish the symptoms of psychological illness (including sex problems) without worrying too much about what's causing the symptom.

Many people are familiar with at least some of these 'behaviour techniques' through seeing films like *A Clockwork Orange*: that was the one in which a violent young man was 'de-conditioned' against violence by showing him violent films – and at the same time making him sick (yuk!).

Obviously, *that* particular technique isn't used in the treatment of sex problems (though people with anti-social sex deviations, like child-molesting, do sometimes consent to undergo a similar 'de-conditioning' process).

When treating the common sex problems like impotence and loss of desire, behaviourists use much gentler methods to try to abolish the basic symptom. For example, techniques used include group therapy, helping people to 'shape' their sexual fantasies, rôle-playing, carrying out sexual 'tasks', and very often exposure to erotic material (pictures, films, books, tape recordings) so as to condition them to respond to sexual stimulation.

Behaviourist psychologists and psychiatrists may encourage patients to masturbate to specific fantasies – a simple but effective system pioneered by the American Dr Lo Piccolo. Or they may try a useful manoeuvre called 'systematic desensitisation'.

This technique was mainly developed at St Bartholomew's Hospital, London (a fine institution, where my wife trained as a nurse). It depends on helping patients to relax while they imagine various situations, starting with ones that only worry them a little – and later moving up to the big worries (like having sex).

This kind of treatment developed because some years ago it became clear that people with various types of phobia and anxiety states could be treated by inducing them to relax while imagining the situations in life that they feared most. It then became apparent that this principle could be applied to certain common sexual disorders in which the main problem (though he or she may not know it) is the person's intense anxiety about sexual intercourse: as we've seen, it's anxiety that makes the impotent man's penis droop or the vaginismal woman's vagina tighten up.

So, doctors and psychologists working in this field began to get patients to lie on a couch and imagine themselves in a sexual situation. As anxiety built up, various means were used to create relaxation – most commonly the slow injection of a short-acting sedative into a vein. After perhaps half a dozen sessions of such therapy, many patients were completely cured. Desensitisation therapy isn't a cure-all – but it can certainly help quite a few people with sex problems.

Psychoanalysis and other Freudian treatments

The idea of psychoanalysis is to explore the conflicts in the subconscious which so often produce tensions – and hence all sorts of psychological symptoms – including sexual ones.

The subconscious is usually explored in the way you've seen in thousands of cartoons: with the patient lying on a couch and talking (a) about whatever drifts into his mind, and (b) about his dreams. The psychoanalyst sits on a chair – normally out of sight of the patient – and takes notes; he refrains from making judgements or issuing instructions, and simply helps the patient to interpret his thoughts and dreams.

It's a common myth that the Western world boasts a vast supply of psychoanalysts and that huge numbers of patients are treated by them. Indeed, outside the USA it's widely believed that a large proportion of Americans are 'in analysis'!

In fact, this is nonsense. Even in the United States – which has more psychiatrists than any other country on Earth – there are only 25,400 psychiatrists of *all* types – about one for every 10,000 people. And the number of actual analysts is far, far less. In Britain, Canada, Australia, New Zealand and other Commonwealth countries, there are scarcely *any* psychoanalysts outside the major cities. Each psychoanalyst can only treat a surprisingly small number of patients, because:

★Full analysis takes a patient two to four years;
★It involves each patient in several sessions of an hour or more a week – so that each analyst may well have only a dozen or so patients under his care in (say) a thirty-six hour working week.

218

So I wasn't surprised when I heard recently that a well-known psychoanalyst had only ever treated about 100 patients in his entire professional life of forty years!

Clearly, therefore, full analysis is only for the very few (mainly the rich few). Even in the US, it's quite difficult to obtain unless you're well off and live in the large Eastern cities or California. In Britain, there are very few analysts, and most of them are concentrated in the South-East – even there, full analysis, as I've said, is likely to be very expensive. You are unlikely to obtain it on the NHS, though it can be done occasionally.

Having said all that, some form of psychoanalytic therapy may help patients with sexual problems dating from early childhood, particularly those in which there have been deep conflicts with the mother or father.

When I say 'some form of psychoanalytic therapy', I mean that since *full* analysis is so expensive and time-consuming, many therapists try to offer a greatly-modified form, in which the periods of treatment are very much shorter – and may indeed be taken in groups.

This kind of briefer, and less expensive, psychoanalytically-orientated therapy may well help you if you feel that your sex hang-ups are closely bound up with your feelings about your parents. Most people agree that it's quite nice (and quite therapeutic) to pour out all your troubles to someone. What a pity that the parish priest is no longer the force he was. . . .

The 'Balint' or 'Seminar' method

Very popular in the United Kingdom, parts of Ireland and some Commonwealth countries, this is a simple and commonsense form of psychotherapeutic counselling developed by doctors who worked with the late Dr Michael Balint, a distinguished general practitioner, who was Hungarian-born but later moved to Britain.

Basically the idea is for the doctor to try to use a relatively short series of interviews with the couple to help them see the causes and possible solutions of their problems. Very often, the relationship (whether it's hostile or friendly) that they make with him can actually be used to help them find a way through their difficulties. If a case is particularly difficult, the doctor will seek aid by discussing it with colleagues whom he meets at a regular seminar session.

Perhaps the most significant discovery of the Balint school of sex therapy has been the fact that vaginal examination of the woman patient who has a sexual problem often produces a 'moment of truth' in which she feels able to reveal information that points to the hidden causes of her difficulties.

Balint psychotherapy is largely practised by women doctors, and tends to work very well with women patients, specially those with vaginismus. So far, I don't personally believe that there is a lot of evidence that male difficulties such as impotence and premature ejaculation respond quite so well to it.

In Britain and various Commonwealth countries, some hundreds of doctors have been trained or are in training in the method. Most of them work in Family Planning Clinics, but some practise outside. If you want to see a Balint-trained doctor outside a clinic, fees are usually moderate, compared with what plumbers or electricians charge. In the UK *don't* contact a doctor directly: the correct procedure is to get a referral note from your GP – if he doesn't know of a Balint-trained doctor, he can write to the Institute of Psychosexual Medicine (see next chapter).

Marriage guidance counselling

Where the main element of a sex problem seems to be the basic *personal* relationship between the man and the woman, then it may well be worth seeking Marriage Guidance Counselling. In Britain, we have that splendid organisation the National Marriage Guidance Council, and similarly-named organisations have sprung up in various Commonwealth countries such as Australia and New Zealand.

In all these countries, the MGC has done a lot to help couples (married and unmarried) with sex problems to talk their difficulties out, especially where there's a background of family strife. Some counsellors are doctors, but most aren't.

A new departure has been the introduction of Masters–Johnson sex therapy (see above), but only a small number of MGC therapists are under training so far.

Hormone therapy

Nearly all patients with a sex problem vaguely hope that hormone injections or tablets will help them. But I'm afraid that this is rarely so – except in the unusual circumstances where someone is suffering from a real hormone deficiency.

I must report that at the beginning of the 1980s, Dr Spark and his colleagues in Boston, Mass., reported that they had found thirty-seven out of 105 impotent men with low male sex hormone levels – and that thirty-three of these were helped by hormone therapy.

Also, in a very small number of men, impotence is due to excessive production of a fairly recently-discovered hormone called 'prolactin'. Treatment with an 'anti-hormone' called bromocryptine will usually cure them.

Otherwise, hormone therapy for men whose potency is flagging is regarded by most doctors as a complete waste of time unless there is genuine evidence of male hormone deficiency. Indeed, some physicians do think that giving a man male hormones could possibly damp down his pituitary gland (which responds to *low* levels of male hormone through a 'feed-back' mechanism) and so have a counterproductive effect. Other doctors do give injections of male hormones, often in the hope that they will have some placebo – that is, psychological – action.

However, in Britain, there has been renewed interest in hormone therapy for *women* recently – largely as a result of the work of the doctor in charge of 'The Clinic' at the Bradford Group of Hospitals. He claims that 'frigidity' (either lifelong or recent) can be helped by giving a weekly injection of male (not female) hormone for four weeks, followed by male hormone tablets if the response is good.

Note that there can be side-effects: acne, hair on the face, a husky voice, and interference with periods. If you want to try this therapy, it's probably best to start with your GP, who may perhaps be willing to adminster it to you rather than refer you elsewhere.

Hypnotism

Hypnotism is now quite often used to treat sex disorders, especially where there is a strong element of anxiety. Avoid non-medically qualified hypnotists, e.g. those who advertise in the local paper. Your doctor will probably know of another physician who practises hypnotism – a few GPs carry it out in their surgeries, and quite a lot of psychiatrists try it. It's not usually a magic remedy – but it's worth bearing in mind.

Treatment by a urologist

Urologists (or urological surgeons) are doctors whose field includes, among other things, the surgery of the male genital organs. Urologists haven't been involved in very much sex therapy in the past, and they tend to get rather fed up when large numbers of impotent men are sent to them – since impotent men only very rarely have anything wrong with their genital organs.

But urologists can help sex problems in a few ways:

(i) carrying out circumcision on a man whose foreskin won't go back;

(ii) inserting a plastic splint into the penis of one of those few men who become impotent for *physical* reasons;

(iii) where possible, using surgery to correct abnormalities of the penis such as hypospadias (a common condition in which the 'pipe' opens onto the underside of the penis, and not the tip):

(iv) providing a plastic testicle for 'cosmetic' purposes where one is missing;

(v) treating Peyronie's disease or 'bent penis'.

If you want to see a urologist, there should be one at a hospital not too far from you: in Britain, Ireland and many Commonwealth countries you'll need a letter of referral from your GP.

Note: there's a new invention which a urologist can instal in certain men with impotence – especially those whose problem is due to physical causes, such as injury. This is an inflatable splint *inside the penis*. A US invention, it's blown up by pressing a little 'bulb' which the surgeon places inside the scrotum (the pouch which holds the man's testicles).

I have to say that this is *not* a minor operation – and the possibilities of things going wrong (for instance, infection) are appreciable – so you should think for a very long time before undergoing this kind of surgery. It's expensive too. Some North American urologists have recently tried to treat impotence by surgery on the blood vessels of the penis, but at present this is a *very* uncertain technique.

Treatment by a gynaecologist

Gynaecologists (or gynaecological surgeons) are doctors who deal specifically with disorders of the female genitals; usually they practise obstetrics as well. Until recently, they haven't been very much orientated towards sex problems, but that's changing fast. However, a woman is bound to find that some gynaecologists are very interested in these problems and others aren't.

In the US, you can consult any gynaecologist you like. But in Britain, Ireland and many Commonwealth countries, in order to consult a gynaecologist, you need a letter from your family doctor. Normally, GPs refer patients to the gynaecologist at the local NHS hospital. However, in the UK a disquieting trend recently has been that women have got so fed up with the long delays of the NHS (sometimes four or five months for an appointment) and the short time available for consultation that they're tending more and more to consult private gynaecologists. If you do this, you should certainly take your GP's advice on whom to consult.

Gynaecologists are obviously best at treating physical disorders of the female genital organs, ranging from uncommon structural abnormalities to genital tract diseases, infections, and hormone problems. *Some* have now taken advanced training in psychosexual medicine – but not nearly enough of them!

Treatment by the 'SAR' method

'SAR' stands for 'sexual attitude restructuring'. It's a fairly new form of therapy which originated in California and which has come into prominence in the US, Canada, Britain and other large Commonwealth countries in very recent years. The theory behind the method is that most of us – whether doctors or patients – must inevitably have certain sexual inhibitions.

So SAR groups meet in weekend seminars at which therapists and patients are shown explicit videotapes which depict almost every conceivable form of sexual activity.

This produces a considerable sense of shock in many therapists and almost all patients, especially as it is the custom to show two different videotapes simultaneously on adjoining sets! Between tapes the participants discuss what has been shown and their own reactions to it. Doctors who are strongly in favour of this method claim that these weekends have helped them greatly in the understanding of their patients, and that the patients themselves benefit considerably from the 'liberating' effect of the process.

The SAR method has attracted a good deal of criticism, together with inevitable and unwelcome attention from the sensational popular press. But it has already established itself at several medical schools, and it may well gain further ground if it can show that its results are really impressive.

Surrogate partner treatment

Treatment with partners provided by the clinic (who are often paid for their services) has inevitably attracted enormous criticism – particularly as the whole thing seems a bit too akin to prostitution for some people's tastes! However, it's often forgotten that Masters and Johnson used volunteer partners (including at least one sympathetic female doctor) in their pioneering work on helping people with crippling sex difficulties. Surrogate therapy is clearly of use only where a patient has no current sexual partner – or perhaps an uncooperative or totally inept one.

I make no comment about the moral issues involved. But I'd stress that because of the legal difficulties, only a few clinics (mainly in the US) now offer surrogate partners. In the UK, there is just one – see next chapter – which openly offers surrogates – though I suspect from what I've heard that a few more do so discreetly.

Self-help treatment

Partly because of the difficulties and expense of getting treatment, there's been a bit of a move to self-help sex therapy in recent years, particularly in the USA. Indeed, for obvious reasons, self-help is becoming a big thing in many fields of medicine. In Britain, because of dissatisfaction with NHS treatment, some feminist groups are trying to follow the example of their American sisters and set up facilities for examining and treating each other for thrush and similar minor infections.

Also important for women who find that cystitis and recurrent bladder and vaginal infections screw up their sex lives, is the system of treatment pioneered by the famous Angela Kilmartin and her U&I Club. Unfortunately the Club itself is no longer active but you can find out all about her admirable work from her self-help books and booklets. Write to Hamlyn Paperbacks, Astronaut House, Feltham, Middlesex, UK, if you'd like more details. In the USA, write to Warner Books, 666, Fifth Avenue, New York, NY 10103.

Finally, an encouraging development of the last few years has been the emergence of feminist groups in which women who have not yet reached orgasm meet and discuss their problems. This work was pioneered in the US by Betty Dodson of New York and Eleanor Stephens of Berkeley, California – and later in the UK by Anne Hooper of London. With the help of masturbation and the use of vibrators, a lot of these women do eventually find that they can reach a climax. Addresses of these 'Women's Pre-Orgasmic Workshops' and 'Bodysex Workshops' (I'm not responsible for the names) are in the next chapter.

CHAPTER TWENTY-ONE

Where To Get Help And Sex Advice

Keep trying and don't give up • *Help in the UK* • *Help in Eire* •
Help in the USA • *Help in Canada* • *Help in Australia and New
Zealand* • *Help in other countries* • *Useful books and cassettes.*

Keep trying and don't give up!

A lot of people who need a bit of advice or counselling about sex
difficulties find – to begin with – that it's still not all that easy to get
help. (I still get quite a few letters from people who've been
assured by nurses – or even by doctors – that 'no treatment is
available for this sort of thing'.)

But don't be put off! If you live or work in any Western country,
then help and advice *are* available. You may have to travel a bit in
order to obtain it, and you may have to put yourself to some
inconvenience. (Obviously, if you're not willing to travel or to put
yourself to inconvenience, then you're not all that bothered about
sorting out your sex life, which is fair enough – as long as you
accept that fact.)

In short, if you're determined enough, you *can* get advice and
treatment. If you're in doubt, I'd suggest kicking off by asking
your family doctor if she or he knows where help is available. A
useful alternative is the Family Planning Association (or equivalent organisation) in your country.

Anyway, here's rather more detailed information, country by
country.

Help in the United Kingdom

In Britain, there's now a wealth of clinics offering advice of all
types on sexual matters. A recent survey which I conducted for
the medical journal *General Practitioner* showed that only in the
north of Scotland should there be any real difficulty in obtaining
help – which most of the time is free on the National Health
Service.

Much of the sex therapy work which is done in the UK is based
on the superb network of clinics set up by the Family Planning
Association in the 1960s and 1970s; the National Marriage Guidance Council too have set up a nationwide organisation of clinics

225

– in a small but increasing number of which it is now possible to obtain Masters–Johnson therapy.

Here are the main sources of sex therapy and plain ordinary advice available in the UK at the time of writing:

Family Planning Clinics: all family planning clinics will try to help with commonsense advice, but at the time of writing, specific therapy is available from the following FP clinics:

London: Raymede Health Centre, W10 (01-960 0942); Caryl Thomas Clinic, Harrow Weald (01-863 7004); Hampton Wick Clinic (an amazing name for connoisseurs of Cockney rhyming slang), Middlesex (01-977 6552); Finsbury Health Centre, EC1 (01-837 6363)

Sussex: Avenue House, Eastbourne (Eastbourne 27121)

Kent: Dudley Road Clinic, Tunbridge Wells (Tunbridge Wells 30002)

Surrey: Ashstead Clinic (Ashstead 72529); Croydon Clinic (01-684 2802); Weybridge Health Centre (Weybridge 48388); Woking FPC (Woking 4160)

Devon: Freedom Fields Hospital, Plymouth (Plymouth 68080)

Bucks: FPA Clinic, High Wycombe (High Wycombe 26666); Slough FPC (Slough 26875)

Herts: Hoddesdon FPC (Hoddesdon 66351/60864)

Cambridge: Town Hall FPC, Peterborough (Peterborough 51634)

Norfolk: Norwich FPC (Norwich 21872)

Notts: FPA House, Nottingham (Nottingham 40431)

Lancs: FPC, c/o Maternity Unit, Stockport (Stockport 483 8687); Family Planning Clinic, East Cliff, Preston (Preston 59344)

Liverpool: FPA, Gambier Terrace, Liverpool (Liverpool 709 1938)

Manchester: FPC, Palatine Road, Manchester (Manchester 434 3555)

Birmingham: Family Planning Service, Edgbaston Centres (Birmingham 454 5694)

Yorkshire: Sheffield FP Clinics (Sheffield 731661 and 26773); Brinsworth FPC (Rotherham 78249); Doncaster FPC (65071); Barnsley FPA (Barnsley 3989)

Humberside: Grimsby FPC (Grimsby 79246)

Cleveland: Cleveland FP Service (Stockton 66047)

Cumbria: Whitehaven FPC (Whitehaven 5551); Workington FPC (Workington 2244)

Edinburgh: Family Planning Centre (Edinburgh 322 7941)

Glasgow: Family Planning Centre (Glasgow 332 9144)

Important note: up-to-date information about all Family Planning Clinics offering advice and/or sex therapy can be obtained from the excellent Family Planning Information Service on 01-636 7866.

Marriage Guidance Council Clinics: all National Marriage Guidance Council clinics will try to help with the sexual aspect of marital difficulties, but the following clinics have especially trained staff.

South: Croydon (01-680 1944); Southampton (Southampton 29761); Kingston-upon-Thames (01-549 3318)

West: Bristol (Bristol 312316); Bath (Bath 65593); Oxford (Oxford 42960); Yeovil (South Petherton 40636); Bournemouth (Bournemouth 27545)

London: London MGC (01-580 1087)

Midland: Birmingham (Birmingham 643 1638); Burton on Trent (Burton 61697); Chesterfield (Chesterfield 31010); Coventry (Coventry 25863); Derby (Derby 49177); Hereford (Hereford 6023); Kettering (Northampton 34400); Leicester (Leicester 543011); Lichfield (Lichfield 52760); Northampton (Northampton 34400); Nottingham (Nottingham 57836); Rugby (Rugby 65675); South Warwicks (Leamington Spa 24899)

North-west: Manchester (Manchester 834 9163/4834); Preston (Preston 717597); Chester (Chester 42747)

North-east: Rotherham (Rotherham 77644); South Humberside (Grimsby 54392); Sheffield (Sheffield 20778); Bradford (Bradford 26096)

Northern Ireland: Belfast (Belfast 23454)

Note: Up-to-date information about Marriage Guidance Council treatment can be obtained from their HQ in Rugby (tel: 0788-65675).

A quite separate, but very worthwhile, organisation is the **Catholic Marriage Advisory Council**, 15 Lansdowne Road, London, W11.

Hospital Clinics: These addresses have all been sent to me by NHS authorities, and treatment at them is therefore free.

Scotland

Grampian Region: Therapy (including Masters–Johnson) at Royal Cornhill Hospital, Aberdeen

Fife Region: One clinic at Loughborough Road, Kirkaldy. Additional help available at Clinical Psychology Department, Dumfermline

Greater Glasgow Region: Four clinics: Glasgow FP Centre (non-specific approach) 332 9144; Duke Street Hospital (non-specific) 554 6267; Gartnavel Royal Hospital (behaviourist, M & J) 334 1734; Stobhill General Hospital (female hypnotherapy) 558 0111

Lothian Region: Six clinics: Astley Ainslie Hospital; Bangour Village Hospital; GP Centre, 18 Dean Terrace, Edinburgh; Royal Infirmary of Edinburgh; Lothian Marriage Counselling Service, 9A, Dundee Street, Edinburgh

Ayrshire and Arran Region: Treatment available by clinical MOs at FP clinics

Dumfries and Galloway Region: Sexual advisory service based on Crichton Royal Hospital. Some health centres staffed by specifically interested GPs

England

South Western Region: Exe Vale Hospital, Digby (multidisciplinary); Nuffield Clinic, Plymouth (M & J behaviourist); Shrublands Day Hospital, Torbay (behaviourist and advisory); Cambray FP Clinic, Cheltenham (M & J and Balint); Southmead Hospital (psychotherapy); Rikenel FP Clinic, Gloucester (Analytic and Hypnosis); Glastonbury Health Centre (Balint, M & J, and couple counselling); Cheltenham General Hospital Psychiatric OPD (behaviourist); Musgrove Park Hospital, Taunton, Yeovil Hospital and Bridgewater General Hospital (all Balint and M & J)

Wessex Region: Old Manor Hospital, Salisbury (patients seen by psychologists and nurse behavioural therapists); Seymour Clinic, Swindon (M & J); Knowle Hospital, Fareham (behaviorist and M & J); Hythe Hospital, Southampton (behaviourist and Balint); Central Health Clinic, East Park Terrace, Southampton (Balint and behaviourist)

SW Thames Region: St George's Hospital, Tooting (eclectic, based on M & J and Lo Piccolo); Netherne Hospital, Coulsdon (behaviourist, based on M & J)

NE Thames Region: The London Hospital, Department of Psychiatry; Antenatal Tower Block, North Middlesex Hospital; GP Clinic, Stuart Cres Health Centre; Enfield War Memorial Hospital; Moorfield Road Health Centre (all Balint mixed with M & J)

NW Thames Region: The Whittington Hospital FP Clinic; Finsbury Health Centre, Pine Street, EC1

East Anglian RHA: Riversdale Clinic, Westgate, Sleaford (Balint)

West Midland Region: Birmingham Maternity Hospital; Department of Psychiatry, Birmingham Medical School (both believed to be M & J)

Trent Region: Barnsley: seven sessions a month by a doctor and a senior clinical psychologist – details from Barnsley Health Authority. Doncaster: Doncaster Sexual Advisory Clinic recently closed owing to doctor's resignation; some patients seen by clinical psychologists at Doncaster Royal Infirmary.

Note: No replies were received to my enquiries from other NHS Regions.

Miscellaneous NHS or private clinics: many of the following are National Health Service, and therefore free. But check *first*, as private fees range up to £50 an hour.

Throughout the country: Institute of Psychosexual Medicine; contact headquarters c/o The Referrals Secretary, 10 Peterswood Hill, Ware, Herts – all treatment Balint-orientated;

Association of Sexual and Marital Therapists, Whiteley Wood Clinic, Woofindin Road, Sheffield

London: Lincoln Memorial Clinic for Psychotherapy, SE1 (01-928 7211); Margaret Pyke Centre, W1 (01-580 3077); Psychosexual Clinic, University College Hospital, WC1 (01-388 0321); Institute of Behaviour Therapy, PO Box 4AR, London, W1A 4AR; West London Hospital, W6 (01-748 3441); London Centre for Psychotherapy, NW3 (01-435 0873); Psychosexual Clinic, St Olave's Hospital, SE16 (01-237 622 ext. 5225); Maudesley Hospital, SE5 (01-703 63333); York Clinic, Guy's Hospital, SE1 (01-407 7600 ext. 3428); Psychiatric Department, The London Hospital, E1 (01-247 5454); Marriage Research Centre, Central Middlesex Hospital, NW10 (01-965 5733 ex 277); Psychosexual Clinic, Kentish Town, NW5 (01-267 4411); Marital Difficulties Clinic, Royal Free Hospital, NW3 (01-794 0500); Women's Sexuality Therapy, Ravenscroft Park, W6 (01-748 1935); Forum Clinic, c/o 2 Bramber Road, W14 (01-385 6181); Hammersmith Hospital, W12 (01-743 2030); Women's Psychosexual Problem Clinic, Elizabeth Garrett Anderson Hospital, NW1 (01-387 2501 ex 57); Marie Stopes Clinic, W1 (01-388 0622); London Institute for the Study of Human Sexuality, SW5 (01-373 0901); The Tavistock Clinic, London WC1.

Hampshire: Alton Marital/Sexual Dysfunction Clinic, Alton (Alton 84001)

Dorset: Herrison Hospital Psychology Department, Dorchester (Dorchester 3661 ex 373)

Lancashire: Clinical Psychology Dept, Oldham (Oldham 6240420 ex 34); Queen's Park Hospital, Blackburn (Blackburn 55222); Larkhill Health Centre, Blackburn (Blackburn 63611); Psychology Department, Lancaster Moor Hospital (Lancaster 65241)

Birmingham: Counselling Centre, Carrs Lane (Birmingham 6436363); Clinical Psychology Dept. Highcroft Hospital (Birmingham 378 2211 ex 4307)

Manchester: Psychiatric Dept. University Hospital of South Manchester (Manchester 445 8111); Sex Dysfunction Clinic, Withington Hospital (Manchester 445 8111)

Humberside: P-S Clinic, Parkinson Avenue, Scunthorpe (Scunthorpe 3463)

Hertfordshire: Hill End Hospital, St Alban's (St Alban's 51153)

Essex: Psychology Department, Goodmayes Hospital, Ilford (01 590 6060 ex 46); Claybury Hospital, Woodford Bridge (01-504 7171)

Avon: Psychology Department, Barrow Hospital, Bristol (Long Ashton 3162); Bristol Royal Infirmary, Bristol (Bristol 22041)

Leicestershire: P-S Clinic, Woodland Day Hospital, Narborough (Narborough 3265)

Cheshire: Psychosex Clinics, Chester and Merseyside (Both Chester 27161)

Durham: P-S Clinic, Department of Obstetrics and Gynaecology, Shotley Bridge General Hospital (Consett 503456 ex 164)

Yorkshire: Sex Dysfunction Clinic, Royal Infirmary, Bradford (Bradford 42200); Doncaster Area Psychological Service (Doncaster 66666); Sex Dysfunction Clinic, Woodsley Health Centre, Leeds (Leeds 444831); Marital and Sex Difficulties Clinic, Whiteley Wood Clinic and Hallamshire Hospital, Sheffield (Sheffield 30391)

Edinburgh: Andrew Duncan Clinic, Royal Edinburgh Hospital (Edinburgh 447 2022 ex 414)

Specific Masters and Johnson Clinics (all NHS):
Doncaster Royal Infirmary
Claybury Hospital (Woodford)
Carlton Hayes Hospital (Leicester)
Guy's Hospital
St George's Hospital (London)
Whithington Hospital (Manchester)
Warneford Hospital (Oxford)
Rochford General Hospital (Essex)
Whiteley Wood Hospital (Sheffield)
Knowle Hospital (Hampshire)

Surrogate therapy clinics: the only clinic in the UK which openly admits to using surrogates – i.e. therapists who have sex with patients is the Institute for Sex Education and Research, 40 School Road, Birmingham, B13 9SN.

Dr Martin Cole (who is not a medical doctor) is the head of this organisation. He has just claimed highly successful results for his first 150 patients, some of whom he has treated personally.

Youth advisory centres: although this book is *not* intended for young people, it's worth knowing that vast numbers of younger men and women are seen by the network of Brook Advisory Centres. Similar clinics are now run by many enlightened Local Authorities – look up the Local Authority in your phone directory and find the number of the Youth Advisory Centre. Here are some useful addresses:

Brook centres:

Birmingham: York Road (Birmingham 455 0491); Aston Student Health Centre (Birmingham 359 3611 ex 299); City Centre (Birmingham 643 5341); Handsworth (Birmingham 544 7553); Saltley (Birmingham 328 4544)

Bristol: Clifton (Bristol 36657)
Cambridge: Clarendon Street (Cambridge 55003)
Coventry: Coventry and Warwickshire Hospital (Coventry 412627)
Edinburgh: Gilmore Place (Edinburgh 229 5320)
London: Tottenham Court Road (01-323 1522); St Bartholomew's Hospital (01-323 1522); Walworth (01-703 9660); Lewisham Hospital (01-703 9660); Kennington (01-226 5358)
Liverpool: Gambier Terrace (Liverpool 709 4558)

Other youth advisory centres:
Battersea YAC (01-720 9409)
London YAC, Kentish Town (01-267 4792); Westminster YAC (01-969 3825); Young People's Clinic, Haringey (01-444 9754); Beckenham YAC (01-650 0125)
As other YACs are set up, their numbers should be available from local town halls.

If in doubt, ring the headquarters of the Brook Advisory Services at 01-580 2991.

Women's pre-orgasmic groups: contact Anne Hooper, c/o Women's Sexuality Workshop, 58 The Pryors, East Heath Road, London NW3.

Venereal disease: contact any of the 220 genito-urinary clinics which form Britain's superb (and totally confidential) anti-VD network. Just ring the nearest large hospital, and ask for the time and place of the next 'Special Clinic'.

Gay counselling: a wide range of counselling services for gays or bisexuals is now available. Begin by ringing the Albany Trust (01-222 0701) or London Gay Switchboard (01-837 7324).

Help in Eire

It's still not easy to get sex advice in the Republic, but a surprising number of doctors and indeed priests are now taking a very enlightened attitude to sex and sex problems.

For more specific information, contact the Irish Family Planning Association at the wonderfully apt address of 14 Mountjoy Square, Dublin, or try the Marriage Counselling Service at 24 Grafton Street, Dublin. And specifically for Catholics, there is the Catholic Marriage Advisory Council, All Hallows College, Drumcondra, Dublin, 9.

Help in the US

It's recently been estimated that there are now about 3,000 people calling themselves 'sex therapists' in the USA – and that only about 100 of them are properly trained! As fifteen hours of sex therapy has been known to cost up to $4,000, be careful who you go to.

231

In practice, large numbers of universities and medical schools now have entirely reputable departments specialising in sex therapy. And here's a list of outstanding and nationally-famous physicians and psychologists who can be contacted:

Dr and Mrs William E. Masters; Reproductive Biology Research Foundation, St Louis, Missouri

Dr Helen Singer Kaplan; Human Sexuality Program, Payne Whitney Clinic, New York Hospital – Cornell Medical Center, NY

Professor Harold Lears; Human Sexuality Program, Mount Sinai School of Medicine, NY

Dr Bernard Zilbergeld; Human Sexuality Program, University of San Francisco, Ca; 6209, Buena Vista Avenue, Oakland, Ca.

Professor Benjamin J. Sadock, Professor Harold I. Kaplan and Professor Alfred M. Freedman; New York Medical College, Flower and Fifth Avenue Hospitals, New York, NY

Dr Jay Mann; VA Hospital, Palo Alto, Ca.

Professor Jon K. Meyer; Johns Hopkins University School of Medicine, Baltimore, Maryland

Dr Leslie Lo Piccolo, San Francisco, Ca.

Dr Lawrence Pervin; Department of Psychology, Livingston College, Rutgers University, New Brunswick, NJ

Professor John Paul Brady; University of Pennsylvania School of Medicine, Philadelphia, Pa.

Dr Sandra Leiblum; Sexual Counselling Service, College of Medicine of New Jersey, Piscataway, NJ

Jay Haley, MA; Family Therapy Research Unit, Philadelphia Child Guidance Clinic, Philadelphia, Pa.

Dr Andrew M. Mattison; Clinical Institute for Human Relationships, 3821 4th Avenue, San Diego, Ca.

Professor Virginia Sadock; Metropolitan Hospital, New York, NY

Dr David H. Barlow; Department of Psychology, State University of New York, Albany, NY

Professor Philip M. Sarrell; Department of Obstetrics, Gynaecology and Psychiatry, Yale University

Dr Bernard Apfelbaum; Director, Berkeley Sex Therapy Group, 2614 Telegraph Avenue, Berkeley, Ca.

Dr David P. McWhirter; Department of Psychiatry, School of Medicine, University of California, La Jolla, Ca.

Dr Harold I. Lief; Professor of Psychiatry, Director of Marriage Council of Philadelphia, Pa.

Dr Carol R. Ellison, 2938 McClure Street, Oakland, California

Dr Lonnie Barbach, Department of Psychiatry, University of California, San Francisco, Ca.

Dr Arnold A. Lazarus, Director, Multimodel Therapy Institute, Kingston, NJ

Dr Enid H. Campbell, Department of Psychology, Trenton State College, Trenton, NJ

Dr Michael A. Perelman, Chief of Training, Institute for Behaviour Therapy, New York, NY

Dr Albert Ellis, Executive Director, Institute for Rational-Emotive Therapy, New York, NY

Dr Richard A. Stein, Director, Cardiac Exercise Laboratory and Medical Service, State University Hospital, Brooklyn, NY

Even if one of the above experts cannot personally help you, he or she can direct you to someone who can.

Further information on sex therapy and sex advice generally can be obtained from:

The International Planned Parenthood Federation, 105 Madison Avenue (30th Street), New York, NY

The American Association of Sex Educators, Counselors and Therapists, One, East Wacker Drive, Suite 2700, Chicago, Ill.

Your local Family Service Agency or Community Mental Health Center

The American Association for Marital and Family Therapy, 924 West Ninth Street, Upland, California, 91786

The American Association of Marriage and Family Counselors, 225 Yale Avenue, Claremont, California, 91711

Help in Canada

Again, a number of universities and medical schools are setting up sex/marital therapy programs.

Useful addresses include:

Family Services, PO Box 224, Richmond Hill, Ontario

Marriage Counselling, United Church House, 85 St Clare Ave East, Toronto 7, Ontario

Family Life Education Council, 120–13 Avenue SE, Calgary, T2G 183

Family Service Association of Edmonton, 9919 – 106 Street, Edmonton, T5K 1E2

Family Service Association of Metropolitan Toronto, 22 Wellesley Street East, Toronto, M4Y 1G3

Family Service Bureau, 1801, Toronto Street, Regina, S4P 1M7

Family Service Centre of Ottawa, 119 Ross Avenue, Ottawa, K1Y 0N6

Family Services of Greater Vancouver, 1616 West 7th Avenue, Vancouver, V6J 1S5

Family Services of Winnipeg Inc., 287 Broadway Avenue, Winnipeg, R3C 0R9

Ontario Association of Family Service Agencies, 17 Dundonald Street, Toronto, M4Y 1K5

Ontario Association For Marriage and Family Therapy, (OAMFT), 3080 Yonge Street, Ste 5082, Toronto, M4N 2K6

Associated Marriage and Family Therapists, 203–235 Garry Street, Winnipeg

Look also in your local Yellow Pages under 'Marriage and Family Counsellors' (just before 'Martial Arts' and 'Massage Parlors'!) – bearing in mind that the many organisations now advertising in Canada vary from Christian to *extremely* commercial.

Help in Australia and New Zealand

A number of doctors are practising Masters and Johnson, or the more 'British-orientated' Balint-type psychotherapy. It's probably best to start by contacting your GP or the local Family Planning Clinic.

In **Australia**, contact:

The Australian Federation of Family Planning Associations, 500 George Street, Sydney, NSW, 2000

The Australian Marriage Guidance Council, 6 Morton Road, Burwood, Victoria, 3125

The Marriage Guidance Council of Western Australia, PO Box 217, W. Perth, 6005

In **New Zealand**, contact:

National Office, Marriage Guidance Council, PO Box 2728 (154 Featherston Street), Wellington

Family Planning Association, Inc., National Office, 218 Karanggahape Rd., Newton, Auckland, 1

Help in other countries

Facilities in other countries tend to be a bit limited, but you could usefully try:

South Africa: Department of Obstetrics and Gynaecology, University of Cape Town

National Council for Marriage and Family Life, 114 MBA Building, 413 Hatfield Street, Pretoria

Israel: Institute for Sex Education, Counselling and Therapy, Shelta Medical Centre, Tel Hashomer, Israel

Jamaica: Department of Psychological Medicine, University of the West Indies, Mona, St Andrew

Family Planning Board, 5 Sylvan Avenue, Kingston, 5

Bermuda: Bermuda Marriage Guidance Council, Bungalow Bay Cottage, Spanish Point, Pembroke

Kenya: Family Service Council of Kenya, PO Box 9464, Nairobi

Useful books and cassettes

I'd strongly recommend seeking *personal* advice and/or therapy rather than trying to use a book to cure any sex difficulties you may have, without professional help of some sort.

But if you simply *can't* obtain (or afford) professional advice, then some of the following books or tapes may be helpful to you and your loved one.

BOOKS There are some perfectly awful (and ludicrously inaccurate) books about sex on sale. But it's extremely hard for the average person to get adequate information about the subject without consulting books. Here are some I recommend.

(In Britain, if you write to the FPA Bookshop, 27–35 Mortimer Street, London, W1A 4QW they will send you their excellent and up-to-date book order list, which includes all of them.)

General
Conception, Birth, Contraception by Robert Demarest and Dr John Sciarra.

Everywoman: A Gynaecological Guide for Life by Derek Llewellyn-Jones.

ABZ of Love by Inge and Sten Hegeler.

Understanding Human Sexual Inadequacy by Fred Bellinveau and Lin Richter.

For the technically minded
Human Sexual Response by William H. Masters and Virginia E. Johnson.

Human Sexual Inadequacy by William H. Masters and Virginia E. Johnson.

For single women
The Sensuous Woman by 'J'.

CASSETTES   The 'relaxation cassettes' which are now produced by some behaviourist-orientated psychologists are really very good at helping people to unwind and generally become more 'laid back' in their approach to life.

In Britain, they're obtainable very cheaply from the Lifestyle Training Centre, 23 Abingdon Road, London, W8. Similar tapes are available in North America.

Relaxing but more sexually-orientated tapes – with explicit erotic advice – have been made by Anne Hooper and Philip Hodson, and are available from Audiogenic Ltd, PO Box 88, Reading, Berkshire.

Cassettes which give useful and stress-relieving advice about *sex in pregnancy* are available from the National Childbirth Trust, 9 Queensborough Terrace, London, W2.

And for couples for just want sexy stimulation, erotic cassettes of varying quality (and probably varying legality too) are available through sex shops. So too are video cassettes, though some are pretty awful—and could get you into difficulty with the law.

CHAPTER TWENTY-TWO

Keeping Sex Safe

(i)   INTRODUCTION

The troubles that sex (specially promiscuous sex) can bring ● *Cancer of the cervix*

(ii)   INFECTIONS

Avoiding sex infections ● *Thrush in men and women* ● *Trichomonas ('TV')* ● *Other vaginal infections* ● *Discharge due to other causes* ● *Gonorrhoea ('clap')* ● *Non-specific genital infection ('NSU')* ● *Syphilis* ● *Pubic lice ('crabs')* ● *Scabies* ● *Cystitis* ● *Herpes*

(iii)   ACCIDENTAL PREGNANCY

Avoiding unwanted conception ● *Which contraceptive?* ● *The Pill* ● *The Mini-Pill (progestogen-only Pill)* ● *The IUD (loop, coil, etc)* ● *The cap (diaphragm)* ● *The sheath (plus foam or pessary)* ● *The Shot* ● *The rhythm method* ● *Male sterilisation (vasectomy)* ● *Female sterilisation* ● *Abortion; the 'morning-after Pill', the 'morning-after coil', and 'menstrual extraction'.*

(i)   INTRODUCTION

The troubles that sex (specially promiscuous sex) can bring

The great tragedy about sex is that something so very, very beautiful can so often lead to distressing (even appalling) consequences – for instance:

★Marriage break-up
★Far less commonly, cancer of the cervix
★Sex infections
★Unwanted pregnancy

Incredibly, most sex textbooks (and most novels, videos and films which glorify sex) don't even mention these unfortunate consequences – or the fact that they're a good deal more likely to happen if you go in for *promiscuous* sex, with a good deal of partner-swapping and so on.

But, though I regard sex as one of the great joys of this life, I think that I really must devote this chapter to pointing out its potential dangers – dangers which so many people forget!

Marriage break-up: I won't dwell on the first of the four points I've mentioned above – marriage break-up. But anybody can see that 'playing around' and committing adultery is quite likely to be a cause of a broken marriage.

I do accept, however, that:

(a) Very often, the adultery is the symptom of the marriage trouble, rather than its cause;

(b) In today's permissive climate, some *avant-garde* couples do actually accept each other's 'outside relationships' quite happily (and may even encourage each other).

Cancer of the cervix (neck of the womb)

The link between cancer of the cervix and sex keeps hitting the headlines. And there's really no doubt that this type of cancer *is* more likely to occur if you've led an enthusiastic sex life – especially one with multiple partners.

On the other hand, the newspapers rarely mention that there are all sorts of other factors which seem (for obscure reasons) to play a part in causing cervical cancer. For instance, you're more likely to develop it if:

(a) You're poor;

(b) You've had several children;

(c) You live in certain geographical areas – like the North of England.

Heaven knows why these things should be, but the important thing to realise is that cancer of the cervix isn't *only* connected with sex. Women who have led extremely 'moral' sex lives can get it too.

Also, there are two other points which moralistic newspaper articles rarely mention:

★This tumour is actually much less common than people think – lung cancer claims sixteen times as many victims.

★Cancer of the cervix is almost entirely *preventable* if you have regular cervical smears. Every sexually active woman should have these tests regularly.

(ii)   INFECTIONS

Avoiding sex infections

As you know, love-making can pass on various infections. And infections of the sex organs are very common indeed. These days, a young woman is probably more liable to get thrush or tricho-monas (the two most frequent causes of vaginal discharge) than she is to get 'flu. Yet the surprising thing is that very few women (or men) seem to know anything at all about these disorders.

If you make love regularly (and sometimes even if you don't), you're very likely to acquire some sort of genital 'bug' at one time or another during your life, and this certainly applies to men as well as women.

Happily, most of these disorders are not of any great consequence, *provided they're diagnosed and treated fairly rapidly*. So, whether you're male or female, I advise you to look through this chapter and get to know the warning signs of 'trouble down below'. If symptoms arise in you or your partner, go and get treated by a doctor right away.

Thrush, in men and women

This is the commonest by far of all infections of the sex organs, and sometimes it seems as though practically all younger women get it these days.

Also known as Monilia or Candida, thrush is a tiny fungus. You can see what it looks like in Figure 43. Babies get it in the mouth and adult women usually get it in the vagina, where it causes pain, soreness, itching and a thick, white discharge (rather like blobs of cottage cheese). The diagnosis is confirmed by taking a vaginal swab and examining it under a microscope. In men, thrush may produce no symptoms at all – or else moderate soreness and redness of the penis, though this is relatively uncommon.

Where does thrush come from? Well, obviously it can come from other people's sex organs (or occasionally their mouths), but I hasten to add that if it suddenly attacks you this doesn't mean that your partner has been unfaithful. You see, a very high proportion of human beings go through life carrying thrush in their bowels. It's very easy for bugs from the intestine to get across the couple of inches of skin that separates the back passage from

239

FIG. 43

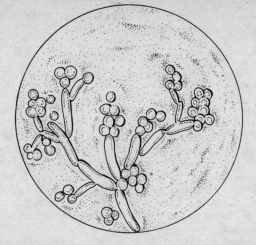

the vulva, and this is probably what has happened in many cases of vaginal thrush.

A woman is more likely to have an attack of thrush if she's on the Pill; if she's recently had a course of antibiotics; if she's pregnant; or if she's diabetic. If you get *recurrent* vaginal thrush, it's best to have your urine checked for sugar, just in case. This also applies to men who keep getting thrush infection round the foreskin.

TREATMENT   Thrush can often be absolute hell for a woman, but treatment is usually very simple indeed, since drugs like the commonly-used nystatin produce about 95 per cent cure if used properly. Instructions for medication should always be followed exactly, right to the end of the course, even if the symptoms have disappeared. In my opinion, the man should always be treated with anti-thrush cream too. (If he's *not* treated, he may re-infect the woman.)

Some doctors also give their patients nystatin tablets to take by mouth, with the object of wiping out the 'reservoir' of thrush in the bowel, and this practice may be useful in delaying recurrences. However, I'm afraid that a lot of women do go on getting thrush two or three times a year whatever therapy they have – though after a while they mysteriously seem to develop some immunity to the fungus.

In *recurrent* cases of thrush, it may be a help (since the fungus loves warmth and moisture) to avoid:

FIG. 44

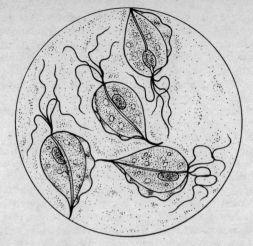

★tights (pantie-hose)
★nylon underwear
★hot baths (a cool shower is preferable to a warm bath)
      If you're desperate, it's worth trying the traditional
remedy of vaginal yogurt (p. 63).

Trichomonas ('TV')

The second most common cause of vaginal discharge is called
Trichomonas vaginalis. This is a rather cumbersome name, so the
bug is often known as 'TV' for short. (And you can imagine what
confusion *that* causes.)

You can see what trichomonas (pronounced tri-ko-MON-ass)
looks like in Figure 44. There are literally millions of people (both
men and women) going around with this tiny parasite in their
bodies. Indeed, some investigators have suggested that as many as
23 per cent of all women carry it, so it's not surprising that the
infection it produces is one of the most common disorders of our
time.

In women, trichomonas can cause a very painful and irritating
discharge. Usually, the fluid is yellowish or greenish and bubbly,
and some women complain that it has an offensive smell.

Characteristically, the opening of the vagina (the vulva) is
bright red and so sore that intercourse is pretty well impossible.
The diagnosis can be confirmed by taking a vaginal swab. And
sometimes 'TV' is found on a cervical smear – a 'cytotest' or Pap

smear for early detection of cancer of the cervix, described above.

In men, trichomonas may produce slight irritation within the urinary pipe, though most commonly the male partner of a woman with 'TV' has no symptoms at all. *But he will very probably be carrying the bug without knowing it.*

This fact is very important, because it means that unless a woman's husband or boyfriend is treated, he will keep on re-infecting her.

TREATMENT   Happily, treatment of trichomonas is pretty easy: traditionally, both partners are usually given a course of metronidazole (Flagyl) tablets to take by mouth three times a day for about a week or so. Flagyl can produce headaches and sickness, but these side-effects are unlikely to occur as long as the couple avoid alcohol during the period of treatment. They should also avoid intercourse, though (as in the case of vaginal thrush) the woman is most unlikely to be remotely interested in sex until this painful and trying condition has cleared up.

Newer drugs such as clotrimazole and nimorazole are now used if metronidazole fails.

Other vaginal infections and causes of discharge

Most women with a sore or itchy discharge have either thrush or trichomonas, but there are other causes of discharge. Let's look at them one by one.

Normal vaginal secretion   It's very common for young girls to think that they have a discharge when they haven't. Every healthy woman has quite a considerable flow of vaginal secretion, the quantity of which varies from day to day and at various times of the menstrual cycle.

The flow increases rapidly during sexual excitement, to provide lubrication for intercourse. The presence of the 'love-juices' is just a sign that everything in your reproductive equipment is functioning normally. As long as the fluid is either clear or milky, there's nothing to worry about.

Don't be concerned about the slight aroma of vaginal secretion either. The 'love juices' do have a definite perfume, the biological function of which (though you may be surprised to hear it) is to attract and excite the male. Women don't usually like this fragrance very much, but it isn't meant to appeal to *them*!

Unfortunately, intensive advertising of vaginal deodorants (particularly in the USA) has convinced a lot of women that they oughtn't to smell of anything except something like 'Cupid's

Quiver' or 'Fragrance of Raspberries' (there genuinely were vaginal deodorants with these names).

Those ideas are nonsense. If you want to go round with your pelvis smelling like the Perfumed Garden, then good luck to you – but it certainly isn't essential to your vaginal health. And bear in mind that you could easily get a sensitivity reaction from the chemicals in vaginal deodorants and scents.

Douching isn't necessary either. If you think you've got too much secretion, don't try to treat yourself, but see a doctor for proper examination and investigation.

Discharge due to other causes

DISCHARGE CAUSED BY FOREIGN BODIES   A common cause of a discharge in women is the presence of a foreign body, usually either a forgotten Tampax or a piece of tampon that has broken off. Objects introduced into the vagina while masturbating or during love play can also get temporarily 'lost' and set up an irritation that causes a discharge. This is why popping things inside (a curiously widespread practice) is really extremely unwise. It's OK to pop a clean vibrator in – provided you don't leave it there all week.

DISCHARGE CAUSED BY DISORDERS OF THE CERVIX   Various disorders of the neck of the womb (the cervix) may produce a discharge. The fluid tends in general to be 'catarrhal' in appearance, or brown, or blood-stained. If you get a brown or bloody discharge, it's *essential* that you are examined internally. The doctor may well be able to tell you exactly what's wrong simply by looking at the neck of the womb. Most often it will be a simple condition (like an erosion or a polyp) which a gynaecologist can usually deal with (e.g. by cautery), without even admitting you to hospital.

DISCHARGE CAUSED BY GERMS   Vaginal discharge can be due to the germs of gonorrhoea, a condition which we'll deal with in a moment.

Discharge may also be caused by bowel germs, and Masters and Johnson have pointed out that where a discharge persists and where investigations by means of vaginal swabs are negative, the patient should be discreetly asked about her sexual hygiene. Often it will turn out that she and her husband are having first rectal and then vaginal intercourse, without washing between, which is very unwise indeed – as explained earlier in this book.

243

DISCHARGE DUE TO 'NEW' INFECTIONS   Recent work, mainly in the USA, has shown that a number of cases of vaginal infection – some of which cause discharge – are due to germs which hadn't previously been recognised as possible causes of illness. For instance, a germ called Gardnerella has lately been indicated as a very common cause of a greyish, unpleasant-smelling discharge.

Fortunately, they can usually be cleared up with antibiotics. But this must be done promptly – for there's a risk that infections can affect the Fallopian tubes and cause sterility. Two of the germs – called 'chlamydia' and 'mycoplasma' – are discussed later in this chapter.

Gonorrhoea ('clap')

This sexual infection is very, very common, and its incidence has been rising rapidly in almost all Western countries since the 1950s. In Britain for example, it is now far more common than measles – though admittedly Britain's superb system of confidential VD clinics has kept the incidence much lower than in many other countries where gonorrhoea is practically reaching epidemic proportions. Indeed, in the last few years, there has been a slight, though probably temporary, fall in the UK's gonorrhoea figures. This doesn't seem to be happening in other countries, and in the USA, for example, the figures are still very high.

The disease is caused by a tiny germ called the gonococcus. Like other forms of VD, it is to all intents and purposes acquired only by having some form of sex contact with an infected person. This need not amount to actual sexual intercourse, and oral or rectal sex can pass it on.

Someone having sex with an infected partner is not absolutely certain to catch the disease, but the probability of getting it is generally reckoned to be around 70 per cent. The risk is reduced a little if the male wears a sheath.

In men, the symptoms are usually very clear cut. About two to four days after contact with a carrier of gonorrhoea, the man gets a *pus-like discharge* from his penis and finds that he has *severe burning pain on passing urine*. These symptoms are usually so unpleasant that he will have the sense to go and have medical treatment, which is just as well, since the late complications of gonorrhoea are not much fun. They include joint troubles, eye inflammation, painful swelling of the testicles and narrowing of the urinary pipe, so that the flow of urine is obstructed.

In women the early symptoms are far less definite. There may *possibly* be pain on passing water and a vaginal discharge but anything up to 50 per cent of infected women have no idea that anything is wrong until the disease is quite far advanced.

This 'hidden' gonorrhoea poses a very serious problem. There are tens of thousands of women around who have no idea that they are incubating the disease, and many of these infect a number of men before their symptoms finally become apparent. By this time, a lot of harm may have been done to their reproductive organs. Gonorrhoea causes severe inflammation of the Fallopian tubes and ovaries, the symptoms of which include lower abdominal pain, fever, menstrual irregularity and vaginal discharge.

This kind of *advanced* gonorrhoea can sometimes respond very badly to therapy, and the woman may finish up sterile or in a state of chronic ill health. I have worked in a tropical city where the incidence of gonococcal infection was very high, and in the port area especially there were thousands of unfortunate women whose pelvic tissues had been almost destroyed by this cruel disease. I sincerely hope that most countries don't find themselves in the same boat in a few years' time.

TREATMENT   The unpleasant complications of gonorrhoea need never occur *provided therapy is started early*. This treatment should preferably be given by a specialist in VD (not just by any old doctor), and in Britain and a number of other countries this means going to a 'Special Clinic' or 'Genito-urinary Clinic'.

The doctor at the clinic will do various tests and, if you prove to have gonorrhoea, he will simply give you an injection of penicillin, and ask you to come back later for further checks. Disregard those scare stories you've probably heard about having umbrella-like scraping devices pushed up the urinary passage. These instruments went out when penicillin came in many years ago!

Don't attempt to treat the condition yourself with 'borrowed' antibiotics. Unskilled treatment often fails: furthermore, it tends to lead to the emergence of *penicillin-resistant* strains of gonorrhoea. It was probably inadequate 'do-it-yourself' treatment of 'clap' during the Vietnam war which led to the spread of penicillin-resistant gonorrhoea from South-East Asia to the US and Australia – and thence to the rest of the world.

If you think you might possibly have gonorrhoea (or any other form of VD), please steer clear of sex until you've had your check-up, and get down to the clinic as fast as you can! Remember that if the infection is treated *early* it's certain to be cured. Even penicillin-resistant varieties can be cured if treated soon enough, because there are certain other drugs available.

Non-specific genital infection or urethritis (NSU)

The initials NSU indicate the condition called 'non-specific urethritis'. Maybe you've never heard of NSU, but at the rate it's increasing you certainly will do in the future.

In Britain and most Western countries, NSU is now by far the commonest form of VD (more common even than gonorrhoea) and it's rapidly becoming one of the biggest health problems we're facing. If we're not careful, before long the majority of young men will acquire NSU at some time in their lives.

NSU is mainly a disease complained of by males, rarely producing obvious symptoms in women, who are thought in most cases to carry it, rather than have actual symptoms. But in the last few years, I've become increasingly interested in the possibility that the germ responsible for NSU may be responsible for the many thousands of cases of tube infection and sterility which occur in women.

Which germs? At present, it seems likely that 'bugs' called 'chlamydia' are responsible for many cases. Others may be due to germs called 'mycoplasmas' – indeed, one gallant British VD expert has actually given himself NSU by putting mycoplasmas into his penis (brave man!).

Other germs may also be the cause of this alarmingly common infection, whose upsurge is undoubtedly linked to the promiscuous society of today.

What are the symptoms? In men NSU develops about a week or ten days after having sex. The symptoms are very similar to those of gonorrhoea (see above), but the discharge may persist for quite a long while despite treatment. Serious complications of NSU are fairly uncommon, but the disease still needs treating as soon as possible.

TREATMENT Tests are taken to rule out other forms of VD (especially gonorrhoea) and the patient is then given antibiotic tablets (usually tetracycline) to take by mouth. Repeat courses of tablets may be necessary, and follow-up visits to the clinic are always essential.

Syphilis

Syphilis is a very serious form of VD, caused by a germ called *Treponema pallidum*. The coming of penicillin (back in the 1940s) provided a complete cure for the disease, and it became very much less common after the Second World War. But then things started to go wrong. . . .

FIG. 45

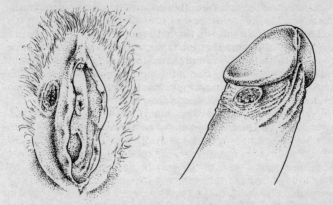

The incidence of syphilis has been rising very sharply in many parts of the world in recent years, though in Britain, and other countries with first class venereological services, it remains, thankfully, a fairly rare disease – except in very promiscuous male gays.

What are the symptoms of syphilis? Between ten and ninety days after having some form of sex contact with an infected person, the patient develops what's called a 'chancre' at the point of contact (most commonly, the penis or vagina). You can see what a chancre's like from Figure 45. It's a hard painless sore, which later develops into a 'raw spot'. In a woman, it may be hidden deep within the vagina and therefore go completely unsuspected.

If the patient doesn't get treatment, the chancre goes away after a variable period, and the unfortunate person usually assumes that he's cured. This is the devilishness of syphilis, because he or she usually *isn't*.

Within the next few weeks, secondary syphilis will probably develop. This usually takes the form of a slight skin rash or an outbreak of mouth or throat ulcers. These symptoms too go away in time – but the germs may very well be still in the body and twelve, fifteen or even twenty years later they may drive the patient mad, cause him intense pain, paralyse him, or destroy his heart and blood vessels.

Furthermore, any woman who has undetected syphilis will probably pass it on to her children, causing them terrible deformities, which is why routine blood tests for syphilis are done on all expectant mothers.

So, you can see that (if untreated) this disease is a pretty nasty customer.

Therefore, even though you don't seem to have any symptoms, if you have the remotest suspicion that you might have exposed yourself to the disease, and especially if you've had casual or commercial sex with someone, follow the advice given in the section on gonorrhoea and go straight to a doctor or – where available – the nearest 'Special Clinic' for tests.

Treatment for early syphilis, which usually means a course of high-dose penicillin injections – nearly *always* cures this once-terrible disorder.

Pubic lice ('crabs')

Sadly and unromantically, 'crabs' are very frequently picked up during intercourse. These little pubic lice produce intense itching in the pubic hair. Before very long the person can usually see the tiny crab-like creatures scuttling around, which is a pretty alarming experience!

You can go to your own doctor or to a 'Special Clinic' for treatment, which is by means of a skin application. As crabs are exceptionally infectious, see your doctor or the Clinic as early as possible; avoid sex at all costs until you've been cured.

Scabies ('the itch')

Another very common parasite, often passed on while having sex with an infected person (though acquirable without actual sex contact), is scabies.

This is a little mite, which burrows under the skin and produces most intense itching, often between the fingers – though it can be in any part of the body.

Happily, treatment by a doctor with an anti-scabies ointment or application will produce a complete cure.

Cystitis

Cystitis isn't strictly speaking an infection of the sex organs (the word 'cystitis' actually means inflammation of the bladder), but attacks of it are closely related to sexual activity and cystitis is quite uncommon in girls who are still virgins; hence the old name of 'honeymoon cystitis'.

248

The reason for this association with sex is quite simple. If you look at the drawings in the chapter on female anatomy, you'll see that the distance between the urinary opening (the urethra) and the back passage (anus) is very short indeed. Cystitis is usually caused by the common bowel germ (*E. coli*), which gets across the little space and finds its way up into the bladder. The germ can get across on sanitary towels, on the material of pants or as a result of lack of care in wiping the bottom after a bowel action; but in practice it does seem that it is likeliest to be transferred during the rough-and-tumble of love-making.

The symptoms of cystitis are: intense pain on passing water; having to rush to pass urine very frequently; having to get up at night; and sometimes passing blood.

Doctors used to regard the condition as being as unimportant as a cold, and indeed some older physicians still take this view, but since the 1960s it has been generally felt that if cystitis isn't properly investigated and thoroughly treated there is at least some risk of the infection leading on to kidney inflammation (pyelitis), with the possibility of long term damage to the woman's health.

So I would recommend that if you get a bout of cystitis you should take a pain-killer, drink plenty of fluids and *go to the doctor within twenty-four hours to ask him to send a mid-stream specimen of your urine (an MSU) to the local pathology lab*. From the result of this test, he'll be able to tell whether the antibiotic he is treating you with is the right one. Even though your symptoms go away, continue with your antibiotics for the full course and if possible go back to the doctor for a check MSU in about a month to ensure that all germs have gone.

Can I also mention that there are quite a lot of women who get recurrent cystitis, but whose mid-stream urines show *no* bowel germs. Why this should happen we just don't know. It could perhaps be that these episodes are due to germs that we don't know a lot about yet (like chlamydia and mycoplasma – see above). Or it could be that the problem is due to some sort of allergy – or to rather unskilled love-making on the part of the man.

Sufferers from recurrent cystitis should read Angela Kilmartin's famous 'self-help' book *Cystitis* (London: Hamlyn Paperbacks; New York: Warner Books).

Herpes

'Herpes genitalis' is one of the most alarming of the sex diseases which have come to the fore in recent years. In some places (like

San Francisco) it's caused a good deal of panic in the 1970s and 1980s.

It's a virus infection, which is passed on by sex, and which causes painful blistering round and in the sex organs. The blisters go away in roughly two weeks.

Unfortunately, the virus itself *doesn't* just go away. It lurks in the nerves which supply the sex organs – and re-emerges from time to time, again causing painful blistering.

More importantly, two points:

★There have been suggestions – so far unproven – that the virus could cause cancer of the cervix (see above). Women who've had herpes should certainly have very regular smear tests, even though there's no *proof* that herpes causes cancer.

★Tragically, some women who have been infected by herpes have given birth to 'herpes babies' – newborn infants who have been very seriously (and sometimes fatally) affected by these blisters. Fortunately, this disaster *can* be avoided by delivering the woman by Caesarian operation.

At the moment of writing, no *really* effective treatment for herpes is available. But happily, it does seem that new and efficient drugs are on the horizon – and possibly a vaccine too. Very promising results have been obtained with a drug called Acyclovir.

(iii)   ACCIDENTAL PREGNANCY

Avoiding unwanted conception

Safe sex has arrived at last – thanks to the Pill and other modern methods of contraception. In theory at least, *no one need ever have an unwanted baby again*. For the first time in human history, it's possible for a man and a woman to have a splendid time making love whenever they want to without any real danger of a pregnancy occurring.

Well, this is absolutely great, of course – or it ought to be. With completely safe contraception, there just shouldn't be any un-loved babies, shotgun marriages or abortions. Sex ought to be just sheer beauty and fun.

But unfortunately all the problems I've mentioned still exist. For hundreds of thousands of girls and women (married and unmarried) the act of love, which should be the most marvellous and satisfying of experiences, ends in the frustration and misery of an unwanted pregnancy.

Why is this?

There are two basic problems. The first is that, despite all the talk of a 'Permissive Society', most people are still fairly ignorant about sex and family planning.

I know that looking around at the casual way that films, books and television treat sex, one would think we were all experts at the love-making game. But the fact that our cinemas show daft films with titles like *Can You Keep It Up For a Week?* doesn't mean that the average boy or girl (or adult, for that matter) has more than the vaguest idea of what *safe* sex is all about – hence all those unwanted pregnancies.

Why are so many people so lamentably ignorant about how to make sex not only fun, but safe as well? Well, of course, it's because they haven't been told anything like enough about sex and its responsibilities either at school or at home.

The other reason, I think, is that people are so plain cussed! They won't believe that it'll happen to *them*. However much they know about unwanted pregnancy, they think that it's something that happens to other people.

The best example I know of this obstinate trait in the human mind is a study, done by a gynaecologist, of the occupations of 1000 women who'd asked him for abortions. Incredibly ninety-nine of them were nurses – and eighteen were women doctors! You could hardly think of a group who know more about avoiding unwanted pregnancy – yet they got pregnant.

So remember: it *can* happen to you – and unless you take precautions, IT PROBABLY WILL.

Which contraceptive?

What kind of contraception are you going to use? The choice is yours – not your doctor's nor anybody else's but *yours*.

Of course, your GP may tell you that a particular method of contraception wouldn't be good for you because of some medical reason; he might also have a personal preference towards some form of contraception – for instance, the great majority of doctors tend to be rather pro-Pill these days because it's so reliable. But unless there is some medical contra-indication, then *you* choose for yourself the method you want to use.

Do bear one thing in mind, though: the choice of a contraceptive is in many ways an emotional decision – and it's important not to let your emotional reactions to a particular form of birth control blind you to the facts.

What I mean is this: if a doctor describes the five basic 'temporary' forms of family planning to a couple, the doctor often sees the woman (or sometimes the man) shudder or wrinkle up her nose in disgust at the very mention of one or other of them. Yet sometimes it turns out in the long run that that particular method is actually the best one for them – and once they understand it and know how to use it, they may come to prefer it above the others.

So don't turn down a method out of hand just because your first reaction is one of revulsion. It's an odd thing that we do often feel initially repelled or worried by particular kinds of contraception, forgetting that these same methods are very enthusiastically accepted by other people.

Very commonly, for instance, women feel frightened or disgusted by the cap (or diaphragm). They may dislike the rubbery appearance or feel of it, or (very often) be scared of pushing something inside themselves. Yet the fact is that millions of other women world-wide are very happy indeed using the cap – and a few will even discreetly admit that they derive a certain amount of sensuous pleasure from slipping it in!

So though you must of course take your emotional reactions into account when choosing a method, *don't* turn any technique down until you've had a really good look at the possible advantages. It's amazing how many women who are scared stiff of going on the Pill become happily established on it once they realise what complete peace of mind it can give them.

What methods are available that will let you and your partner enjoy really satisfying and happy love-making without much risk of pregnancy?

Well, apart from female sterilisation and vasectomy, which are obviously pretty permanent, there are five good 'temporary' methods of contraception.

The choice is between the Pill, the Mini-Pill (progestogen-only Pill), the IUD, the cap and the sheath. How good are they at giving you effective protection against pregnancy while letting you enjoy love-making to the full?

Expressed as a percentage, the approximate safety factor with each of these methods is as follows:

Pill	100 per cent	Cap	96 per cent
Mini-Pill	98 per cent	Sheath	96 per cent
IUD	98 per cent		

252

Now let me just explain what these approximate percentages mean, because a lot of people don't understand them. I've known men to look at these figures and say, 'Hey, doc – does that mean that if I have it off 100 times using the sheath, my girl will get pregnant *four times*?'

The figures *don't* mean that at all. What they're intended to show is that:

If 100 couples use the Pill for a year, probably *none* of the women will get pregnant.

If 100 couples use the Mini-Pill for a year, roughly *two* women will get pregnant.

If 100 couples use the IUD for a year, again roughly *two* women will get pregnant.

If 100 couples use the cap for a year, roughly *four* women will get pregnant.

If 100 couples use the sheath for a year, then again roughly *four* women will get pregnant.

I must stress that word 'roughly', **because these figures really are only approximate**. While the safety rate of the Pill tends to be pretty nearly 100 per cent in all trials that have been conducted, results with the other methods of contraception vary very widely, depending on who is using the method and even who is prescribing it! In one recent piece of research quite different results were obtained when the investigators looked at two groups of women, both of whom were using the same kind of IUD, but who lived in two different towns not all that far away from each other.

Then, of course, there's the question of *how well you yourself use the method*. The Pill is the safest of all these contraceptive techniques, but if you're like the girl who says: 'It keeps on falling out, doctor' (or if you just forget to take it) then you certainly won't have 100 per cent protection! That's even more true with the Mini-Pill (progestogen-only Pill); as we'll see in a moment. Being more than a few hours late with this preparation could be critical.

There isn't much that you, the patient, can do to make the IUD go wrong (unless your husband suddenly takes it into his head to pull it out with the sugar-tongs), but if you don't check with your finger from time to time to make sure it hasn't fallen down into the vagina, then you could be running a slightly increased risk of pregnancy.

And as far as the cap and sheath are concerned, 'user error' largely accounts for the wildly differing figures which are quoted by different authorities. Some people have claimed, for instance, that the 'success rate' of the sheath can be as low as 85 per cent in some cases. Personally, I doubt this very much and think that you'd only get such a figure if you studied a group of couples who were so vague (or, I suppose, so horny) that half the time they never managed to get the sheath on before having intercourse!

One thing that nearly all doctors are agreed on is that the success rates I've quoted above for the Pill, Mini-Pill, IUD, cap and sheath are far better than those of all the other methods – or, of course, the 'success rate' of just having sex without any protection at all!

That's why it's so crazy to say (as quite a few people do), 'Oh, but I've heard of women getting pregnant on the IUD/cap/ sheath . . .'. *Of course* women get pregnant occasionally with these methods – but they're far more likely to do so if they're using idiotic manoeuvres like withdrawal ('being careful'), or if they're using nothing at all!

Now let's just run briefly through all those five really reliable methods and list their main advantages and disadvantages. When you've looked at the pros and cons of each technique, you may find one or more of them that you might be interested in for your own use.

The Pill

Advantages   Virtually 100 per cent reliable. Can improve love-making by giving both partners complete peace of mind about risk of pregnancy. Gives woman the chance to be in complete command of her own fertility. Offers superb control of periods, which are usually *more regular*, *lighter*, *shorter* and *much less painful*.

Disadvantages   At present needs to be prescribed by a doctor. May cause minor side-effects (nausea, breast tenderness, etc) in early stages. Uncommonly, may cause more significant side-effects (severe migraine, high blood pressure, etc). Very, very rarely, may cause serious thrombosis. *Not* suitable for a small number of women, especially those who have had a thrombosis. Of *doubtful* suitability for most women over thirty-five, specially if they're smokers, are overweight or have other risk factors present.

The Mini-Pill (progestogen-only Pill)

Advantages   About 98 per cent safe, if you don't miss any. Free from many of the side-effects of the Pill. *Probably* (not certainly) little or no risk of thrombosis, especially with norgestrel-containing Mini-Pills. Can be taken whilst breast feeding.

Disadvantages A small number of pregnancies occur. Has to be prescribed by doctor at present. Doesn't have Pill's superb period control – in fact periods may well be irregular. Dangerous to miss taking tablets, or to be late with them, as pregnancy may occur. Possible slight risk of ectopic pregnancies (pregnancies outside the womb).

The IUD (intra-uterine device)

Advantages About 98 per cent safe. Requires no action by you once it's in except to attend for check-ups – though it's preferable that you (or somebody) pop a finger in once a month to make sure it hasn't fallen out into the vagina.

Disadvantages A small number of pregnancies occur. Device has to be inserted by a doctor. Periods may be heavier, and perhaps more painful. Uncommon side-effects include infections (admittedly rather alarmingly common in women who haven't had babies – particularly ladies who have a number of boy-friends), and rarely perforations of the womb. Difficulties may also arise if prompt action isn't taken should pregnancy occur. Also possible that frequency of ectopic pregnancies (pregnancies outside the womb) may be increased.

The Cap (diaphragm)

Advantages Pretty safe, especially if put in every night. Lets the woman control her own contraception. Virtually no side-effects, except possibly an increased tendency to cystitis. May well help protect against cancer of the cervix.

Disadvantages Usually has to be fitted by a doctor. Repels women who dislike the idea of putting something in themselves (but this problem can be overcome); also repels those who dislike the feel and appearance of rubber. Insertion can interfere with the spontaneity of love-making (but not if woman pops it in every night before going to bed, or if man puts it in as part of love play).

The Sheath (plus foam or pessary) (French letter, rubber, 'johnny' or condom)

Advantages Available in many places and without a doctor's prescription. Fine for the man who likes to take control of things himself. May be a slight help to the over-excitable male who tends to reach a climax too quickly. *Very good results when used with the*

255

added protection of contraceptive aerosol foam, or pessaries.

Disadvantages   Small number of pregnancies occur. Sheaths occasionally break or leak, especially if damaged by fingernails or teeth. Many people dislike rubbery appearance and feel – but newer, more attractive coloured sheaths are now available. Others dislike lack of sensitivity – but very thin sheaths may help. Some couples feel sheath interferes with spontaneity of love-making – but not if woman rolls it onto man's erect penis as part of love play.

'The Shot'

Finally, there's *another* method of contraception – but it's not easily available to most women in Western countries. 'The Shot' (like the Pill) gives you very nearly 100 per cent protection against pregnancy. It's been in use for over fifteen years and is now employed in some sixty-five different countries. But at the moment it still *isn't* widely used in the UK or most larger Commonwealth countries (and scarcely at all in the USA), partly because of uncertainties about long-term safety – and partly because of understandable opposition by feminist groups to the practice of 'conning' women into having the Shot.

However, a number of doctors *have* decided, after thinking the matter over carefully, that there are certain of their patients to whom it's justifiable to give the Shot – after full discussion with the woman herself. These are mainly women for whom no other contraceptive is suitable – and who desperately don't want to get pregnant because of difficult social conditions or a poor medical history.

What is the Shot?   It's an injection of a female-type hormone called a 'progestogen'. (You may remember that the two hormones in the Pill are an oestrogen and a progestogen – and that it's a progestogen which is used in the 'Mini-Pill'.) The Shot is a long-acting jab, and a single dose will last a woman for three months, with a double dose lasting for about six months. The main such preparation in use is called 'Depo-Provera'.

How does it work?   Depo-Provera works mainly by stopping you from ovulating (releasing eggs) – which is what the Pill does. It also has other anti-fertility effects, including the capacity to make the mucus around the neck of the womb (the cervix) thicker, so that sperms will find it harder to penetrate.

What are the advantages?   Advantages of Depo-Provera include the following:

1. It's convenient to use: no daily Pill-taking – just a three-

monthly or six-monthly jab in the bottom.

2. There's no fear of forgetting it.

3. Breast feeding isn't interfered with, so the jab can be given shortly after childbirth; to date there have been no reports of ill-effects in children who have been breast-fed by mothers receiving Depo-Provera – though feminist groups are understandably worried about the level of the hormone in breast milk.

4. Unlike the Pill, Depo-Provera contains no oestrogens – the hormones which have been blamed for many Pill side-effects, including thrombosis.

5. Unlike the IUD, it doesn't usually produce very heavy periods (but it may well make them *very* irregular – see below).

What about disadvantages? Everything in medicine has its disadvantages, and Depo-Provera is no exception. The main problems are:

1. Menstruation tends to become irregular, often with periods far apart, or with a lot of 'spotting'.

2. By the end of two years, 40 per cent of women may be having no periods at all – though this probably doesn't matter if they don't want any more children, *and* if they've been warned in advance so that they're not alarmed.

3. Return of fertility may be delayed after coming off Depo-Provera.

4. Slight weight gain may also occur.

5. The other worry about Depo-Provera is *whether it could cause cancer*, especially of the cervix (neck of the womb). It's because of uncertainty about this that the United States Food and Drug Administration (FDA) have for so long delayed approval of the drug as a contraceptive. The main problem is that research work published in the 1970s suggested that early cancer of the cervix was more frequently seen among American women who were using Depo-Provera. The flaw in this argument was that these were mainly poorer women with many children – and cancer of the cervix is known to be much commoner *anyway* in women who are poor and who have had a lot of babies, making the figures very difficult to interpret. Better-controlled (i.e. more scientific) trials in Thailand have not yet shown any proven increase in cancer rates.

New versions of the Shot, which are claimed to be less likely to cause side-effects, are now coming into use.

The 'Rhythm Method'

I hope I won't offend anybody's religious feelings by saying that the rhythm method or 'safe period method' (sometimes known irreverently as 'Vatican roulette') really isn't all that good.

The Catholic Church still allows *only* this particular form of birth control, though I very much hope that this attitude will change in the next few years. Maybe it will – because there's no doubt that many Catholics (including a lot of doctors and, indeed, some priests) are now in favour of far safer methods of contraception, like the Pill or the IUD.

Statistics suggested that in Western Countries only about 5 per cent of married couples try to use the rhythm method these days, though unfortunately a very large number of young *unmarried* couples do take the most hair-raising chances each month in the belief that, if they make love only during the so-called 'safe period' all will be well. Sadly, they're very often wrong.

What is the safe period? The basic idea of the rhythm or safe period method is that a woman usually ovulates (that is, releases an egg) somewhere about fourteen days before a period. So, a woman with an average twenty-six-day cycle tends *as a rule* to be 'ripe' for conception at about the twelfth day of her cycle – that is twelve days after the start of a period.

Because a man's sperms can probably survive inside the woman's body for not more than a few days, you might think that it's only possible to get pregnant during the time just before and just after the twelfth day of the cycle. But the trouble is that you *can't* say for certain that ovulation will occur fourteen days before a period. There are some women who release it a week earlier. Furthermore, plenty of women vary from month to month – ovulating at totally different times in each cycle. There's also the problem of the fact that lots of women don't have clockwork-regular periods anyway. *If you don't know precisely when your next period's going to be, you can hardly pinpoint a time fourteen days before it!*

Add to all this the fact that emotional upsets (including worry about pregnancy) can alter the time of ovulation, and the safe period method begins to look decidedly less safe after all. I know there are people who claim that it works for them, but frankly I am always rather suspicious that those for whom this method is successful could be among the 10 per cent of couples who are subfertile anyway.

If you don't have sex all that often, and if you have periods that are regular as clockwork, then one of the variations of the rhythm method described below may work reasonably well for you. But for the average young couple, who are highly fertile and highly sexed, *this really isn't a good method* – and it's particularly

help. I'm afraid that I personally don't think that the ovulation method is ever going to be much use to the great majority of couples, who are going to find it all too much fuss and bother.

In the United States, some couples are being taught an even more complex variation of the 'ovulation method' which involves doing litmus paper tests on the vaginal fluid. I suppose this is OK if you like that sort of thing.

More seriously, there is now a chance that we will soon have a cheap and effective method of detecting a woman's ovulation day, by means of a hormone test. *That* would really put the 'rhythm method' back in business with a bang (if you'll forgive the phrase).

Summary If you're making love, then if possible use some *safe* method of contraception – not the rhythm method, even in its most complicated forms.

However, I do recognise the very real difficulties that Catholics have as far as contraception is concerned, and I know how upsetting it can be for a Catholic woman to go against her Church's teachings. All I can say is that if you go to your parish priest and discuss the Pill or IUD with him, you may well find him far more understanding than you expected.

However, if you feel you have to use the rhythm method, then pick the temperature chart or the Billings variants (or a combination of the two).

And if irregular periods make this difficult, then there *is* a solution: every now and then I hear about ladies in just this situation who have nevertheless made a tremendous success of the rhythm method, keeping their charts with such skill and precision that never *once* have they fallen pregnant when they didn't want to.

The trick, of course, is to use the Pill to keep your periods regular. Somehow, the rhythm method just seems to work much better that way. . . .

Sterilisation

Note: Any surgical operation can occasionally go wrong, so obviously any man (or woman) contemplating sterilisation should discuss possible complications with the surgeon beforehand.

Almost certainly, you know somebody who's had the male sterilisation (vasectomy) or female sterilisation operation. These days lots of people decide after two, three or perhaps four children that enough is enough: they've completed their family and they don't particularly want to go on using the Pill or the IUD, or having to bother with the sheath, until the wife is fifty or thereabouts. (Most women who reach the menopause under fifty are potentially fertile for another two years afterwards; women who reach 'the change' *at or after* fifty are usually regarded as potentially fertile – and therefore need to take contraceptive precautions – for *one* more year.)

So, to avoid having to use contraceptives for another fifteen or twenty years after the last child is born, many men and women decide on sterilisation. Happily it's a lot easier to obtain now than it used to be: surgeons are generally very much more liberal in their outlook, and whereas a few years ago it was true that even a man of thirty-five with four children might have a lot of trouble in getting a vasectomy, the position now is that almost any man or woman over about twenty-eight ought to be able to obtain a sterilisation operation *if they and their spouse really want it.*

Male sterilisation (vasectomy)

What exactly *is* a vasectomy? Well, you can see precisely what happens in Figure 46. The surgeon simply cuts through the slim spaghetti-like tube (the vas) that carries sperms upwards from the testicle to the penis.

Only a tiny nick on each side is required: indeed the operation can often be done through just *one* tiny cut. (There is no question of cutting the testicles or the penis as so many people seem to think!)

All this is usually done under a local anaesthetic, though a few surgeons do prefer you to have a whiff of gas and go to sleep for ten to fifteen minutes while the operation is being carried out. Generally, though, the procedure is for you just to lie on a couch and chat with the doctor and nurse while the job is being done. The very brave may be allowed to lie slightly propped up so that they can watch the whole process!

You'll feel no pain during the operation apart from the slight jab at the start as the local anaesthetic is put into the skin of the scrotum (the pouch). And immediately afterwards you'll probably feel astonishly well too, and wonder what all the fuss was about. However, don't be tempted by the lack of pain into disregarding the precautions outlined below under the heading *After the Operation.*

FEARS ABOUT VASECTOMY   Virtually every man who undergoes a vasectomy is secretly terrified – unless he is totally and utterly devoid of any imagination whatever. The reason for this is the good old Freudian one that we men are very frightened of anyone damaging our proudest possessions. The symbolic relationship between vasectomy and castration is all too obvious!

But it *is* just a symbolic relationship: in reality, vasectomy *isn't* anything whatever to do with castration and there is certainly no need at all to fear that undergoing the operation will make you start singing soprano in the church choir.

Vasectomy and sex
Nor, I can assure you, will vasectomy spoil your sex life. Indeed, far from it: many men report that, because the fear of unwanted pregnancy is removed, sex seems even better than before.

FIG. 46

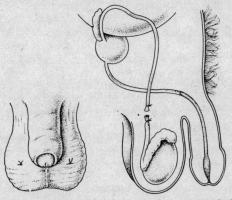

At one time, in fact, vasectomy was recommended as a treatment for failing sexual powers – but any effect it had must have been purely psychological, because there is no physical reason why it should affect sex in any way.

The only people who report lessened sexual desire after vasectomy are a tiny group of men who have deep psychological problems: these chaps should in theory be picked out prior to the operation by the counselling process.

Do you ejaculate afterwards?
This is one of the questions most asked by worried men who are thinking of having a vasectomy. The answer is *yes – you do*. And it's most unlikely that your or your partner will notice the slightest difference in the volume of the fluid which is produced when you 'come'.

That may seem a bit puzzling, but the fact is that most of the seminal fluid which squirts out when a man 'comes' is actually produced *not* by the testicles but by glands higher up the pipeline. So after vasectomy you will still produce what appears to be absolutely identical seminal fluid, but it won't contain any sperms.

Warming: However, it takes time to 'clear out' all the sperms after the operation – see below.

Immediately afterwards You'll probably feel fine after the operation, but nevertheless you should go straight home, lie down, and remain flat on your back for the rest of the day. You'll almost certainly begin to feel bruised and sore by the evening, and *this feeling will be a lot worse if you haven't rested.*

It's a good idea to have some aspirin, paracetamol or codeine to take if needed during the first twenty-four hours, because the bruised feeling will take a little while to wear off. (And you'll almost certainly look like a blue baboon down below for a few days.) If pain is troublesome, it's a welcome relief to get into a warm bath, in which your testicles will gently float upwards, thereby relieving the strain on the bruised area.

Resuming work Many men go back to work on the day after the operation, but others prefer to arrange to have it on a Friday so that they can rest till Monday.

In general, if your work is heavy, do try and take a day or two off: humping shovelfuls of coal around could just possibly damage the stitches (see below). But men with desk jobs can usually get back to work next day.

Resuming sex Very often people come away from the operating theatre with no very clear idea of when they can resume love-making again, and some don't have sex for weeks out of fear about what might happen.

All this is quite unnecessary. An American surgeon, when asked by the patient on the table how soon he could have sex, replied, 'Better wait till you get home!' And a patient of the famous Marie Stopes Clinic in London is believed to have set up a new world record for Britain by making love *only two and a half hours after the operation* – not bad when you consider that he had an eighty-mile train journey home.

Two words of caution though:

1. Over-athletic sex (like over-energetic work) could possibly loosen your stitches, so just take it a bit easy in the early days.

2. You aren't safe against conception (and must take some form of contraceptive precautions) until you've passed your tests – see immediately below.

When are you safe? A lot of sperms are often present in the piping *above* the point at which the surgeon has cut through the tube (the vas). *It takes time to clear these out* – and how soon you do it depends largely on how often you make love.

In practice, about twelve climaxes will usually get rid of pretty well all the sperms in the seminal fluid in most cases. So the regular arrangement is for the man to have two 'sperm tests' about three months after the operation. The test involves nothing more than ejaculating into a little sterile bottle (the doctor or clinic will give you this) and sending it in for the lab to have a look át the fluid under the microscope.

If they can't find any sperms in two successive tests, they'll let you know that you are 'all clear'. From then on it is most unlikely that you can get anybody pregnant, and so you can dispense with contraceptive precautions.

ARE THERE SUCH THINGS AS SPERM BANKS? Yes, in America and the UK it is sometimes the practice for men who are going to have a vasectomy to 'make a deposit' in a sperm bank beforehand. The idea is that some sperm would then be available if the man later changed his mind and wanted more children or if he gets divorced and re-married, or if his family were killed in an accident.

The system is that the man visits the sperm bank shortly before the operation. Slightly unbelievably, he is led to a comfortable room and left alone with a sterile bottle and even possibly a pile of copies of *Playboy*. When he has produced his specimen, it is immediately deep-frozen and (presumably) kept in a very secure place until the day when he might need it. Naturally this service is quite expensive.

Such sperm banks are not at present widely available in most other countries largely because of fears that the freezing method – which admittedly works pretty well with bulls' seminal fluid for artificial insemination purposes – might damage the sperm. And it's widely felt that men shouldn't undergo vasectomy unless they're sure that (barring some calamity striking their family) they'll never want any more children.

POSSIBLE COMPLICATIONS OF VASECTOMY Serious complications arising from the operation are very rare. However, as with any surgical procedure, things can occasionally go wrong. These are the main problems which may arise:

Severe bruising or bleeding Sometimes a stitch 'gives' a few hours after the operation (which is why you should take things easy afterwards). The result may be either *bleeding* through one of the tiny cuts or (more likely) *internal bleeding* into the scrotum (pouch).

If this happens, you'll probably feel something 'go' and either notice some external blood loss or find that your scrotum is fast swelling up in a rather sinister and painful manner.

What to do   Lie down, with your bottom up on a pile of pillows so that your hips are higher than your head. Grab a large pad (a towel will do) and press it hard over the area of your testicles. This may look undignified, but *firm* and *continuous* pressure will stop the bleeding. Stay lying flat till a doctor has seen you.

After an episode of internal bleeding, your scrotum and penis are likely to be very much more swollen and bruised than is the case after an ordinary uncomplicated vasectomy. Having an enormous great black football between your legs is no fun, but usually the only thing to be done is to stay in bed till it all goes down – though some surgeons do believe in operating to remove the clot. Your doctor will probably give you tablets to try to speed up the resolution of the bruising, and possibly pain-killers as well.

If the pain is bad even while lying in bed *get into the bath for a bit*. This can be an immense relief, as the water will provide gentle support for the swollen scrotum.

Infection   Infection after a vasectomy is not common, but is more likely to occur if there has been bleeding inside the scrotum (see above). If you start feeling feverish and have a temperature after your vasectomy, contact your doctor, who will probably put you on antibiotics. And don't worry – despite what *every* man fears, I have never heard of a case of anybody losing his testicles as a result of a post-vasectomy infection!

FAILURE OF VASECTOMY   Although vasectomy is usually a very successful operation, occasionally men are found to be still fertile afterwards. This should be picked up at the three months sperm. test, but very rarely it isn't.

Reasons for the operation failing include:

1. The man may have a third vas (tube) – most people only have two.
2. The tubes may manage to rejoin somehow (Nature, if she possibly can, will keep trying to ensure that children are born!)
3. A *sperm granuloma* may develop – this is a little swelling, caused by leaking sperm, which in effect creates a bridge between the two cut ends of the tubes.

But let me emphasise that these complications are *rare*. Most people get on very well indeed after a vasectomy and need have no further worries about unwanted children. Indeed, if a man's wife becomes pregnant after he's had a vasectomy, one's first thought is whether this might be a case of the 'milkman syndrome', rather than any fault of the operation.

Finally, a word about those much-publicised fears that vasectomy might give men artery disease, high blood pressure and so on. At present, these fears are only based on experiments on crab-eating Macaque monkeys – not on men.

As a vasectomised man myself, I'm not worried – though I shall have my blood pressure checked a little more frequently in future, just in case.

Female sterilisation

What happens when a woman is sterilised? Well, the basic idea is shown in Figure 47. The surgeon's object is simply to tie or cut through the two Fallopian tubes which, as you can see, normally carry the tiny eggs from the ovaries to the womb. This effectively prevents the sperms (shown as little 'tadpoles' in the drawing) from getting to the eggs and fertilising them. Incidentally, the unfertilised eggs disappear inside the abdomen without doing any harm at all.

How is the operation done?   Basically, there are three types of operation, and new ones are being developed. The introduction of laparoscopic sterilisation (see below) has made the operation much more acceptable to many women, because it's a much less upsetting procedure.

FIG. 47

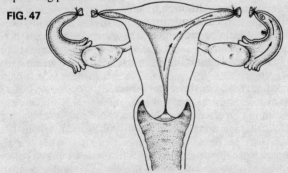

'Traditional' sterilisation   The 'old' way of sterilisation involves quite a long stay in hospital – usually about a week or so. It's almost always done under a general anaesthetic.

The surgeon makes a longish cut in the lower abdomen (about 4–7 in or 10–18 cm in length). Usually he does it transversely, fairly low down (even occasionally below the line of the pubic

267

hair) so that the woman will be able to wear a bikini afterwards without embarrassment. Then he finds the Fallopian tubes, and cuts and ties them in much the same way as shown in the picture.

Because this operation involves quite a big cut in the abdomen, you tend to get some pain and discomfort for a few days afterwards. Serious complications are fortunately rare, though of course things can very occasionally go wrong with *any* surgical operation.

The gynaecologist who does the operation (or one of his medical or nursing staff) should tell you how soon you can resume normal physical activity. But as a very general rule, it will probably be possible to drive a car within about three weeks of the sterilisation and to do normal housework within about four weeks.

Love-making can usually be resumed about a week or so after returning home from hospital, but obviously nothing too athletic should be attempted in the first month or thereabouts, so as not to put too much strain on the parts that have been operated on.

Laparoscopic sterilisation   This is the new operation which has become so popular in the last few years – the reasons being that firstly it causes very much less upset for the woman, and that secondly recovery is very much quicker so that you spend very little time in hospital. However it does usually require a general anaesthetic.

What *is* a laparoscopic sterilisation? It's just one which is done without making a big cut in the abdomen. After the patient has been given an anaesthetic the surgeon pushes a slim telescope-like device through a little nick made just at the lower edge of the navel, which allows him to see the ovaries and tubes. Then another tiny nick is usually made on one side of the stomach, and through this hole the surgeon pushes an instrument which can crush and coagulate the tubes or clip them.

The two little cuts in the belly usually require only about one stitch each, and as a rule they heal so as to be virtually invisible. And because the incisions are so tiny, you're usually out of hospital in one to two days. Normal physical activity and normal love-making can usually be resumed within about a week or so.

Disadvantages of laparoscopic sterilisation   Though this operation sounds a great idea, there are one or two possible drawbacks:

a) The technique can't be used for a sterilisation immediately after childbirth – though it's perfectly suitable for sterilisation done at the same time as a termination of pregnancy.

b) It's not suitable for *all* women, especially those who are very fat, or who have adhesions inside the stomach as a result of previous surgery. Sometimes the surgeon finds it too difficult to perform and has to decide to change over in midstream to the 'traditional' operation instead.

c) There's a rather higher incidence of *complications* and *accidents* with laparoscopic sterilisation, which should only be carried out by very experienced operators.

While you certainly don't have to worry about having the operation done by a reputable surgeon, there are one or two private clinics whose surgical standards are regulated by nobody, and where it would seem to be a trifle dodgy to have a laparoscopic sterilisation done.

Vaginal sterilisation It's possible to get at the tubes through the vagina, and so perform the operation without making any incisions in the stomach at all. This operation is not all that easy to perform (especially in a woman who has had no children).

New forms of sterilisation New techniques of sterilisation are being developed, including a 'mini-laparotomy' which can be done under local anaesthetic with the woman going home the same day; this technique is so far only in very limited use.

AFTER THE OPERATION Here are the answers to a few commonly asked questions about the after-effects of sterilisation.

Will it affect your general health? No – there are no generalised effects at all. All the operation does is stop you getting pregnant.

Does it stop your periods? No, these continue as before. However, recent reports have suggested that there is some evidence that periods might be heavier or more painful after sterilisation. Most women, however, don't complain of this problem. It may be that the heavier periods which have been reported are simply due to the coming off the Pill.

Is it foolproof? No, not entirely. There is a small failure rate after sterilisation (round about 1 per cent at most centres) but very few couples feel there is any point in using any contraceptive precautions once the operation has been done.

Will it affect your sex life? No – except perhaps to make it *better*, because of peace of mind about unwanted pregnancy.

HOW TO GET A STERILISATION There are slightly different procedures, depending on whether you're pregnant or not at the time you decide on sterilisation.

When you are not pregnant Perhaps because the operation is a 'bigger' one than vasectomy, getting it arranged is a slightly more

269

formal business than fixing up a sterilisation for a man.

Some gynaecologists may still be applying rather stringent criteria and refusing to sterilise younger women with only a small number of children; indeed, not too long ago there was a rather strange scheme in some parts of the world whereby you wouldn't be 'allowed' a sterilisation unless your age multiplied by the number of your children totted up to more than 120!

But most surgeons are now much more accommodating and it shouldn't be all that difficult for any really determined woman over the age of about twenty-eight to get a sterilisation – though she may have to see more than one gynaecologist in order to obtain it.

When you're pregnant   Sterilisation is very often first discussed when a woman is pregnant – either with a wanted or an unwanted pregnancy.

If you're having a baby, the obstetrician/gynaecologist may well be happy to sterilise you a day or two after delivery. But *do* arrange this with him when you first go to ante-natal clinic – if you don't say that you want to be sterilised until you've had the baby it may be too late to arrange it. Anyway, you shouldn't be making important decisions like this in the emotional time just after you have given birth – it's far better to make the decision with your husband well beforehand.

If you're having a termination, the surgeon may offer you a sterilisation (usually laparoscopic – see above) which could be carried out at the same time; if you're in a private clinic, this will obviously add considerably to the cost of the bill.

While it is certainly often convenient and sensible to get sterilisation over and done with so that you don't have the unpleasantness of any more terminations, the gynaecologist should *not* tell you that he will only terminate your pregnancy if you agree to be sterilised at the same time. This occasional practice has been widely described as 'blackmail' and that's just what it is.

Abortion; 'The Morning-After Pill', the 'Morning-After Coil', and 'Menstrual Extraction'

Warning: If you think you may have an unwanted pregnancy, DO NOT get involved with attempts at ILLEGAL abortion. Instead, read the section of this chapter devoted to abortion, and then see your own doctor right away.

I hope that I've made clear by now that modern techniques of contraception are so safe that any couple ought to be able to make love in the knowledge that an unwanted pregnancy is very unlikely indeed. But unfortunately, disasters do occur – and usually they happen not through any failure of a contraceptive method, but because the couple 'trusted to luck' and didn't use anything. Personally, I look forward to the day when we'll have taught both adults and youngsters enough about contraception to make sure that this doesn't happen any more.

But in the meantime, what can be done after the event if you've been unwise enough to make love without protection? Well, there are post-conceptive methods, and I'm going to describe them here. But I'd like to make clear that I am not advocating the widespread use of these methods – I'm simply telling you what they are in case you're ever in desperate need of them. There are actually four 'after-the-event' means of fertility control, and these are:

★The morning-after pill
★The morning-after coil
★Menstrual extraction (interception)
★Abortion

The morning-after pill and coil are used the day after intercourse, and menstrual extraction is used within about two weeks or so of having unprotected sex. I find it quite impossible to say with any confidence whether these three methods really constitute abortion, since no one knows with absolute certainty how soon the fertilised egg 'implants' in the womb – though it's probably about five days after intercourse.

But, in practice, few doctors would feel that the use of a *morning-after pill* or *coil* really produces an abortion: even if the egg and sperm *have* united by the morning after love-making, then it seems most unlikely that the resulting fertilised egg has managed to attach itself to the lining of the womb.

The position is rather more difficult with *menstrual extraction*. Again, if it's carried out within a day or so of intercourse it would be very hard to regard it as producing an abortion. But if it is done two weeks or more later (that is, when the woman's period is already overdue) then most people would see it as being an early abortion. It seems likely that in Britain and most countries with Anglo-Saxon legal traditions, the law would view it in that light (see below).

Now let's have a look at these four methods in detail.

THE MORNING-AFTER PILL For generations now, some doctors have tried to help women who've had unprotected sex by giving

271

them 'something to bring on a period'. Whether their prescriptions often worked or not is hard to say. But a true morning-after pill does now exist. It is widely prescribed in the USA (particularly by university and college doctors), and now in the UK and other countries.

The morning-after pill is either (a) a high dose of a female hormone; or (b) two tablets of one of the high-content contraceptive Pills, followed 12 hours later by a further two tablets. Given within a matter of three days after unprotected intercourse, it will usually bring on a period. Unfortunately, it has two main drawbacks:

Nausea In the dosage required, it often produces nausea and vomiting in many women. Advocates of the morning-after pill claim that this can be prevented by giving an anti-nausea drug at the same time. Fortunately method (b) above *doesn't* usually produce much nausea.

Possible effect on the foetus If giving it *weren't* successful, the effect of the drug on the foetus might be harmful. Because of the possibility of such a tragedy, advocates of the morning-after pill say that a woman who has used it must be offered a termination of pregnancy if it doesn't work.

THE MORNING-AFTER COIL   The controversial *morning-after coil* is an ordinary IUD which is inserted a day or two after unprotected sex, and which is thought to work by preventing implantation of the egg. The advantage of this method over the morning-after pill is that the woman is left with a reliable method of contraception for the future, once the device has been inserted, and the chance of side-effects is lessened.

MENSTRUAL EXTRACTION (interception or menstrual regulation) The third 'after-the event' method is called either 'Menstrual Extraction', 'Interception' or 'Menstrual Regulation'. It's simply a technique (developed in the USA) in which the contents of the womb are sucked out, thus 'bringing on a period'. Doctors who carry it out slip a thin tube up the vagina and through the cervix (or neck of the womb); they then attach a suction device, such as a large syringe, to the end and draw out the womb contents. This takes only a minute or two, and is usually pretty painless – so there's no need for general anaesthetic.

Menstrual extraction is successful in the vast majority of cases in which it is used. Not surprisingly, it's become very popular in the USA and in many other parts of the world. But in Britain and quite a few other countries it just hasn't caught on – and at present it's very unlikely that this is a service your GP will ever provide.

Why are there reservations about menstrual extraction? Mainly because of the feeling that, unless it's done within a few days of the unprotected act of intercourse, it's really just a very early abortion – and of course strict rules govern the availability of abortion (see below).

However, advocates of menstrual extraction claim that it is done so early that it falls into a 'grey area' between contraception and abortion, being really neither one nor the other; that's why they use the term 'interception' to describe the technique.

Whether they're right or wrong, worldwide interest in menstrual extraction is obviously immense. In the USA, some feminist groups actually use it on each other – though I certainly don't think this is a good idea healthwise since it could lead to infection.

In Britain and elsewhere it seems unlikely that menstrual extraction will ever be offered routinely in family doctors' surgeries until the precise legal position about whether it does or doesn't constitute an abortion is sorted out. At present, it seems that a GP who did a menstrual extraction on a girl who was already overdue with her period would be inviting prosecution for illegal abortion. I think that if he did it *before* she was overdue (and therefore long before anyone could know whether she was pregnant or not) then it would be very difficult to bring any kind of case against him. But at present, few doctors would be willing to take the risk.

Abortion

Please re-read the warning at the beginning of this section about ILLEGAL abortion before you read any further.

Abortion isn't a method of contraception – it's a disastrous *failure* of contraception. Yet every year, millions of women all over the world undergo the experience *legally*. Heaven knows how many more have *illegal* abortions.

Some of these women are dealt with very badly, either by people who want to exploit them for money, or by people who treat them with rudeness and cruelty in some sort of misguided effort to show them how 'wicked' they have been.

If you have the misfortune to have an unwanted pregnancy, then I'm sorry to say that there's a very real risk that you'll run into just these problems. Trying to cope with exploitation or unkindness when you're lonely, confused and pregnant can be a pretty miserable experience – and that's why I'm going to try to deal with the whole subject of abortion as fully and as clearly as possible in this section.

I'm simply going to state the facts and *not* take moral attitudes. I do realise and understand that in the present controversy over the rightness and wrongness of abortion, there are perfectly sincere and decent people who hold diametrically opposing views on the moral aspects of this subject. But what worries me is that so very often the *actual medical facts* about abortion are distorted or suppressed in order to promote a particular point of view.

So I take no sides on the moral question. All I propose to present here are the facts.

ILLEGAL ABORTION

Please have nothing at all to do with illegal abortion. Back-street abortions are, by and large, carried out by people who don't really know what they're doing – and the havoc they wreak of women's bodies is absolutely appalling.

A high percentage of back-street abortions cause intense pain, severe bleeding, and dangerous infection of the reproductive organs. Before the introduction of more liberal abortion legislation (which gave qualified gynaecologists a much freer hand to carry out terminations in cases of need), hospitals admitted a terrifyingly large number of women who were suffering from the after-effects of an amateur abortionist's efforts.

Nowadays, things are far better and we don't see anything like as many cases of the 'back-street syndrome'. But attempts at illegal abortion still go on, especially in areas where people find it hard to get a *legal* termination of pregnancy. And even today, quite a few women still die as a result of crude attempts at illegal abortion. *I'm sure that many more will die if legislation is brought in to make it more difficult to obtain a legal abortion carried out by a doctor.*

So, if you really want a termination, get one done *legally* by a competent and reputable surgeon. This section will tell you how to go about it.

LEGAL ABORTION

The Law   In recent years, many countries have introduced laws that allow doctors to perform termination of pregnancy in certain circumstances. These laws have, on the whole, tended to follow the pattern set in the abortion legislation which was adopted in Britain and in New York State in the late 1960s.

The usual basis of this legislation is that a pregnancy can be terminated if doing so would lessen the risk to the woman's health (physical or mental).

In fact, it can be shown that it is actually much safer to have an *early* termination of pregnancy than it is to go on and have a baby (motherhood still carries some risk to life and health even today). So some doctors actually interpret the law in this light and are more or less willing to give an abortion on request to any pregnant woman, provided she comes to see them early enough.

So, if you're pregnant and don't want to be, then you don't need to be terrified about asking a doctor for advice. However, *be extremely careful whom you consult* (see below). As long as you go to a reputable doctor, he will see that the requirements of the law are complied with.

Far and away the most important thing to remember is that you must act with considerable speed. Don't hang about for weeks hoping that things will put themselves right somehow – they probably won't. And a late termination can be difficult, dangerous or impossible.

Having a doctor to advise you from the start is very important indeed, which is one reason why I recommend starting with your own GP if at all possible. He or she will be able to interpret the result of the pregnancy test for you (by and large, they're right about nine times out of ten), and he should be able to help you sort out what you want to do, and (if you definitely want a termination) to tell you where it is best to try to obtain one in your area.

Only a very few family doctors are uncooperative and unhelpful in this respect. Most GPs, even if they are strongly against abortion, will do their best to make sure you get into safe hands and not into those of back-street operators or commercial exploiters. However, a tiny majority of doctors refuse to give their patients any information at all about getting a termination, and leave them to take their chances.

If this is the case with you, then not a bad idea would be to call in at your local Family Planning Clinic, or Family Service Clinic in the USA, where the doctor will certainly be willing to give you sympathetic (and free) advice about what facilities are available in your area.

Where to go for the operation As I've said above, your GP should be able to advise you about this. It may well be best if he refers you to the gynaecologist at your local hospital. (But when you're ringing for an appointment, make sure the hospital know it's a termination you're enquiring about: otherwise in the UK they may give you a date to see the gynaecologist in two months' time.)

Be careful where you go I stress the need for caution because the abortion scene is a very strange one indeed – and one in which vast sums of money have been made by certain gentlemen (including, I'm sorry to say, a tiny handful of doctors) during the last few years.

It's a world in which very odd things happen, in which deception is far from unknown, in which women get mysteriously hi-jacked by taxi-drivers while on the way to one surgeon – and end up on another one's doorstep! It's a world in which the organisation that cuts corners and skimps on the standard of care which it gives to women will get rich faster than its competitors – provided *they* don't find some way of driving it out of business first.

Be guided by a reputable doctor, and you shouldn't get into difficulty.

The Operation   Once you've been legally 'accepted' for a termination, you'll be given a date (usually a few days later) on which to attend the hospital or licensed clinic. You should also be told what sort of operation will be done.

Operation in early pregnancy   If no more than about twelve weeks have passed since your last period, it will be very easy to terminate the pregnancy by the vaginal route – that is, without making a cut in your abdomen.

There are two main methods of doing this – by vacuum aspiration, and (rarely these days) by scraping the womb.

Vacuum aspiration   Most women have terminations by the suction method these days. You go into the hospital or clinic some hours before the operation, and you're carefully examined by a doctor to see if you're fit for a general anaesthetic. Then you're given a pre-med injection and prepared for the theatre. Finally, you're put to sleep (usually by means of a jab in the back of the hand), and when you wake up fifteen minutes or so later, it's all over.

While you were asleep, the gynaecologist passed a slim suction catheter through the neck of your womb, and sucked out the contents. In early pregnancy, there is so little material in the womb that this takes only a minute or so, and is unlikely to cause any serious physical upset. However, you stay in hospital until the next morning.

Womb scrape   A 'scrape' of the womb is simply the well-known 'D&C' (dilatation and curettage) procedure. It too is done under a general anaesthetic, but what happens is that the surgeon passes an instrument through the neck of the womb and uses it to scrape the womb lining. This operation is slowly falling into disuse, because of the fact that the suction procedure is so much easier – and less traumatic to the womb.

'Lunchtime abortion'   This is the frivolous media term applied to abortion done by vacuum suction in early pregnancy without

276

need for an overnight stay in hospital – *and often without need for a general anaesthetic*. Because the vacuum suction method is so 'mild' it can readily be used on a patient who is awake – though of course many women feel much happier emotionally if they can be asleep during their termination.

'Lunchtime abortions' are not trivial procedures, however, and good medical aftercare is necessary.

Operation in later pregnancy   (After about the twelfth week.) Ideally, every woman who is going to have a termination should have it done well before the twelfth week, since after that time the operation is much more difficult and the risks increase considerably. (If you're paying for it yourself, the costs are probably going to be higher too.)

Happily, fewer late terminations are now being done. If somehow or other you have failed to get to a gynaecologist until you are more than twelve weeks pregnant, then it *may* still be possible to do a vacuum suction or a 'scrape' via the vagina.

More likely, you will have to have either an abdominal operation (in which the doctor opens the abdomen in order to be able to empty the womb) or one of a variety of procedures in which certain solutions are injected in order to make the womb contract, and so produce a sort of miniature labour.

I'm afraid that none of these operations in later pregnancy is much fun. All of them involve some days' stay in hospital and a period of convalescence. Complications such as bleeding and infection are common, and the death rate (though still very low) is much higher than that associated with the operation performed in early pregnancy.

The conclusion is obvious. If you really want a termination, *get it done early*. Delay may hazard your health – or even your life.

Aftercare

The great majority of women who've had an ordinary vaginal termination (carried out in good time) feel completely fit and well within a couple of days of the operation. Many of them go back to work the same week.

But in fact it *is* best to take things a bit easy for a week or two after the operation. While the risks of bleeding, infection, and psychological trauma have been wildly exaggerated by certain strict anti-abortionists (you're more likely to run into these troubles if you go on and have a baby than if you have an early termination), nonetheless these things can happen.

So, if you have any sudden or heavy bleeding, or if you have abdominal pain, discharge and a temperature, *then go to bed and*

277

ring your doctor. Similarly, in the unlikely event that you feel very depressed after the termination (instead of feeling the profound sense of relief that most women experience), then talk to somebody, and particularly your family doctor, about it.

After a *later* termination (one done after twelve weeks), even more care is necessary, and the surgeon who does the operation should advise you about this.

Contraception   But one of the most important aspects of after-care is simply *making sure you don't get pregnant again*. You may say, 'Oh, that won't happen to me!' – but, alas, it may well do. Ideally, either the surgeon or your own doctor should raise the subject of contraception with you. If they don't, for heaven's sake ask them! Provided you enquire in time, it's possible to have an IUD fitted at the end of the termination – or indeed to have a sterilisation carried out if you don't want any more children.

Alternatively, as soon as you come out of hospital you can start taking the Pill or Mini-Pill, or have a cap fitted. Or you could tell your husband or boyfriend that it's high time he started using a sheath, or had a vasectomy.

Please, at all costs, don't subject yourself to the trauma of having another unwanted pregnancy, because this certainly may be damaging both psychologically and physically. Furthermore, there's evidence that repeated terminations of pregnancy can damage the neck of the womb and thus cause problems (such as miscarriage) when you *do* want to have a child.

You shouldn't resume love-making for three weeks after the operation. And when you *do* start again, make sure that it really is SAFE love-making – because, honestly, that's the only kind that's really worth having. Let me repeat the deeply intellectual verse we quoted earlier in the book:

> 'Don't trust to luck,
> When you have a fuck!'

AFTERPLAY

One final thing about sex: don't take it too seriously.

Ignore people who think that you should have orgasms in some particular way or with some particular frequency. Do what you and your partner enjoy most – and have fun.

Above all: remember that laughter in bed is a precious gift – more valuable than 1,000 orgasms. You can survive without orgasms, but you can't survive without laughter.